THE GHOST OF '66

MARTIN PETERS was born in Plaistow in 1943 and made his debut for West Ham at eighteen. He played 364 games for the club before being transferred to Tottenham Hotspur for a record £200,000 in 1970. In 1975 he moved to Norwich City, where he spent nearly six years and was voted the finest player in the club's history. He had a brief spell as player-coach and then manager at Sheffield United. He won 67 caps for England between 1966 and 1974. He now lives in Shenfield, Essex.

MICHAEL HART, who worked with Martin Peters on the writing of this book, is the football correspondent for the *Evening Standard*, and has written numerous other books, including the autobiography of Geoff Hurst. He lives in Earls Colne, Essex.

THE GHOST OF '66
MARTIN PETERS

with Michael Hart

An Orion paperback

First published in Great Britain in 2006
by Orion
This paperback edition published in 2007
by Orion Books Ltd,
Orion House, 5 Upper St Martin's Lane,
London WC2H 9EA

1 3 5 7 9 10 8 6 4 2

A CIP catalogue record for this book is available
from the British Library.

ISBN 978-0-7528-8149-2

Printed and bound in Great Britain at
Mackays of Chatham plc, Chatham, Kent

The Orion Publishing Group's policy is to use papers
that are natural, renewable and recyclable products and
made from wood grown in sustainable forests. The logging
and manufacturing processes are expected to conform to
the environmental regulations of the country of origin.

www.orionbooks.co.uk

CONTENTS

ACKNOWLEDGEMENTS

I would like to express my sincere thanks and gratitude to those who have helped and encouraged me. These include my mum and dad, Mary and William, my wife Kathy, who has given me 42 years of love and support, our children Lee Ann and Grant, who have given us both so much happiness and joy and two wonderful grandchildren Hannah and Meg.

My thanks also go to Michael Hart for his time and diligence over the past eighteen months and for his help in producing a book that I am very, very proud of.

I would also like to acknowledge the debt I owe my sports master at Fanshawe School, Mr Hooper. From the professional game I'd like to thank: Ted Fenton, Ron Greenwood, his scout Wally St Pier, and all the West Ham players; the manager at Tottenham, Bill Nicholson and all the Spurs players; and the manager at Norwich, John Bond, and coach Ken Brown, and all the Norwich players.

And, of course, I can't forget the other 21 players who made the summer of 1966 special not just for me but the entire nation. Forty years later I'm still reminded of that achievement every day. Whether I'm in the high street, the railway station or airport, someone will come up to me at least once a day and ask: 'Are you Martin Peters?'

Finally, I'd like to remember some of those I've met along the way who are no longer with us: Bobby Moore, Alan Sealey, 'Budgie' Byrne, Harry Cripps, Noel Cantwell, John Dick, Dave Bickles, John Charles, Cyril Knowles, Justin Fashanu, Les Cocker, Harold Shepherdson, Ron Greenwood, Peter Osgood and last but certainly not least . . . Sir Alf Ramsey.

1

'ENGLAND EXPECTS'

On the evening before the most important game in the history of English football I went to the cinema. You might have thought that on such an occasion, only hours before the World Cup final, the England squad would be closeted away from public view, concentrating solely on the challenge ahead, but you would be wrong. I went to the cinema with Bobby Moore, Bobby Charlton and the rest of Alf Ramsey's squad.

We were staying at the Hendon Hall Hotel in a discreet corner of north London, not too far from Wembley, and had been together as a group for almost two months, preparing for the finals. Alf liked to keep his players safe from distractions whenever we played at Wembley. That's why we stayed in Hendon at the ivy-clad former home of the great eighteenth-century English actor and director David Garrick. This quiet, old-fashioned, cloistered hotel, with its dark panelling and thick carpets, was close enough to Wembley Stadium to be convenient and far enough from the temptations of the West End.

The downside was the distance from the hotel to Alf's favoured training base, which was the Bank of England ground at Roehampton in Surrey. On some days, when the traffic was bad, we'd spend three hours sitting in the coach, travelling to and from the training ground. One day, the players asked Bobby

Charlton to suggest to Alf that we train at a ground nearer the hotel. When the team bus was stuck in traffic, Bobby went to the front of the coach and put the suggestion to Alf.

'I'll give it some consideration,' he said, but before Bobby had returned to his seat, Alf turned round and shouted down the bus, 'Bobby, I've considered it. We'll stay as we are.'

Travelling apart, Hendon Hall was a familiar, comfortable and welcoming base camp for us. We could easily saunter down to the local high street to do some shopping, buy a newspaper or kill an hour or two. Even so, I was slightly surprised that, less than twenty-four hours before the World Cup final, going to the pictures to see *Those Magnificent Men in their Flying Machines* was considered top of the agenda of things to do. On that July evening in 1966 we attracted few glances from curious passers-by as we strolled down the hill to the local cinema. People didn't make the fuss they make today and there was no police escort. No one bothered us in the cinema, although the presence of the England squad the night before the World Cup final did turn a few heads. Before we went to our seats Alf ushered me to one side in the foyer.

'I don't want you to repeat this to anyone,' he said quietly. 'I haven't told the others the team, but I want you to know that you'll be playing tomorrow.'

A few weeks earlier I would have had no logical reason to suppose that I'd be playing for England against West Germany at Wembley in the World Cup final. I'd had some experience of international football at the lower levels but Alf had ignored my claims for a place in the Under-23 team for nearly two years. I'd played at Schoolboy and Youth level and had five Under-23 caps when my international career suddenly ground to a halt.

Then, in April 1966, Alf selected me to play against Turkey at Blackburn for the Under-23s. We won 2–0 and George Armstrong, the Arsenal winger, scored both goals. I remember sitting down before the match with George and Alan Birchenall, who was playing for Sheffield United at the time, discussing our prospects, at that late stage, of convincing Alf that we were worth a place in his World Cup squad. As I recall, none of us thought the World Cup was a realistic prospect. All three of us would have settled for a single senior cap. For a professional footballer in those days, there was no greater honour than playing for England. Sadly, neither George nor Alan achieved that ambition, but I was lucky. My chance came a month later when, out of the blue, Alf picked me to make my senior debut against Yugoslavia at Wembley. That match was played on 4 May, just seven weeks before the World Cup kicked off.

Afterwards I still assumed I'd be watching the World Cup on television and reading about it in the newspapers. Even when I was named in his provisional squad of forty for the tournament, I didn't believe I'd be a contender when he named his final twenty-two. Then, when he did pick me, I knew, I just *knew*, that I wouldn't be selected to play. I was only twenty-two, although not quite the baby. That distinction went to Alan Ball, who was eighteen months younger than me.

Alf had so much talent to pick from – Gordon Banks, Bobby Moore, Bobby Charlton, Jimmy Greaves and Ray Wilson were widely acknowledged as being among the best in the world. Ron Flowers, George Cohen, George Eastham, Jimmy Armfield and Nobby Stiles had vast experience. Where would I fit in? My shirt, with No. 16 on the back, hardly suggested that I had a high ranking in the pecking order.

I wasn't surprised when he didn't select me for the opening game against Uruguay but I was surprised when he told me I would be playing in the second game against Mexico. Although I kept my place against France, Argentina and Portugal, I wasn't sure whether I'd retain it against West Germany. In terms of status within the squad, some players were automatic selections but I wasn't one of them. So that evening when Alf told me I was in the team, I had to take a couple of deep breaths to suppress my feelings of relief – and elation – although, to be honest, I don't remember feeling any more pressure than I'd experienced in a club match on a Saturday afternoon.

For a start, the media interest in those days wasn't quite the same as it is now. These days, the media is often responsible for fuelling a quite unrealistic level of public expectation and the burden must be something of a handicap to today's players. I feel a little sorry for some of them. I don't remember ever feeling that kind of pressure when I played for England.

I was quite relaxed that summer evening as we all walked back to the hotel from the cinema. I noticed a lot of whispering among some members of the squad, and a lot of suppressed giggling. Perhaps they knew they were playing – or not playing! Perhaps I was not the only one Alf had taken into his confidence.

Anyway, I wasn't going to tell anyone my news. At least, I wasn't planning to tell anyone. My lips remained sealed until we got back to the hotel. I was sharing a room with my good friend and West Ham club-mate Geoff Hurst. Once in the privacy of our room, Geoff and I looked at each other and started smiling. We had been friends for a long time. Our wives were friends. We spent a lot of time with each other.

'Are you in?' he asked me.

'Yes,' I said. 'Are you?'

He nodded, and our smiles got wider. If anything, Geoff was more concerned about his place than I was about mine. He was a latecomer, like me. He made his debut against West Germany in a friendly in February 1966 and hadn't played in the opening three World Cup games. He got his chance when Jimmy Greaves suffered a badly cut leg against France. Geoff was called into the side, scored against Argentina and kept his place for the semi-final with Portugal. Jim reckoned he was fit to play in the final but Alf boldly decided to keep the side that had beaten the Portuguese 2–1.

I believe Alf had seen something in the 1–0 win over Argentina that he believed was worth keeping. Bobby Moore, Geoff and I had played together at West Ham many times but the controversial game against Argentina was the first occasion on which the three of us played together for England, and so was the first time we had been able to use the near-post cross. The classic execution of that goal, using the tactic perfected by West Ham manager Ron Greenwood, won wide acclaim at the time.

In the seventy-seventh minute I gathered a pass from Ray Wilson on the left and drove the ball to the near post. I knew that Geoff would be running to meet it. The move came straight out of the Ron Greenwood coaching manual, and was something we'd done many times for West Ham. Geoff's header was enough to put England into the World Cup semi-finals for the first time.

So that night, on the eve of the final, Geoff and I both felt a mixture of relief and delight. Our celebration involved nothing more than a cup of tea and an early night but before going to bed we phoned our wives. That summer, my wife Kathy and I had decided to move back to Barkingside from Hornchurch. I wasn't expecting to be involved in the World Cup and, as it turned out, we had to move during the tournament. The timing was unfortunate because it meant that Kathy had to move without me. I knew I had no hope of getting away during our eight weeks of preparation. Alf would have frowned upon it and the competition for places in the starting line-up was such that no player would have done anything to jeopardise his chances. Kay Stiles, Nobby's pregnant wife, suggested he return home for the birth of their child. Nobby, vastly more experienced than I was, knew that if he went away for a couple of days, he could return to find that his place in the pecking order had gone to another player. He stayed with the squad.

Kathy coped magnificently. Her twenty-first birthday fell on the day after we'd beaten the French and I'd sent her twenty-one red roses. I rang her on her birthday and said, 'Did you get the flowers?'

'They're lovely, Martin,' she said, 'but you wouldn't believe it – someone nicked three of them before they were delivered.'

'What d'you mean?' I asked her.

'There are only twenty-one,' she said. 'There should have been two dozen.'

'No, I sent twenty-one – one for each year!'

The next morning, Geoff and I decided to have breakfast in our room while reading the papers. We called room service. I had my usual cereal, toast and tea. When we eventually went downstairs, you could feel a little anxiety among the players. We weren't the only guests staying at the hotel. Other people, commercial travellers, businessmen, were also there and that helped to keep the morning as normal as possible.

These days the England team is locked away in seclusion. If they are in a hotel preparing for a tournament, they have the place to themselves. The idea is that only in isolation can the players focus properly on the job ahead – at least, that's the theory.

That morning Geoff, Bobby and I loitered around the hotel with the rest of the lads. Some of them wandered down to the high street. Nobby Stiles went off to church. Geoff had a walk. I stayed in the hotel chatting with anyone who wanted to talk. Jimmy Greaves, who knew by now that he would miss what would have been the greatest game of his career, was packing his bags. He was twenty-six and the finest England goalscorer of all time, but he would play only three more games for England.

Alf wandered in and out of the lounge as the morning un-folded. At a brief meeting he told us what was expected of us. We treated him with great respect. No one would question his decisions. I was a newcomer to the squad but it was immediately apparent how close Alf was to his players. I'd had a little experience of his style of management with the Under-23 set-up but, viewing it at close hand with the senior squad, it was possible to assess the strength of the bond between the manager and his players.

Initially, I felt I was on the fringe of things. I was probably still a bit naive and I had a lot of respect for Alf and the people around me. There was an obvious pecking order, with the two Bobbys at the top, but when we were playing, everyone had equal responsibility.

I'd learned about squad etiquette during three weeks of intensive training at the end of the 1965–66 season. Lilleshall was the venue, an imposing country estate in Shropshire that had once belonged to the Duke of Sutherland. The period we spent training in those marvellous grounds was vital to our preparation. The work was unrelenting but it created a sense of unity and harmony that was the platform for our later success.

I'd roomed with Gordon Banks, who was a senior player. He had a very positive attitude and made me feel at home. He was always joking about the peacocks you could hear screeching during the night.

Bobby and Geoff were as important as 'Banksie' in helping me settle into the squad. The fact that we played together in the same club side was a great help. Bobby was almost in a class of his own, status-wise, and there was some reflected glory for me in being his club-mate – but even the big stars had to take their plates back to the serving counter at the end of each meal when we were at Lilleshall. Can you imagine them doing that today?

After an early lunch, just four hours before kick-off, we climbed into our motor coach for the trip to Wembley. The police escorted us via a back route. As we got closer to the stadium, the crowds deepened and cheered us on our way. I remember sitting in the bus, wondering what was in store for me. Kathy was going to be in the stadium. Friends would be there, too, and the world would be watching on TV.

My main hope was that I wouldn't let anyone down, especially Alf. He'd shown great faith in me and I thought I had a debt to repay. The pressure I felt was largely self-induced. I wanted to do well and represent my country with pride.

Perhaps without realising it, Alf had placed a great burden on his players, although no one seemed troubled by it. In 1963, shortly after his appointment as manager, he predicted that England 'would win the World Cup'. There may have been occasions when he regretted those words but that afternoon, as we climbed down from the bus and walked into the cool of the Wembley dressing rooms, we all wondered whether his prophecy would be proved correct.

I was waiting for nerves to seize me but it didn't happen. I was quite relaxed. I always took my time getting ready and this match was no different. It usually took me about an hour. That was the way I got my mind right for the challenge ahead. I always put my kit on in the same order. The shorts went on last. Bobby Moore always put his kit on in the same order, too, with his shorts last. He also wanted to be the last of the eleven to put his shorts on.

In the dressing room that day I waited until 'Mooro' put his shorts on and then I slid into mine. Triumph – or so I thought. Mooro took his off again and waited until we were walking up the tunnel before putting them back on.

I also always preferred being last to leave the dressing room. I liked to be at the end of the line as we walked on to the pitch. Unfortunately, so did Jack Charlton. As the newcomer – and Jack's a bit bigger than me – I had to concede that privilege to him on that day.

Mooro finally led us out of the dressing room into the great cavernous tunnel that led up to the pitch. We filed up to the top of the tunnel and stood in line, Mooro at the head, Jack at the back. I was third from the back. We stood there for two or three minutes waiting for the Germans to emerge from their dressing room.

We could hear the crowd growing impatient as they waited for the players to leave the tunnel. All sorts of thoughts raced through my head. I remember thinking how lucky I was to be playing in the World Cup final at the age of twenty-two. I was desperate not to let the side down. Was it going to be our day? Or was it going to be their day?

We'd waited for what seemed several minutes when suddenly we could hear them coming, their boots resounding on the concrete surface of the tunnel. It was a chilling moment as the Germans filed up to the mouth of the tunnel. I glanced across – Seeler, Weber, Beckenbauer, Haller, Schnellinger, Overath. Yes, they had some great players.

Before that thought had time to take root, we were ushered forward. Both teams walked together into the sunshine to be greeted by a wall of noise. My life was about to change.

2

THE LURE OF THE RIVER

My dad, William Peters, was a Thames lighterman and I was very proud of the fact. When you lived in the East End of London in those days, your dad having a job at all was something that gave the family status and respectability, and being a lighterman was no ordinary job. It wouldn't have suited everyone but it was the job of my dreams. I wasn't going to be shut away in an office or factory. I was going to be on the river. Like a lot of Cockney families, we were dependent on the Thames for our livelihood and, when I was a kid, it was always assumed that I'd follow my dad on to the river. I loved the idea.

The Company of Watermen and Lightermen, among the oldest of the London livery guilds, produced some of the most colourful workers in the docks during the heyday of the Port of London. My dad was one of them.

It's hard to imagine today but London was once the busiest port in the world with wharves, extending for eleven miles, handling cargo from something like 60,000 ships a year. My dad worked on the barges in all the great docks – the East India, the Royal Albert, the King George V and the Millwall.

I was born in my grandmother's little house in Egham Road, Plaistow, just off the East India Dock Road. As a kid I could scamper down Prince Regent Lane for about half a mile to reach the Royal Victoria Dock. In the school holidays, my dad would take me on the great flat-bottomed barges that ferried the cargo between the ships and the quay or riverside factories. I soon discovered that he was a very popular figure with the other lightermen. They all seemed to have a very relaxed attitude to life despite the precarious nature of their trade.

They'd line up early most mornings at some pre-arranged venue – usually a pub – and wait for the foremen to come along and pick the men they needed. The riverside pubs played a big part in the lives of the lightermen, who were always at the mercy of the tides and currents. The barges relied solely on the river's current for motive force, and on long oars, or sweeps, for steering. The lightermen would ride the currents – upstream when the tide was coming in and downstream when it was going out. If the current wasn't favourable, they'd wait in the riverside pubs for the tide to turn. Sometimes they had to wait a long time. My dad had to be fished out of the Thames more than once, having fallen from his barge after a long period of spectacular relaxation in some distant pub down river.

The more I saw him work, the more I realised that it was an extremely skilled job, requiring an intimate knowledge of the river's current and tides. It also needed considerable strength to steer the barges and help with the loading and unloading.

It wasn't very highly paid but these were tough, uncomplaining, working-class men who had a sense of camaraderie that was similar to what I experienced later in football dressing rooms. Jerry Wright and one or two other old mates of my dad keep in touch with me but, sadly, their craft has all but disappeared.

The beginning of the end came in the sixties when the shipping industry adopted the newly invented container system of transportation. The London docks couldn't cope with the huge container ships and the industry moved to deep-water ports at Tilbury and Felixstowe. By 1980 the docks had closed, leaving a vast area of derelict land, unemployment and poverty. Eventually, it was all redeveloped when the Government created an Enterprise Zone and kick-started a property boom. What were once warehouses, piers, cranes, jetties and rows and rows of little terraced houses became high-rise office blocks, luxury apartments, Canary Wharf and the Millennium Dome. That's progress for you! It's just as well that I showed a talent for football. Otherwise I'd have been out of work like all the other lightermen. Back in the fifties, though, I wanted to work on the river. I didn't want to do anything else with my life.

I was born in November 1943 at a time when the East End, and particularly the docklands, remained a target for Hitler's bombers. My nan's little two-up two-down terraced house with outside toilet escaped the worst the Luftwaffe had to offer but there were times when the family had to retreat into the Anderson shelter in the backyard.

My grandmother, Daisy, shared her house with my mum, dad and me until we moved into a council house in Dagenham. My mum, Mary, worked as a waitress in a Lyon's cornerhouse in the West End and my dad worked on the river throughout the war. He'd had a bad accident on a motorbike, breaking a leg in two places, and this spared him military service.

My nan had been a widow for years. Her husband, Stanford – that's my middle name – had died in the First World War. Nan didn't have a job but she was a money-lender, which was not unusual among East Enders in those days. People were poorer than they are today and she'd lend a few shillings to the neighbours and collect a few pence interest.

Not long after I was born, Mum and I were evacuated to a village called Roden in the Shropshire countryside. Most children were taken out of London during the war. My mum's two sisters, Gladys and Phyllis, went as well, but my dad stayed in London to continue working. Fifty years later, when Mum was very ill, we took her back to the same place in Shropshire. She'd often said how much she wanted to revisit the 'big house'. I had no real memories of it. When we got there, the family in residence invited us in. It was an end-of-terrace house and certainly not big, although it must have seemed so at the time – or perhaps it was her memory playing tricks. Anyway, she was very happy to go back. She died not long after that.

After the war, we returned to London and I grew up playing football and cricket in the street with all the other kids. I remember racing up and down on my little tricycle, or in one of the go-karts we used to build from soap boxes, old pram wheels and planks of wood scavenged from bombsites.

I was sparely built as a youngster – there weren't many fat kids in those days – and my mum used to insist on giving me a spoonful of cod liver oil every day to build me up. I loathed that moment when she took the bottle out of the pantry and, even now, I shudder when I think of it.

My big treat in those days was a visit to the speedway to watch West Ham. Speedway was enormously popular in the years immediately after the war and attracted huge crowds to White City, Hackney Wick, Wimbledon and Custom House. I loved the noise and excitement and was fortunate because West Ham had one of the great riders of the day, Jack Young, an Australian who in 1951 beat Split Waterman and Jack Biggs to become the first rider to win the world title twice.

I had no thoughts of becoming a professional footballer although I loved playing and by the time I was about fourteen had started to build a bit of a reputation. One or two Football League scouts turned up on the touchlines to watch our games. I always assumed they were watching other players.

By this time the family had moved to the vast East London overspill estate in Dagenham and one of my teachers at Fanshawe School, Archie Hooper, had taken a particular interest in my progress on both the football and cricket fields. A tall, thin, amiable man, he was the sports master and gave up a lot of his spare time to escort boys from the school to football and cricket matches. I enjoyed cricket. I was a bit of an all-rounder and once won a Jack Hobbs bat for taking nine wickets for 17 runs for my school one lovely summer afternoon. I often wonder whether schoolteachers today devote the same amount of time to encouraging pupils to play football and cricket. Mr Hooper was a great influence on me at that stage of my young life. I stayed in touch with him until he died.

It was partly due to Mr Hooper that I was invited to take part in a trial for the England Schoolboys football team. I survived the first trial and was picked to play for the South against the North at West Bromwich Albion's ground. I did well enough to be selected for the final trial match, to be played at Ipswich between England and the Rest. I was picked to play at left-back for the Rest, which meant I had a bit to do. Alf Ramsey, who was manager of Ipswich at the time, was in the crowd at Portman Road. He had played at full-back for England and I was really pleased with myself in the dressing room afterwards when one or two adults said that my performance had reminded them of a young Ramsey.

In those days I played mostly at centre-half, although the schoolboy selectors tried me out at full-back and left-half. I didn't really mind where I played. I just enjoyed playing. I never pushed myself forward. I'd just wait and be happy if I was picked. I felt I was just a bit-part player on the schoolboy scene. The starring role belonged to someone else.

It was while playing for Dagenham Schoolboys that I first met a confident young man who was destined to become manager of England – Terry Venables. Even at that stage, Terry was a clever and highly promising midfield player. We became good friends despite being opposites in many ways. He was an extrovert while I was quiet and kept myself to myself. I suppose we were the two outstanding young players in Dagenham at that time. His dad, Fred, and my dad used to stand on the touchline comparing notes about their sons. They didn't live far from us and

I'd often go to Terry's house for tea. He'd stand in front of a mirror and, having checked that his hair was right, he'd do a Perry Como impression. He hasn't changed much over the years.

There's no doubt that he was an outstanding player and everyone predicted that he'd play for England one day. They were all correct. He played at every level, from schoolboy, youth, Under-23 and amateur to full senior international. To date, this is a unique achievement. No other footballer has played for England at every level.

Terry's talent as a creative player was obvious. I think mine was subtler and perhaps took a bit longer to develop but, even as a centre-half, I favoured playing my way out of trouble rather than simply hoofing the ball away. I think I had a bit more flair than the average central defender. I can remember flicking the ball over the centre-forward I was marking, running round him and instigating an attack. That was the kind of thing he was supposed to be doing to me!

Although I was playing in an age group that was a year above me – Terry is ten months older than me – I was clearly making an impression. The first scout to come to our house was from Fulham. He told my dad that I was good enough to go on the groundstaff at Craven Cottage, but he thought I was fifteen when I was only fourteen. My dad suggested he return the following year. I think Dad was quite relieved because he had made it clear that he didn't think professional football was a suitable career for me. He wanted me to follow him on the river.

Then, after the England Schoolboy trials, I was selected to play at left-back against Scotland at Derby. The local papers made a big fuss about it. They reminded their readers that Alf Ramsey and Jimmy Greaves were Dagenham boys who'd made the grade as professional footballers. They pointed out triumph-antly that Dagenham had produced an England Schoolboy for the second consecutive year. The previous year Terry had been capped. He was as pleased with my elevation as I was. I still have the telegram he sent me at the Baseball Ground on the day of the match.

However, I have to say there was an element of disappointment about my international debut. I didn't play badly, but the Scots beat us 3–2. England's goals that day were scored by another player who was to become a professional – Brian Dear, a left winger from East Ham. He and I later played together for West Ham in the First Division.

In all, I played six times for England Schoolboys and was particularly proud to be part of a half-back line that was given enormous credit for the 2–0 win over West Germany on a spring afternoon in 1959. The schoolboys from the two countries had met just three times before, with England winning twice and the other game drawn. This was the first time the two nations had met at Wembley and the game attracted a record crowd for a schoolboy international of 95,000. I'd never seen so many people in one place. The gate receipts were also a record for a schoolboy match – £18,950, which, in those days, was a small fortune.

Wolfgang Overath was in the opposition's team for the first of what would prove to be a series of encounters. He went on to become a great midfield player and we faced each other many times, most notably at Wembley in the 1966 World Cup final. Incidentally, the England captain that day was Chris Lawler, who went on to play 500 games for Liverpool, winning the league title and UEFA Cup with them, and to win four senior caps.

That Schoolboy international match was an unforgettable experience, made all the more pleasurable when the German manager Dettmar Cramer selected right-half Bobby Smith and me, at left-half, for special praise. 'They were England's match winners,' he said. Well, after that I was suddenly hot property. Some clubs, Fulham for instance, already had a file on me. Others knew more about me than I realised. The telegrams sent to me at Wembley that day included one from a Mr St Pier, who was keen that I should join his club.

Wally St Pier was perhaps the most famous and certainly the most successful scout of his day. At the time he was in his thirtieth season at West Ham, having started as a player. A big, smiling man, he had a crushing handshake that left your fingers numb.

He made a good impression when he met my father, who was slowly coming round to the reality that I was unlikely to become an apprentice lighterman. My dad came to trust Wally completely, and West Ham was in our neck of the woods. Tottenham came to see me and Arsenal invited me to Highbury. I remember being shown around the ground by the manager, George Swindin, and sitting in the directors' box to watch a match. Fulham were still in the background and, personally, I was inclined to favour Chelsea because Terry Venables had gone there and they had a good reputation for developing young players.

It wasn't as if I was a West Ham fan. I didn't really support any team. I certainly didn't watch West Ham as regularly as I watched the amateurs of Dagenham, my local club, which was just a bike ride away from home. I can remember going to watch Blackpool play at Upton Park in an FA Cup match specifically to see the great Stanley Matthews in action. I had no real boyhood footballing heroes but everyone acknowledged Matthews as one of the sporting icons of the time. These were the days before television, so all I knew of Stanley Matthews was what I read in the newspapers or was told by other boys in the school playground. There was still some mystery and intrigue attached to football and any kid who was lucky enough to see a match was pumped for information by all the other kids afterwards. Today there is no mystery – everyone knows everything about football because the TV coverage is so comprehensive.

At forty-three with thinning hair, Matthews was past his best when I saw him that day in 1958 but, for a youngster like me, it was still a privilege to watch him run along the wing with the ball at his feet. He had little influence on the outcome of the match. West Ham won 5–1 and Vic Keeble, whom I still see from time to time, scored a hat-trick.

As I discussed what to do with my life with Mum and Dad, Wally St Pier was the most influential outsider. My parents were still not totally convinced about the wisdom of football as a career when we went to see the West Ham manager, Ted Fenton, at Upton Park for an interview. Wally was present in Mr Fenton's office and he could see I was anxious. My dad had to be cajoled into allowing me to join the club and Wally was clearly delighted when Dad finally said, 'Well, if that's what you really want, Martin, you'd better sign the forms.' So that afternoon in May 1959 I signed for West Ham United as a ground-staff boy.

Despite what you might have heard about 'persuasion' money being offered to parents of aspiring players, no money changed hands. My parents asked for none and none was offered. We weren't well off, but we were never hungry. We were just an ordinary working-class family. My dad always had enough cash for his cigarettes and a bet on the horses. I used to run the money down to the 'man on the corner' – he always wore a hat and was a suspicious-looking character – in the days before betting offices became legal.

My first wage was £6 a week – £5 in the summer – and my duties included scraping the mud from the boots of the first-team players and helping to keep the dressing rooms tidy. Occasionally, we'd have to do a bit of painting around the ground. Among those who joined the club at the same time as I did were John Charles, Dave Bickles and Brian Dear, who all progressed to the first team.

I can remember cleaning boots in the dressing room in my first week at Upton Park, wondering whether I'd rather be sitting in the prow of a lighter, heading down river with the wind in my face and the Thames lapping at the bow. I realised that this was a great opportunity, one that most boys of my age could only dream about, and it was an exciting time but I was realistic. I knew, because Dad had pointed it out repeatedly, that within two years I could be out on my ear looking for work somewhere else if I failed to make the grade as a footballer. I had to knuckle down, work hard and listen to members of the coaching staff. I'd always played above my own age group so I felt I was ahead of the game in schoolboy football, but I quickly found out that among the West Ham groundstaff boys, I was just another hopeful.

3

A FAMILY AFFAIR

The West Ham playing staff reflected the local community, much as the playing staff today reflects the global nature of modern football. Most of the club's players in the early sixties came from within about ten miles of Upton Park and many were former groundstaff boys. Jackie Burkett, Harry Cripps, John Lyall, Joe Kirkup, Eddie Bovington, Ken Brown, Geoff Hurst, Mike Beesley, Bobby Moore, John Cartwright, Tony Scott, Andy Smillie and Derek Woodley had all preceded me through what was becoming one of the most productive youth schemes in football.

For the first few months, I sat quietly in a corner of the dressing room, carried out my duties diligently, trained hard, listened and learned. Despite my dad's liking for the attractions of the riverside pubs, home life was orderly and stable, and the values my parents had drummed into me and my younger brother David stood me in good stead. I was polite and willing, and increasingly able to do whatever was asked of me on the training pitch.

David was born seven years after me, so although we kicked a ball about in the back garden when he was a toddler, we never played serious football together. Once I went to watch him play in a Sunday morning league final in Dagenham. I arrived five minutes late to be told that he'd just been sent off, which was most unlike him. He was an amiable youngster who wore glasses and played the guitar, so I knew it had to be a miscarriage of justice.

Each day I travelled by bus from our house in Dagenham to Upton Park where a van took us boys to the training ground at Grange Farm in Chigwell. Occasionally, while I was waiting for the bus, Andy Malcolm would drive by and give me a lift. It was quite an honour for a groundstaff boy to arrive at training in the company of a first-team player.

I soon began to realise what a tough, competitive profession I'd chosen, but my dad had prepared me for this kind of challenge in life. He had instilled a work ethic in me and I made sure that no one worked harder than I did in training.

As Wally St Pier had told my parents, Ted Fenton had great faith in me. I will always be grateful to him for that. He clearly believed I had a chance of making it and signed me as a full professional in November 1960. He watched me in most defensive and midfield positions. I normally played right-half for the reserves and captained the Colts from right-back. Eventually, Ted encouraged me to settle at right-half.

He was one of the old-style football managers. A big, endearing character with a warm smile, he wore a Trilby hat and smoked a pipe. He was another East Ender, from Forest Gate. He had played for the club until the outbreak of the Second World War when he served as a PT instructor in North Africa and Burma. After the war, he managed Colchester, then in the Southern League, and was lured back to West Ham in 1950.

Remarkably, in the first half of the century the club had just two managers – Sid King (1902–32) and Charlie Paynter (1932–50). Ted remained as manager until 1961 when he left in circumstances that were never satisfactorily explained. The club said that he was suffering from strain and had been granted 'sick leave', but he never returned to Upton Park.

He looked after me in my early days with the club. Under his watchful eye I progressed through the junior ranks and was eventually chosen to play for the England Youth team. I made my debut against Scotland on a cold winter afternoon at Newcastle. Terry Venables and I filled the two wing-half positions and I was fortunate enough to set up England's equaliser for Tottenham's Frank Saul in a 1–1 draw.

Terry had postponed signing professional forms with Chelsea on his seventeenth birthday, as most youngsters did in those days, in order to qualify for a Youth cap. He'd already made his Football League debut when he played for the England Youth side. A week later, he played for the England amateur team against West Germany.

The Youth team coach was Billy Wright, the former England and Wolves captain and the first man to play 100 times for his country. He had been given charge of a young squad of England players of immense promise. He was one of the big names in the game at the time and it was a thrill to turn up for training when he was coaching.

As well as Terry, my England Youth team-mates included goal-keepers of the calibre of Gordon West and Jim Montgomery. My West Ham club-mates Ronnie Boyce, John Sissons and John Charles were also in the ranks of the England Youth squad, as were Graham Cross of Leicester City, Neil Young of Manchester City, John Sleeuwenhoek of Aston Villa, George Armstrong of Arsenal, Chris Lawler of Liverpool, and Chelsea's Alan and Ron Harris and Bert Murray. All these players worked their way through football's youth ranks and became top professionals. We were among the first to benefit from the facilities and amenities developed for young footballers in the years after the Second World War.

It may surprise you to know that before the war, organised competitive football for youngsters was practically non-existent. Then the Football Association appointed a 'minor' committee to promote football for youngsters, and in 1944–45 this committee suggested the introduction of the County Youth Championship, which was the forerunner of competitive youth football. The far-sighted Stanley Rous, then the FA secretary but later president of FIFA, inaugurated the International Youth Tournament in London in 1948. It was an immediate success and laid the foundations for competitive youth football worldwide.

I'm a great believer in the benefits of organised sport for youngsters and wish that more could be done to encourage young people to play competitive sport today. Too many kids seem to be more interested in sitting in an armchair, or pub, watching football on TV.

I rarely watched football purely for entertainment. That was time wasted. I'd rather be playing. Even Kathy, who was to become my wife, had to accept that our social life couldn't be allowed to disrupt my playing career. Luckily for me, she became my biggest supporter.

I'd seen Kathy Doris Winifred Ward a couple of times before I actually plucked up the courage to talk to her one night in the bowling alley in Dagenham. Bowling was just another of the sports I enjoyed, although I was never very good at it. She was a very attractive young lady – still is! I've never forgotten the evening I first talked to her. I remember it so well because it was the night before England played Portugal at Wembley in a World Cup qualifying tie in October 1961. She thinks it's typical of me that I remember the occasion because of a football match.

When we first met she asked me what I did and I told her that I played football.

'But what do you do for a job?' she asked.

I explained that I played football for West Ham and got paid for it. She didn't realise that you could play football for a living. Having got over that hurdle, I asked her out the following night. I was going with an official West Ham party to watch England at Wembley but suggested that we could meet later in the evening. She agreed and we went to a local dance in Key's Hall, Dagenham. I was in a particularly good mood because England had won 2–0, with Bobby Charlton and Ray Wilson in the team. I walked Kathy home that night and she came to watch me play for West Ham reserves the following Saturday. That was the beginning of a love affair that continues to this day.

She didn't much like football at first but her interest grew during our courtship. Most Saturdays she'd leave her job as a telephonist in the city at lunchtime and travel by tube train to watch me play for the reserves in the afternoon. We used to go everywhere together by bus or tube, but by the time I was selected to play for England in a Youth international against West Germany at Northampton in March 1962, my family had invested in our first car. My wages helped and between us my dad and I bought a blue Ford Popular for £450.

I was already in Northampton with the squad of England players when Kathy set out for the match with my mum and dad. As far as driving was concerned, my dad's 'comfort zone' was confined to the East End. Anywhere much farther afield and he risked getting lost. Well, he did on this occasion. North-ampton could have been on the other side of the world.

Kathy remembers him stopping the car on the outskirts of the town to ask a passer-by the way to the County Ground. My dad wound down the window and the pedestrian leaned in to the car to point out the route on a map. Dad had stopped the car on an incline and it started rolling backwards.

'William! William! Brake,' cried my mum from her seat in the back. 'Put the brake on, William.'

They got to the match in time to see me score in the eighteenth minute with a drive from about twenty yards. It was the only goal of the game but had it not been for the excellence of the German goalkeeper Sepp Maier, who would later play for the senior side, we would have scored a lot more goals. Billy Wright, who was developing a team to play in the International Youth

Tournament in Romania the following spring, was delighted with our performance. I still have a newspaper cutting at home with a headline that reads: 'Tireless Peters is Youth Star'. Happily, we all drove home together in the blue Popular.

My dad drove that car for years, although he never took a driving test. I have to be honest and say that, on occasions, I drove the car without a full licence, which, looking back now, was a stupid thing to do. I particularly remember one evening when a neighbour knocked on our door. We had no telephone in the house – people didn't in those days – and as this lady lived by the telephone booth a little way down our street, she would often answer if she heard the phone ringing.

On this occasion she answered and took a message for my mum from a pub in the Mile End Road. It was from Dad, who had simply said, 'Pick me up in the car.' He was obviously incapable of getting home on his own, so my mum and I climbed into the little Popular and set off for the Mile End Road. When we arrived, he was standing on the pavement arguing animatedly with a policeman. I was driving, but I hadn't passed my test. Mum sensed my unease and, as I drew the car up to the pavement, she leaned out of the window.

'William. Get in the car immediately,' she shouted. 'I'm sorry officer. I'll look after him now. Rest assured, I'll look after him good and proper!'

The policeman could tell from my mum's tone that Dad was in big trouble. He helped bundle him into the car, with me pretending to be outraged by such behaviour.

My mum and dad had lots of adventures in that little car as they monitored my progress with West Ham and England. I was a regular in the England Under-18 team until I was too old to qualify and by that time I was pressing for a place in West Ham's first team. By that time, Ted Fenton had been replaced by a man who was to have an enormous influence on my development as a footballer. Ron Greenwood took over as manager of West Ham in April 1961. I've always remembered his arrival because it coincided with the Russian cosmonaut Yuri Gagarin becoming the first man in space.

Ron was a north country man, from Burnley, and had played for Bradford, Brentford, Chelsea and Fulham, winning a League Championship medal with Chelsea in 1954–55. I was told at the time that he'd been a thoughtful centre-half and those who knew him were not surprised at the progress he'd made as a coach. Before he came to West Ham, he'd been coaching at Arsenal and looking after the England Under-23 team. I remember Bobby Moore saying, 'You want to learn? Well, there's no better teacher,' but as far as I was concerned he was an unknown quantity and, like any young player awaiting the arrival of a new manager, I was anxious. Although I had a pedigree at youth level, I still had a lot to prove and I hoped the new manager would give me a fair chance.

To start with, he gathered the entire playing staff on the pitch at Upton Park. We all lined up against the Chicken Run stand, a primitive but much-loved construction of timber and corrugated iron, now long gone, as he explained what he expected from us and what he hoped to achieve. Changes were evident within days, especially on the training pitch. The running spikes were binned. They're not used these days but when I was a youngster running spikes were an essential part of a player's training equipment. Ron told us that in future everything we did would be in football boots. All training, he said, would involve the use of the ball. This suited me perfectly. I was naturally fit and, if not particularly fast, I had great endurance. I didn't really need fitness work. I wanted to devote more time to my ball skills.

Under the previous regime, training had been more about running and fitness than technique and ball control. The exercise session I most disliked involved rising from a sitting position suddenly, on the whistle, and then sprinting. It was a race. I was almost always last. Having long legs, I was like a new-born foal getting to my feet and I didn't have the speed to catch up with the others. The cross-country races in Hainault Forest were a different matter. I'd often finish among the leaders.

We often lifted weights, too. They were not particularly heavy but when I began to develop back problems I wondered whether it was because we were lifting weights before our bodies were fully formed – we were still in our teens. Geoff Hurst, Ronnie Boyce and Jackie Burkett also suffered with back problems, and I think we were using weights too early.

It was soon apparent that Ron was a brilliant, innovative coach, and that he could improve any player who wanted to improve. I was one of them. It was an exciting, stimulating time and I couldn't wait to get on the training pitch each day.

I was eighteen, a regular in West Ham's reserves and captain of the England Youth team when the manager called me to one side on the training pitch in April 1962. It was just three weeks after I'd scored for the England Youth side at Northampton, but I had still to make my first-team debut for West Ham. He told me that he thought I was ready and that there was a chance I'd be playing in the next game – against Cardiff at Upton Park on Good Friday. I'd ricked my neck in training that week but I didn't say anything. I didn't want to jeopardise my chance of playing.

West Ham were comfortably placed in the middle of the old First Division, although we were struggling to score goals and had just lost 3–0 to Everton at Goodison Park. The following morning, waiting for the bus to take me to training, I saw the newspaper headlines: 'Greenwood axes six!' The boss, it seemed, had been planning a bit of a shake-up.

One or two big names, the papers said, had become complacent. He dropped the captain Phil Woosnam, centre-half Ken Brown, right-half Geoff Hurst, right-back John Bond, inside-right Ron Tindall and outside-left Malcolm Musgrove. I read that I was to play at right-half, taking Geoff's place in the side. It was too good an opportunity to miss. Ricked neck or not, I intended to play at Upton Park the next day.

A crowd of 25,459 watched the match. It wasn't a classic but if Cardiff, fighting against relegation, thought that a team packed with reserve-team players was going to be accommodating opposition, they were wrong. Every one of the reserves had something to prove, as did the man who was to become West Ham's greatest player. With Woosnam on the sidelines, Ron Greenwood made Bobby Moore captain that day. Bob presided over a 4–1 victory and the manager was so pleased that he strode into the dressing room immediately after the match and announced, 'Same team tomorrow, lads.'

Over the Easter holiday period, clubs would play three games in four days. So, twenty-four hours after beating Cardiff, the same team faced Arsenal at Upton Park in front of a crowd of 31,912. Bobby was captain again and I kept my place at right-half. This time it was an exhilarating match. Bobby was our inspiration. George Eastham was outstanding for Arsenal.

Tony Scott gave us the lead in the sixteenth minute but by the seventieth we were 3–1 down – and without our goalkeeper. After three minutes of the second half, Lawrie Leslie, Scotland's first-choice goalkeeper at the time, dived bravely at the feet of Geoff Strong and broke a finger. With no substitutes allowed, John Lyall, later to become manager, had to go in goal. I moved from right-half to fill John's place at left-back and Lawrie, clutching his broken hand, finished the match in my position on the right. He did exceptionally well, forcing two fine saves from the legendary Arsenal goalkeeper Jack Kelsey and, after John Dick had headed in my centre to make it 3–2, Lawrie won a corner on the right six minutes from time. From the corner Bill Lansdowne scored our equaliser.

Next day's newspapers made a big fuss of Lawrie – 'Keeper Leslie dazzles on the wing' read the headlines. He was our hero and deserved the acclaim. I was mentioned at the bottom of one report. I cut it from the pages of the paper and stuck it in a scrapbook. It read: 'Geoff Hurst may have the hardest job winning back his place, for eighteen-year-old Peters, at wing-half, showed all the promise and poise expected of an England Youth-team skipper.'

We had Easter Sunday off but on the Monday we made our way to Paddington railway station to catch a train to Cardiff. Lawrie Leslie was obviously ruled out of the game at Ninian Park because of his broken finger, so Ron called up his under-study, Brian Rhodes. Brian was a former Essex Schoolboy goal-keeper who had few first-team opportunities during his ten years at Upton Park. He was to die tragically young of leukaemia.

Sadly, the game against Cardiff didn't go well for him. We were already losing 2–0 when he fell heavily in the sixty-fifth minute, dislocating his right collar bone. As we gathered round poor Brian, prone on the pitch, I heard one of my team-mates say, 'Go on, Mart! You go in goal. You've played in goal before.'

It was true. I had played in goal, replacing Brian when he was injured during a reserve match. So I volunteered and was given the green goalkeeper's jersey. I did my best and made three saves that I was quite proud of, but there was nothing I could do to keep out Derek Tapscott's diving header from Dai Ward's cross. That goal gave Cardiff a 3–0 victory, although it only delayed the inevitable. They were relegated the following week and were to spend most of the next fifty years trying to regain their place among the game's élite.

As I was soaking off the Ninian Park mud in the communal bath after the match, Ron Greenwood was telling reporters that 'Young Peters is a real player, one of the most versatile I've come across.' In the space of four days I'd made my first-team debut and in three games played at right-half, left-back and goalkeeper. I played in the two remaining matches that season, against Bolton and Fulham, at right-half.

The die was cast. I was versatile. I could use either foot. I could play on the right side or the left side. I could even play in goal. I was useful to have in the squad. Being versatile had great advantages but it also had drawbacks, as I would discover in the years ahead.

4

THE UPTON PARK INNOVATOR

No individual contributed more to my development as a professional footballer than Ron Greenwood, so you will understand my sadness when he died in February 2006 at the age of eighty-four. We never enjoyed the warmest of relationships but I have to acknowledge that his coaching opened my eyes to what could be achieved with hard work and self-belief. Ted Fenton gave me my chance but it was Ron who helped me develop into an international-class player. I found his coaching ideas fresh and challenging. He liked to work with players who wanted to learn, and I was one of them.

The 'kick and rush' football that I'd grown up with had no place in the Greenwood coaching manual. Thoughtful and patient, he introduced new training ideas and then challenged us to use what we had learned in match situations.

He was a quiet, scholarly sort of coach, who valued his privacy away from football. When he was teaching a new skill or tactical concept, he was a great communicator, but other areas of his life remained a closed book to the players. He rarely mixed with us away from the training pitch.

To outsiders, he gave the impression that he was totally immersed in his world of training and tactics. Some interpreted this as aloofness and, at times, you sensed an air of superiority about him, but he was obviously the man the club wanted because bringing in an outsider went against long-held tradition. He was West Ham's fourth manager and the first not to have had a previous association with the club. I wonder now whether his appointment was an admission by the board of directors that they had not got it right with Ted Fenton, and they felt that Ron was the man to restore the club's stature.

The truth was that West Ham's immediate past was so mediocre that winning anything was a novelty. Bear in mind, too, that West Ham's supporters were no different from those of any other club. For them, winning was, and still is, what matters. Public relations may not have figured high on Ron's agenda but, provided the team were winning, nothing else much concerned the fans.

For a young player, though, the most important thing was to create a good impression in front of Mr Greenwood. I was a respectful boy – most kids in those days acknowledged the authority of their seniors. He was the manager and I was one of his most junior players. I listened and learned. I arrived on time each morning and trained for as long and as hard as I could. I thought he was a fantastic coach. He taught me more about the game than anyone else. He told me that the good habits I picked up as a young player would stay with me throughout my career – bad habits, too. He was right about both.

Ron's first game in charge was a 1–1 draw with Manchester City at Upton Park in April 1961. Tottenham were about to become the first club that century to secure the league and FA Cup double, while West Ham were embroiled in a fight against relegation. Before Ron took over, we had won just three of seventeen match-es and that might, in part at least, explain the demise of Ted Fenton. Although Ron won none of his first four games at the end of that season, West Ham avoided the drop by four points.

After my first-team debut over Easter 1962, I kept my place for the last five games of the season – we finished eighth – and started the new season at left-back against Aston Villa. We lost 3–1. I was then given Geoff Hurst's No. 4 shirt – he was left out – and asked to play at right-half, where I spent most of the season. I also wore the No. 6 and No. 10 shirts. I remember reading a comment by Ron Greenwood in which he agreed that the fans did not always appreciate my contribution. 'He's not a typical English player but he's the answer to a manager's prayer,' he said.

It was no coincidence that Geoff, Bobby Moore and I all flourished in the environment Ron created at Upton Park in the early sixties. All three of us wanted to learn and improve. Ron liked his players to visualise what it was they were trying to achieve. 'You need to have pictures in your mind,' he used to tell us at training. What he meant was that we should all be able to envisage what was happening around us. This was an essential element in the fast, one-touch football he tried to encourage. To play that way successfully – a bit like Arsene Wenger's Arsenal – you have to be totally confident in the whereabouts of your team-mates. You need to know where they're coming from, and where they're going to.

When Ron was showing us a new tactic or passing move-ment, he'd walk us through it a few times until we got the hang of it. He encouraged us to play forward passes rather than pass sideways. He taught us the value of the wall pass and we devel-oped passing strategies that carried us through the heart of opposing defences.

Much of what he taught us remains relevant today. So many of Ron's ideas are still applied successfully in the modern game and, over the years, top coaches such as Sir Bobby Robson, Don Howe, Dave Sexton and Terry Venables have acknowledged the debt they owe him.

In the sixties he was looked upon as something of an inno-vator, but we couldn't always get it right on the pitch. We made a desperate start in 1962–63, my first full season in the senior team. Three straight defeats in our first three games, including a 6–1 trouncing by Spurs, meant extra work on the training pitch.

We were still bottom of the table when Ron demonstrated his ability to recognise what wasn't apparent to others. In this case, Geoff Hurst was the beneficiary of Greenwood's foresight. Geoff had started the season at left-half but Ron dropped him and sent him to play in the reserves. After one particularly poor performance in a reserve match against Shrewsbury, Ron called Geoff to his office. The club had tried to offload him to Crystal Palace some months earlier as part of the record deal that bought Johnny Byrne to Upton Park, so Geoff feared the worst, but he was in for a surprise. Ron told Geoff he was selecting him for the first-team game against Liverpool at Upton Park the following day – at centre-forward. Geoff wore the No. 10 shirt and did well enough to keep it for the rest of the season and for the rest of his career.

We beat Liverpool 1–0 and, five days later, beat Manchester City 6–1. I scored my first West Ham goal at Maine Road, just before half-time, but when Malcolm Musgrove scored our fifth in the seventieth minute, the Manchester City goalkeeper flew into a rage – and when Bert Trautmann flew into a rage, you took notice. A German paratrooper in the Second World War, his reputation as a fearless goalkeeper was due partly to his astonishing performance in the 1956 FA Cup final when, unknowingly, he played the last twenty minutes with a broken neck and helped City to win 3–1.

It was an honour to play against him but I was surprised by his reaction when Musgrove scored. Bert insisted Malcolm was offside and was so angry that he ran to the halfway line and kicked the ball into the back of referee Keith Stokes, who had no choice but to send him off. Alan Oakes went in goal.

If such an extraordinary incident was repeated today, it would fill the headlines for days and bring down the wrath of the football authorities on the head of the culprit. It would have been seen by millions on TV and be discussed and debated at length by the intelligentsia, but in 1962 there was no significant TV coverage of league football. Bert was hugely popular and I don't think the incident did his reputation any serious damage. A former prisoner-of-war, he chose to remain in England when the fighting ended in 1945. He was voted Footballer of the Year in 1956 and was asked to present the award to his countryman Jurgen Klinsmann of Spurs when he won the title in 1995.

Our form in 1962–63 remained indifferent although I felt I was playing well enough. Ron obviously felt the same because he recommended me to the England coach Walter Winterbottom for my first Under-23 cap. Walter had already named his squad to play Belgium at Plymouth in November 1962 but had lost two players who were rivals for the left-half position. Alan Deakin of Aston Villa and Malcolm Beard of Birmingham had been forced to pull out because of injury. Walter asked Ron if he could have Bobby Moore, already an established full England international, to deputise at left-half. Ron said, 'Why don't you have a look at Martin Peters?'

It was my big chance. I played well against Belgium – Alan Mullery and Bobby Tambling were team-mates – and scored two goals in a 6–1 win. Walter Winterbottom obviously liked what he saw because three weeks later he selected me again for the Under-23 team to play Greece in Birmingham. England won 5–0 and Bobby Tambling scored a hat-trick.

That summer I added significantly to my education when I travelled with West Ham's first-team squad to New York to take part in an international club tournament on Randall's Island. Ron was one of the new breed of coaches who believed we could learn from the development of the game in other countries. America wasn't a football hotbed by any means but the prospect of playing against the teams from France, Italy, Mexico, West Germany, Brazil, Poland and Czechoslovakia who had also entered, excited Ron. He loved watching foreign football and always cited the great Hungarian team and their victory over

England at Wembley in 1953 as a defining moment in his own football career.

The journey from London took about fourteen hours and we stayed in self-catering apartments on the corner of East 86th and Madison. I shared my accommodation with Geoff Hurst and Ronnie Boyce. We were the three unmarried members of the squad.

The club gave us five dollars a day spending money. It wasn't a lot but I was determined to save as much of mine as I could because I was planning to get married as soon as I could afford it. The others took the mickey out of me when I refused to go shopping or squeezed three cups of tea from one teabag.

The tournament involved two groups of clubs with the winner of each group scheduled to meet in the final. We lost just one of our group games, to Mantova of Italy, a skilful team who beat us 4–2. Our qualifying record was good enough to take us through to the final where we met Gornik of Poland, who included Wlodimierz Lubanski in their ranks. The unknown seventeen year old was to become one of the all-time greats of Polish football. We won 3–2 over two legs and then met Dukla of Czechoslovakia for the Challenge Cup.

They were a superb team and had five of the Czech side that had played in the World Cup final the previous summer. Although they beat us 2–1 over two legs, the experience we gained from that summer in the United States was to prove invaluable when we began our first season of European competition a year later.

I was nineteen, I'd captained the England Youth team, made my Under-23 debut and had now had a taste of continental football. I was beginning to feel that not only could I cope but that I could actually do quite well in my chosen career. I was taking nothing for granted, though. I knew there was plenty of room for improvement.

In all, I played five times for the England Under-23 team

and, although I was by then an established first-team player at West Ham, I still could not say with honesty which was my best position – nor, for that matter, could anyone else, including Ron Greenwood.

In my first three seasons I wore six different shirt numbers – seven if you include my emergency spell as goalkeeper. By the time I'd finished at West Ham I'd worn all eleven shirts. I even had a short spell at centre-forward where my lack of real pace weighed heavily against me.

As a kid, I was happy to play anywhere as long as I was in the team but, after a while, I began to wonder whether my usefulness was preventing me from establishing myself as a specialist in one position. Ron moved me about regularly between the midfield and defensive positions. I often filled in for players who were injured or suffering a loss of form. At least I was playing. In my first full season I appeared in 36 of our 42 First Division matches. Only Bobby Moore, Ken Brown and Jack Burkett played more often. In my second season I played in 32 games in the First Division and was ever-present until Boxing Day when, suddenly, I came face to face for the first time with the harsh realities of life in professional football.

Over that Christmas holiday in 1963 West Ham played Blackburn Rovers twice in three days. Most West Ham fans of that era will tell you the significance of those two matches against Rovers. For me, they have a special resonance, even now more than forty years later.

I'd enjoyed an almost unbroken run of first-team action for the previous eighteen months when we met Rovers at Upton Park on Boxing Day. They were the First Division leaders, unbeaten in their previous ten games, and had an outstanding player in Bryan Douglas, the little England winger. Even so, few in the 20,501 crowd that day could have imagined they were about to witness West Ham's record defeat. Blackburn's 8–2 victory remains West Ham's heaviest defeat to this day.

The rout on a mud heap of a pitch began after just five minutes when Fred Pickering scored from eighteen yards. Our main tormentor was the mischievous Douglas. After Johnny Byrne had equalised and then hit the bar, Douglas restored Blackburn's lead in the twenty-ninth minute and created goals for Andy McEvoy and Mike Ferguson. In the second half, with Douglas skipping about on the mud, McEvoy made it 5–1, Pickering scored two more to complete his hat-trick and then McEvoy scored his third.

By the time Byrne scored our second goal after sixty-one minutes, a stunned crowd was already streaming home, Christmas ruined for many of the Upton Park loyalists among them. Christmas was ruined for me, too. Losing like that was a bitter experience but I didn't immediately realise the full consequences of the defeat.

The boss didn't appear in our dressing room afterwards. Apparently, he wanted to avoid saying anything he might regret, and he wanted to think about the line-up for the return match in two days' time. Ron decided on just one change but I wasn't aware of it until we got to Blackburn the following day – Eddie Bovington was given my place in midfield.

Although I'd been troubled by a slight knee injury and hadn't played well in the first game – no one had – I felt hurt by the decision to make me the scapegoat for that big defeat. Later, I could understand the manager's decision but at the time I was angry. He wanted Douglas marked man for man and felt that Eddie, who was a tough, efficient midfield player, was better equipped for the job. I had not yet fully appreciated that the very best players were those who could mix clever, creative play with tackling and defensive duties.

With Eddie marking Douglas, West Ham beat Blackburn 3–1 on a soaking wet pitch. It was a remarkable turnaround and the change in fortune was attributed to Ron's tactical acumen. He was delighted. I was still angry, and I would get angrier.

Eddie retained his place in the side for the next match – the third round of the FA Cup against Charlton at Upton Park. We won that 3–0 so naturally Ron wanted to keep an unchanged team again. Eddie kept the No. 4 shirt for the rest of the season. I played only intermittently, a total of eight First Division games, filling in when required. I didn't play in any of the FA Cup ties as West Ham ousted first Charlton and then Leyton Orient, Swindon Town and Burnley before beating Manchester United 3–1 in an epic semi-final at Hillsborough. Eddie played in all of them. I sat in the rain at the side of the pitch at Hillsborough and watched, my resentment at my personal loss mixed with delight at watching my team-mates progress to Wembley. On the train home to London that evening, the players celebrated reaching the FA Cup final in the dining car. I just didn't feel a real part of it. I felt as if I was on the fringe. My place in the Cup final team was disappearing before my eyes.

It was a difficult time for me. As it became increasingly obvious that I wasn't going to figure in the FA Cup matches, I decided to make my feelings clear to the manager. I was not the sort of person to kick up a fuss and was apprehensive when I knocked on Ron's door, having rehearsed what I wanted to say. I told him that I was fed up with being moved from one position to another. I told him that my failure to pin down one position and make it my own had probably cost me my only chance of playing in the FA Cup final. I even asked Ron to say which position he felt was my best. He couldn't answer that. What he did say was, 'I'll tell you one thing – you'll play at Wembley more times that I eat in the stadium restaurant.'

Ron was sympathetic but clearly wasn't going to bend. He was happy with the form of the team and I had to agree that Eddie was playing well. He had a different style from me but was a good player who deserved his chance. I was just a youngster and Ron told me it was a test of character. It was my first set-back, he pointed out. There would be others – better get used to them.

Good professionals, he said, overcame their disappointments.

He was right but missing the FA Cup final in 1964 was the biggest disappointment of my career. I never got another chance and, as with all kids who play football, it had been a long-held ambition. West Ham hadn't played in the final since the famous 'White Horse' final against Bolton Wanderers in 1923, which was the first to be played in the new Wembley stadium. So, inevitably, the 1964 match against Preston North End was a big occasion in East London. I felt I should have been in a starring role, rather than in the supporting cast.

I got tickets for my mum and dad and was part of the squad at Wembley but after our 3–2 win I stood self-consciously on the edge of the pitch as Bobby Moore and the others paraded the Cup. I tried to join in the merry-making but it didn't come naturally. The consolation that day was that our win ensured we'd be playing in the European Cup Winners' Cup the following season – an arena in which Greenwood's style of football would really blossom.

Ron was one of the most influential coaches of his generation – later he became England manager – and although the style of play he developed may not have been conducive to the nine-month slog of the championship, some of the football West Ham played in his time was memorable. Europe was the real prize, the test for which he had worked and waited. Up until then, Spurs had been England's only European winners, but Ron felt sure that West Ham had the players to cope with the challenge and, after my disappointment, I felt quite proud when he told me that my game was ideally suited to European football. First, though, I had to get my place back in the team.

5

FOOTBALLERS' WIVES

I consoled myself in the summer of 1964 by listening to the new offshore pirate radio stations – 'House of the Rising Sun' by The Animals was the big hit – and thinking that if any of eight or nine of my West Ham team-mates had been injured in the build-up to the FA Cup final, I would have been called into the side. Ron Greenwood knew I was versatile enough to have played in all those positions if needed – but did he believe I was good enough to hold down one position regularly?

Kathy and I were looking at houses and planning our wedding for that November so there was plenty to think about. It was good to have her to talk to, because she could help me look at things in a better perspective.

I wasn't as badly off as John Lyall, for instance. The tough England Youth international had seemed to have an excellent career ahead of him as a full-back with West Ham. He'd grown up in a similar environment to me and was making good progress until, at eighteen, he had his first knee ligament operation. In the years that followed he was in and out of the team and in and out of hospital. Finally, after yet another comeback match, this time against the Metropolitan Police at Imber Court, he was told he should never play again. He was twenty-three and had a wife, a son and a mortgage, but he took it all in his stride. Ron Greenwood encouraged him to start coaching at Stepney School and, thirteen years later, John succeeded Ron as manager of West Ham.

John's sadness and my own frustrations were nothing, though, compared to the tragedy that unfolded across London at White Hart Lane that summer. One of the great players of that era, John White, was killed by lightning while sheltering under an oak tree near the first fairway on the Crews Hill golf course in north London. Aged just twenty-seven, he was a Scotland international, had played in the Tottenham double team of 1961 and was one of the big names in the First Division. I remember how shocked I felt when I heard the news. I'd played against him the previous September when he created two of the Spurs goals in their 3–0 win over us.

At least I had some sort of future as a player, and hopefully it would be with West Ham, but I was still bitterly disappointed at missing the FA Cup final. Kathy and many of my club-mates, including John, convinced me that I would have a big role to play at West Ham in the coming season.

When I told the club I planned to buy a house, I was encouraged when they agreed to act as guarantors. This, I explained to them, was one of the conditions demanded by our mortgage company. Kathy and I had been looking at houses on the County Park Estate in Hornchurch, which was a new development of three and four-bedroomed houses that had caught the eye of several players at West Ham. It was a pleasant, unpretentious Essex estate, but not the sort of place today's millionaire players would choose.

We arranged our wedding for 8 November at St Martin's Church in Dagenham. It was my twenty-first birthday. Kathy was nineteen. Too young? Perhaps. That's certainly what my parents thought. They insisted that I wait until I was at least twenty-one before getting married. Initially, they wouldn't give their blessing so Kathy and I decided that, with or without their support, we'd marry on my twenty-first birthday.

Not only did Mum and Dad believe we were too young but they were unhappy that I was marrying a Roman Catholic girl. Kathy had been raised as a Catholic and one of the conditions placed upon us by the church was that our children had to have a Catholic education. My parents weren't happy about any of it and even Kathy, for many years afterwards, felt troubled by the fact that she'd married outside the Catholic faith. Such religious considerations are rare today but were quite common when we married. Kathy's Catholicism presented no problem to me, although I didn't want our children to have to adhere to the restrictions imposed by the Catholic church.

Happily, our love was strong enough to overcome any obstacle, and still is after more than forty years of marriage. That's not to say that the path of true love always ran smoothly. I remember one incident before we were married when a row developed during the course of the evening. We were driving in the little blue Poplar I shared with my dad. She demanded I stop the car and as she leapt out she took off her engagement ring and threw it at me.

'You know what you can do with that,' she snapped.

I didn't know quite what to do, so I drove off a little sheepishly, leaving her on the pavement. She told me later that I was not supposed to do that. I was supposed to get out of the car and beg forgiveness!

When I drove off, she ran across the road, barged past four blokes getting out of a taxi and, in the famous line from the movies, demanded that the taxi driver, 'Follow that car.' As I was drawing up to the pavement outside my parents' house, she jumped out of the cab and ran up to me.

'Mart! Mart! Can I have the ring back?' she said.

I gave it to her and asked her to get into the car.

'I'll walk home, thank you very much!' she retorted. Later, she explained that she didn't want me to think that I'd enjoyed *total* victory that evening.

Anyway, we married as planned. My pal Joe Kirkup was best man. Joe progressed with me through the Upton Park youth ranks and spent eight years at the club before joining Chelsea and later Southampton. When he finally hung up his boots he emigrated with his family to South Africa and succeeded Johnny Byrne as player-manager of Durban City. When he came back to England, he had a variety of jobs running pubs, newsagents and a sports shop. Then he and his wife Jill retired to France. We're still friends and I see him from time to time at reunions.

The day before the wedding, I was in the team to play Blackburn Rovers. We drew 1–1, John Sissons scoring our goal. I was determined there would be no repeat of Rovers' last visit – the costly 8–2 trouncing they gave us the previous season. It was my eleventh consecutive First Division match that season. I had been playing at left-back but that day I wore Bobby Moore's No. 6 shirt. Bobby wasn't selected. We were told he'd gone to hospital for tests. It later emerged that he had a testicular problem that required surgery. He was out of action that season from the beginning of November until the middle of February. When he came back to the club everyone asked him how he was, but no one asked him the nature of the problem. Bobby was a considerable figure at West Ham, even then, and would not have welcomed questions of that nature from young players. 'Mooro', as he was often known, kept many elements of his life off the pitch to himself and everyone respected his wish for privacy. I'm not sure the same would apply today.

Twenty-four hours after drawing with Blackburn, Kathy and I were married and moved into our new house in Hornchurch. The house we had eventually settled on was a semi-detached property, costing about £3000. It had the advantage of adjoining Judith and Geoff Hurst's place. By this time, Geoff had enjoyed two good seasons in the first team and was establishing a reputation as a goalscorer. Judith and Kathy were already good friends. Geoff and Judith got married just before us and

Kathy was Judith's bridesmaid. If Judith was having a coffee morning, Kathy would jump from our coalbunker on to the Hurst's coalbunker and go in through the kitchen door. The lives of footballers' wives in those days were clearly not as glamorous as the lives of the wives of today's stars.

For Kathy and I, it was the start of a lifelong friendship with Geoff and Judith. In the fullness of time we used to babysit for each other and on occasions either Kathy or Judith would cook for both families and dinner plates would be handed back and forth across the fence.

Quite a little clutch of players from Upton Park lived within a few hundred yards of each other on that estate. As well as Geoff and Judith, we spent a lot of time with Ronnie and Dawn Boyce, Brian and Jan Dear, John and Janice Sissons and Jackie and Ann Burkett. I remember going out in a group one night in the car when London was shrouded in the kind of fog we don't see these days. It was so thick that Ronnie Boyce had to get out of the car and walk in front just to keep us on the road.

Although they didn't live so close, we also socialised occasionally with Bobby Moore and his first wife Tina. For a long time, Kathy, Judith and Tina were really good friends. Bobby was a bit older than I was, and already an established England international, on the way to becoming a world-class player. He and Tina had a wide and sophisticated circle of people they mixed with regularly. I remember Geoff telling me once that he sometimes used to say he was a friend of Bobby Moore's just to get a table in a restaurant!

Occasionally, Kathy and I would go out for dinner in an east London pub with John Bond and Kenny Brown and their wives. I remember the night my car was stuck in thick mud in the pub car park. We couldn't move it so John announced that he would push it out. He positioned himself at the back of the car, started to push and told me, sitting in the driver's seat, to press the accelerator pedal gently. The inevitable happened and John was splattered with mud.

I guess that, compared to today's multi-millionaire football stars, our social lives were pretty tame. Some nights we'd go to the cinema and on other occasions a group of us would meet and play cards for a few shillings while the wives sat and gossiped and drank sherry.

It was a relief finally to have our own home. Buying the house had been complicated by West Ham's attitude to the matter of guaranteeing the mortgage. Although they'd agreed this in principle, when it came to signing the paperwork they decided they wanted something in return. Ron Greenwood called me in one day and told me that the club would happily stand as guarantors for my mortgage, providing I signed a new two-year contract.

That took me a little by surprise. I wasn't impressed with their tactics but I accepted their terms and signed on the dotted line. At least it meant that they considered I had a future in football and wanted me to continue with the club.

Kathy and I were very raw in these financial dealings. No one in either family had any experience of mortgages or of buying houses. Fortunately, we received help from Jack Turner, who had an office at Upton Park. The sign on his door said 'Property Manager'. Very few people outside the club had much idea what he did.

A lifelong West Ham fan, Jack was working in the insurance business when Reg Pratt, chairman from 1950–79, asked him to help administer the club's houses. In the years after the Second World War, West Ham bought several houses in East London to rent to their players. They found this was a way of enticing players, particularly those from the provinces, to join the club. Jack's role broadened and eventually he was offering West Ham players financial advice. He set up a scheme whereby money was deducted from weekly wage packets and invested in building societies. A lot of players made use of his advice, although some, notably Malcolm Allison, looked upon him as an outsider and wanted nothing to do with him.

As well as dealing with property and finances, Jack had another, less obvious, role at the club, which involved scouting for young players. Not many people know this, but Jack made the first report to West Ham on the young Bobby Moore. He wasn't very impressed but said that Bobby was worth another look. In fact, he and Bobby had a long association. As Bobby's fame grew, so did Jack's influence. He created Bobby Moore Limited and took care of all his promotional activities. He helped Bobby to set up his sports shop opposite Upton Park and, at one time, Bobby earned more from this than he did from the club.

In later years, I suspected that Jack's success in establishing close ties with individual players irritated Ron Greenwood. The two were never close, but their relationship worsened. Ron clearly didn't want him at the club and, in the end, the chairman asked Jack to leave. The official explanation for his departure was that he no longer fitted in at West Ham. Jack was bitter about it for years afterwards.

In a sense, Jack Turner was the forerunner of today's football agents. He was probably the first to recognise the scope for such a role in professional football. His job initially involved administering club property but developed into a wide-ranging role that encouraged players to gain greater control over their own futures. In such circumstances, clashes with the club management were almost inevitable. Nonetheless, I was very grateful to Jack at the time. Partly due to his advice, by the time Kathy and I married I'd saved nearly £1000 to put down as a deposit on the house. We invited him to our wedding.

Marriage, I must say, did me no harm at all. Six days after the wedding I scored one of our goals when we beat Arsenal 3–0 at Highbury. I scored another one when we beat Leeds 3–1 a week later and again in the next match when we won 3–0 at Chelsea.

At the same time, we were progressing impressively in the European Cup Winners' Cup. In the first round, a Ronnie Boyce goal secured a 1–0 win over the part-timers of La Gantoise in Belgium. It was as well we won because we were terrible in the home leg. The crowd jeered and slow-handclapped. I mis-hit a back pass beyond our goalkeeper Alan Dickie – an own goal that gave La Gantoise the lead. Fortunately, Johnny 'Budgie' Byrne equalised just before half-time, which was enough to put us into round two, where we faced Sparta Prague, the pacemakers at the top of the Czech First Division. By this time we were without Bobby Moore, and Ron Greenwood gambled massively by playing Ronnie Boyce as a sweeper both at home and away. Ronnie was brilliant, and an influential figure in ensuring we didn't concede a goal at home. We won the first leg 2–0, John Bond and Alan Sealey scoring, and although we lost the second leg 2–1 in Prague, we advanced confidently to the quarter-finals.

Lausanne, bristling with Swiss internationals, were our next opponents. We played them after a really bad run of form in the First Division but Bobby Moore was back to bring his authority to bear. We won the away leg 2–1 and beat them 4–3 at Upton Park in a memorable match. I scored, but the night belonged to Brian Dear. He'd had few first-team opportunities that season but scored twice against the Swiss, his winning goal coming in the final minute and giving us a 6–4 aggregate victory.

That win put us in the semi-finals. Our opponents were Real Zaragoza of Spain. Brian kept his place in the team for the first leg at Upton Park because he was on fire and, yes, he scored again, his eighth goal in eight games. 'Budgie' hit the other and we defended our lead for most of the second half. The fans didn't like it.

Brian – 'Stag' to all the lads in the dressing room – was enjoying the best period of his career. A few days after that win over the Spanish side we played West Bromwich Albion at

Upton Park in the First Division. We won 6–1 and Stag hit five goals in twenty minutes, still a record for a First Division match.

A natural goalscorer, Stag could have enjoyed a long and illustrious career at West Ham if he'd had a more disciplined approach to training. He liked to have a laugh and would occasionally overstep the mark. One time he snatched a peach from me and refused to return it. We'd just left a café not far from Upton Park and on the way home I'd stopped to buy some fruit. The peach wasn't important but the principle was. I had a quiet, easygoing nature and sometimes people took advantage of that. I rarely lost my temper but I did on this occasion and punched him hard in the face. You could say he was surprised. He gave me back the peach immediately and never stepped out of line with me again. I suppose my reaction might have been a bit excessive but as a teenager Stag could be a real irritant. He enjoyed teasing people and on this occasion he was being, well, just Stag! We laugh about it today. I've known him since I was ten and I guess he's one of my best friends.

A week after Stag's five goals against Albion we took our slender 2–1 lead to Spain for the second leg of the semi-final. Zaragoza were an outstanding attacking team. Their forward line was known as 'The Magnificent Five'. Ron Greenwood told us they would attack and our chances would be few, so we would have to make the most of any opportunity we got.

Zaragoza scored first but when a half chance fell to nineteen-year-old Johnny Sissons he took it with aplomb. The Spaniards claimed they were denied three penalties, but the match ended 1–1. West Ham had reached another final and, happily, this one was to be played at Wembley.

Our opponents were TSV Munich 1860 of West Germany, and it was our very good luck that the first-team squad had had the chance to watch them in action twice before the big day. During pre-season training, while on tour in Europe, we had passed through Munich where Tommy Docherty's Chelsea were playing them. As we knew then that they would be in the Cup Winners' Cup, Ron suggested we watch them.

Eight months later, after our win over Zaragoza, TSV Munich had to meet Torino of Italy in a semi-final play-off in Zurich. It was typical of Ron that he suggested to the club that he take the entire first-team squad to Zurich to watch our opponents. 'It will be educational,' he insisted when the cost of such a project was mentioned.

Ron got his way. We all went to Zurich where we sat in the open air in a violent thunderstorm as Munich 1860 beat the Italians 2–0. From the players' point of view, it gave us an invaluable insight into the strengths and weaknesses of the opposition and it was also a very useful team bonding exercise.

The final itself was a wonderful occasion, especially memorable for me, having missed out on our last big day at Wembley. Ron's team that day showed several key changes from the one that had been on duty in the FA Cup final. The whole right side changed, with Joe Kirkup taking over from John Bond at right-back, me replacing Eddie Bovington at right-half and Alan Sealey selected ahead of Peter Brabrook on the right-wing. However, perhaps the most significant change was in our attack. Budgie Byrne was missing, having picked up a knee injury playing for England against Scotland at Wembley. His place went to Brian Dear.

Ron Greenwood initially described the loss of Budgie as an almighty blow. It was, too. We all felt it. Budgie was one of the great players of the time. West Ham had signed him from Crystal Palace in March 1962 for £65,000, a record between English clubs. He was already an England international, even though he had been playing for Palace in the Third Division. Geoff Hurst benefited enormously from his arrival. Geoff was happy to shoulder the donkey-work while Budgie employed his pace, ball control and alert mind in the penalty area. He had great balance, good footwork, a wonderful ability to volley the ball and a knack of controlling it on his chest, something that Geoff took note of and, in time, became adept at himself. The two of them developed a really productive relationship on the pitch.

Budgie was so quick, his touch so sure, that big defenders hated playing against him. The quality of his control was in the Bergkamp class and he could touch the ball round one side of a defender and sprint round the other side to collect it. Ron often described him as 'the Di Stefano of British football'.

He had an aggressive streak, too, and he liked to win, but sometimes I wondered whether he took it seriously enough. He loved a party and a good time. He was as sharp as a needle and a chatterbox, hence his nickname. Everyone liked him – including Alf Ramsey. Having named him in his original squad, it must have been difficult for Alf to leave him out of the final party of twenty-two for the 1966 World Cup. I guess including him would have meant leaving out Jimmy Greaves, Roger Hunt or Geoff, and obviously Alf didn't want to omit any of them.

The nearer we got to the European final, the more Ron Greenwood worked to convince us that we could win without Budgie. His tactics, once again, were spot on, with Geoff Hurst in a withdrawn role and John Sissons and Alan Sealey in the wide positions.

I remember Ron saying to me in the dressing room just before the match, 'I thought you said I'd cost you your lifetime's ambition to play in a Wembley final.'

I always tried to control my emotions before a big match but I did feel tense as I walked from the dressing room up the concrete tunnel to the pitch. It was not my first experience of a big Wembley crowd, having played for England Schoolboys, but this was my first final. It was a memorable match and, even now, is ranked as one of the best of all the many Wembley finals. We played really well, winning 2–0. Years of hard work and faith had contributed to our victory. Ron told us afterwards that we had demonstrated that football at its best is a game of beauty and intelligence.

Bobby Moore played brilliantly, as did Jackie Burkett at left-back and Jim Standen in goal. Johnny Sissons struck the bar and a post and I tried to chip the goalkeeper, but the real hero of the night was newly married Alan 'Sammy' (the seal) Sealey, who scored both our goals. His first was a thudding drive from a sharp angle after sixty-nine minutes. His second, just two minutes later, was a classic poacher's goal, the roots of which could be traced back to the West Ham training ground.

We were awarded a free kick after Brian Dear was fouled. Geoff ran over the ball to deceive the German defence and Bobby floated it to the back post where I ran in and got a touch, but the ball squirmed away to Sammy, who drove it into the back of the net.

At the end, as we stood under the floodlights shaking hands, the 100,000 crowd – including Mum, Dad and Kathy – saluted both teams and the West Ham anthem, 'I'm forever blowing bubbles', filled the warm night air. The next day's newspapers claimed that we had restored the public's faith in football after the boring Leeds–Liverpool FA Cup final three weeks earlier.

For Ron Greenwood, it was the fulfilment of a dream. He knew that European football was the way ahead. It wasn't just the result but the manner of our win that pleased him so much. He felt that all his principles had been justified.

West Ham had followed the mighty Spurs side of Bill Nicholson and become only the second English club to win a European title – and Ron Greenwood had done it at his first attempt. It took Matt Busby and Manchester United six attempts to win their first European crown. It took Bill Shankly and Liverpool nine attempts.

For me, it had been a great year. I'd played a total of forty-seven first-team matches, although, once again, I'd worn four different shirt numbers. Still, European football had made others aware that I could flourish at the highest level of the game. One man who had taken note was Alf Ramsey.

6

THE THREE AMIGOS

I guess I was always considered the third man. Some thought that was a problem for me, but it wasn't. Even Ron Greenwood, in his book *Yours Sincerely*, treads carefully when discussing the three of us. He starts one chapter with the words: 'Hurst, Moore and Peters – no order of merit, that, just alphabetical.'

Normally, when the three of us are clumped together, the names appear in this order: Moore, Hurst and Peters. I can't argue with that. I didn't in 1966 or in the years immediately afterwards and I don't now.

Bobby Moore was an iconic figure in the sixties. The captain of England, he stood astride the world game alongside Pele. Unlike David Beckham today, his fame was based almost solely on his ability to play football superbly well. Beckham plays football well, but his fame and popularity are due in no small part to the power of television, self-promotion, his pop-star wife Victoria and the work of agents and publicists.

Bobby did some advertising work but had none of the promotional and marketing advantages that players enjoy today. Nevertheless, he was still recognised worldwide as a great footballer. He was clearly number one in the pecking order, and I'm sure Geoff Hurst would agree with that.

Geoff is second because he, uniquely, scored three goals in a

World Cup final. Some people say, 'But he did nothing else in his career,' but I say that's rubbish and, even if it was true, scoring a hat-trick in a World Cup final ensures his place in the history of the game. Taken in isolation, it's some achievement. Someone has to score four to better it and I think that's unlikely.

I am happy to be in bronze medal position. Only two English footballers have scored goals in a World Cup final and I'm one of them. Had it not been for my goal against West Germany, England would probably have lost 2–1. Geoff often jokes about that.

Geoff says, as Bobby did when he was alive, that of the three of us, I was the best footballer. Naturally, I wouldn't argue with that! Coming from two footballers of their stature, it's a great accolade. I was proud to be the third man in that trio.

The three of us had been friends for some time but it was the 1966 World Cup that made us a 'trio' in the eyes of the public. Before that, we were just three players from the same club.

As they are both a couple of years older than I am, I didn't come across either of them in schoolboy football. I met them for the first time when I started training at West Ham but I was a new boy and they were established players, particularly Bobby.

In my early days, Bobby made an enormous impression on me. No young player learning the basics of the trade could have had a better role model than Bobby Moore. One of the first things I noticed was the way he dedicated himself to improving his game. As others trooped off the pitch at our old training ground in Chigwell, Bobby would stay behind to work on his heading or his sprinting. He was a technically gifted and clever player, but he knew his weaknesses. He wasn't a natural runner, nor was he good in the air. To succeed at the highest level he knew he had to compensate for his deficiencies. He challenged himself to overcome all obstacles, and he became one of the world's greatest defenders.

Bobby was a quick and willing learner and had benefited since the age of twelve from the coaching of Malcolm Allison. Before a long and successful career as a manager and coach with Plymouth, Manchester City, Crystal Palace, Sporting Lisbon and Middlesbrough, Malcolm had spent eight years playing for West Ham. During that time, he devoted two evenings a week, with other senior players including John Bond and Noel Cantwell, to coaching local kids. Can you imagine star Premiership players giving up two evenings a week to coach children? During Ted Fenton's time as manager, Malcolm often took the coaching. Even as a player he was a master tactician and innovator, and has never really been given the credit he deserves for what he did for so many youngsters at West Ham.

Malcolm, himself a central defender, recognised great potential in the young Bobby Moore and took him under his wing. Years later, Bobby told me the best piece of advice he ever received was from Malcolm – always try to know where you are going to play the ball before you receive it. Malcolm told Bobby that was Di Stefano's secret at Real Madrid.

If you watch film of Bobby playing, you will notice that seven or eight times out of ten he clearly knows where he's going to pass the ball before it arrives at his feet. This ability to think quicker than the opposition disguised Bobby's lack of pace and made him, in my opinion, one of the best defenders of all time.

Bobby made his debut for West Ham in a 3–2 win over Manchester United at Upton Park in September 1958. It was just eight months after United had lost so many of their top players in the Munich air crash and Matt Busby was rebuilding his team. For West Ham, it was the club's sixth match in the First Division, having won promotion as Second Division champions the previous season. Bill Lansdowne was injured and Fenton had to decide whether to give the No. 6 shirt to Bobby or Malcolm. Bobby was eighteen, had just signed as a full professional and had no experience of first-team football.

Malcolm was thirty-one and had just spent a year out of the game with tuberculosis. He'd had a lung removed, but had made a full recovery and desperately wanted to play again. His eight years at West Ham had all been spent in the Second Division. So, for both teacher and the pupil the match against Manchester United had real significance. In the end, Fenton chose Bobby and Malcolm never played for West Ham again.

Bobby played nearly 700 first-team games in sixteen seasons with West Ham, winning the Footballer of the Year award in 1964. The more important the game, the better he played. He seemed to thrive on responsibility and that's what made him a natural leader. On the pitch nothing seemed to trouble him. Remember the World Cup final? Only seconds remained of extra time when he found himself in England's penalty area with the ball at his feet. The Germans were desperate to get hold of the ball and Jack Charlton was screaming at him to kick the wretched thing out of the ground, but not Mooro! He dribbled the ball around the penalty area, waiting for the right moment to carry it forward, and then hit the pass that provided Geoff with the shot for his hat-trick.

Some fans, particularly those in the north, thought he was a bit of a soft touch but that was rubbish. The blond hair, good looks and his taste in fashionable clothes disguised a formidable opponent. I remember one training session in February 1963 when I felt the full force of a Bobby Moore tackle during a five-a-side match. I was particularly pleased because I hadn't missed a game that season. Then Bobby ploughed into the back of me. I was in agony and was taken to hospital. An X-ray revealed a fracture of my left leg. I was put in plaster and driven home to my mum and dad.

Every day I used to telephone Kath from the phone booth across the road. On this occasion, because I was struggling to get about, Dad said he'd call. So he went to the call box and with typical male tact shouted down the phone, 'Kath, Kath!

Martin's been injured. But don't worry – it's only a broken leg!'

Kathy, who was at work, immediately decided that she had to race round to comfort me. Running out of her office in London's Fenchurch Street, she got knocked down by a car and ended up in hospital, too. Fortunately, she wasn't seriously hurt and was released later in the day after treatment for bumps and grazes, one leg swathed in bandages.

That night West Ham were playing Fulham at Upton Park in the FA Cup. My dad drove us to the ground and we were helped to the directors' room, where we soon realised that neither of us would be able to sit in the stand to watch the game. We spent the duration of the match in the boardroom, each of us with a leg resting on a stool. People laughed. You couldn't blame them.

I was out of action for two months but missed just five First Division games because for six consecutive weekends matches were cancelled. The pitches were constantly frozen during one of the worst winters of my career.

Bobby was very apologetic and as soon as I started training again took a particular interest in my progress. I returned to the side for a 2–0 win over Sheffield Wednesday. Alf Ramsey, still new to the job of England manager, was in the crowd at Upton Park, watching Bobby, who'd already won about ten England caps.

A few weeks after that game, Alf picked a squad of players for a friendly international in Czechoslovakia, which England won 4–2. It was the first win of his managerial reign. Who captained England for the first time that day? Yes, Bobby Moore.

What Alf liked about him was his calm, his intelligence and his ability to read the game, which he could do better than any other defender. This enabled him to become the best interceptor of a through ball I've seen. He could judge the flight of a ball, anticipate its destination, intercept it and play a pass back upfield before the man he was marking could appreciate what was happening.

His confidence was awesome. He was so sure of his ability on the ball that he always wanted to start attacking moves from defensive positions. He would rather accept the ball from the goalkeeper on the edge of our penalty area than see it kicked long. I can remember Alf instructing Gordon Banks *not* to throw the ball out to Bobby Moore, but to give it to either of the full-backs instead, or kick it long. 'We have to change it sometimes,' he explained. 'We can't always rely on Bobby to start the attacks from the back.'

Bobby was a bit put out by this and would still demand the ball from Banksie. There were even occasions when Bobby completely ignored the goalkeeper and restarted play himself with a quickly taken goalkick.

As dedicated as he was, Bobby loved to socialise and enjoy himself. As the captain of England he had responsibilities, which he took very seriously. He was a great ambassador for professional football and for the country. As his fame grew, more and more people wanted to be seen in his company. We had a great relationship but, off the field, he moved in increasingly different circles from Kath and I. He liked the world of showbusiness and was a particular fan of Frank Sinatra, but he never lost sight of his roots. He was always at ease with people from London's East End. He didn't like people to feel in awe of him and went out of his way to make them feel comfortable.

I remember, for example, how he helped young Frank Lampard feel at home. Frank was unchallenged as West Ham's left-back for sixteen years but, like most youngsters, he felt a bit vulnerable when he first got into the team. His second match, on Boxing Day 1967, was at Leicester and we were on the train back to London after a 4–2 win when Bobby spotted him sitting alone. As usual, Bobby was wearing a Saville Row suit, with shirt cuffs thrust forward to reveal smart cufflinks. In one hand he held a can of lager. With the other he beckoned Frank to join him. Frank sat in the spare seat opposite and Bobby gave him a can of lager and told him how well he'd played at Filbert Street that day. With a few kind words he began a friendship that lasted until the day he died. Bobby and Frank roomed together on trips with the team for eight years. Even today, long after Bobby's death, Frank will walk into a restaurant with his wife Pat and say, 'Mooro would have loved this place.'

Bobby enjoyed lively company. He was great friends with Johnny Byrne, Jimmy Greaves, Brian Dear and Harry Redknapp. Harry refers to him as 'God' and has been heard to shout at his defenders, 'God never did it like that!'

I always referred to him as 'Robert'. It was just a habit. Professionally, there was a very strong bond between us. I had huge respect for him as a player and a person but I was never quite sure whether he felt the same about me – or any of his other team-mates for that matter. Very few people got close to him. He enjoyed a joke and had a dry sense of humour but rarely revealed his true feelings to anyone.

He was at West Ham when I arrived and was still there when I left. During that time, a West Ham team without Bobby Moore was inconceivable, but the day came, as Bobby knew it would, when Ron Greenwood decided he could do without him. He had already turned down one mischievous attempt by Brian Clough to sign him and Trevor Brooking – £400,000 the pair –and, although I was at Tottenham by this time, I knew the relationship between Bobby and the manager was deteriorating.

Ron took great pride in the development of the young Moore and would never have a word said against him. He was thrilled when Bobby became the youngest winner of the Footballer of the Year award and often remarked about the maturity he'd shown during the ludicrous allegations against him about a stolen bracelet in the build-up to the 1970 World Cup in Mexico. Bobby had no bigger fan than the West Ham manager. So you can imagine how Ron must have felt when he was told that his captain was among a group of players who had been seen out drinking in Blackpool the night before an FA Cup tie.

Whatever the rights and wrongs of the case, this became front-page news, one of the great football scandals of the time. It was, in essence, a storm in a teacup – perhaps a storm in a pint glass might be a more apt description. Bobby liked a drink but never allowed it to affect his performance on the pitch. If he turned up for training a bit worse for wear, he would sweat it out on the pitch.

I'd been at Tottenham for about ten months when West Ham were drawn to travel to Blackpool in the third round of the FA Cup in January 1971. The night before the game, Bobby went for a drink in a Blackpool nightclub with Jimmy Greaves, Brian Dear, Clyde Best and the club physiotherapist Rob Jenkins.

The fact that West Ham lost 4–0 put Ron in a foul mood but by Monday he was even angrier because fans had started to call the club to say that Bobby and the others had been seen out drinking the night before the game. Ron wanted to sack all four – could you imagine that happening now? – but the board of directors talked him out of it, insisting that fines and suspensions would be sufficient.

It was, though, the beginning of the end of Bobby's illustrious career at Upton Park. His relationship with Ron Greenwood was never the same again. Ron used to say that he could talk about Bobby Moore the footballer for hours. 'But ask me about Bobby Moore the man and I'll dry up in a minute,' he would say.

Bobby looked after himself well, but he loved being 'one of the lads'. In hindsight, I'm not surprised that Ron Greenwood felt let down. It was Ron, after all, who had given Bobby his first chance with the England Youth and Under-23 teams and recommended him for his first senior cap. He had shaped his understanding of the game and helped him develop into one of the world's greatest defensive footballers.

The inevitable parting of the ways came in March 1974. Ron

obviously felt the time had come to let him go. Alan Mullery, a former team-mate with England, persuaded Bobby to join Fulham where the manager, Alec Stock, was gathering a distinguished collection of former internationals, including George Best, Rodney Marsh and Peter Storey.

After his years of loyal service, Bobby felt he deserved a free transfer but West Ham wanted a fee. Eventually, they agreed to sell him to Fulham for £50,000, but they allowed Bobby to keep half of it. Fulham were delighted to have the former England captain in their ranks. His debut against Middlesbrough attracted a crowd of 18,114. The attendance at the previous home game had been 6731. Bobby spent four happy seasons at Craven Cottage, helping them to their first FA Cup final in 1975. Fittingly, their opponents were West Ham.

As he was the last of the three of us to leave, his departure closed a chapter in Hammers' history. He played his first game in 1958 and his last in 1974. Geoff played his first in 1960 and his last in 1972. I played my first in 1962 and my last in 1970 – eight years during which time the three of us were together and contributed to probably the most successful period in the club's story.

I can't remember the three of us ever having a serious row or falling out. Our friendship survived the years and when we were on the pitch together we had an uncanny understanding. It's amazing that three young players should develop together at the same club and then play such a pivotal role at international level.

Ron Greenwood used to tell anyone who'd listen how lucky he was to have inherited three such players. The fact that we all contributed to three distinct parts of the team – defence, midfield and attack – was a considerable bonus for West Ham and England. Few people can understand how the relationship between Geoff, Bobby and I worked. It's one of those things I didn't really think about at the time. Even now, I wonder how it was that three players from the same club so profoundly influenced the outcome of the 1966 World Cup.

What people will understand is how Geoff and I felt when Bobby died of bowel cancer in February 1993. The disease claims 20,000 lives a year and is the second highest cancer killer in the UK. I was driving to the shops when my mobile phone rang with news of his death. I knew he was seriously ill but it was still a shocking moment, one I will never forget.

Geoff and I had known for a long time that he had a problem. The course of hospital treatment he underwent in 1964 was never fully explained. He became ill again in 1991 but he still lived life to the full with his second wife, Stephanie. For some years, he worked for Capital Gold Radio as a commentator and was revered by football crowds wherever he went. It was typical of the man that he should deal with his illness with such quiet dignity and fortitude. Whenever I saw him I'd ask, 'How are you, Robert?' He'd reply, 'I'm fine, Martin. How are Kathy and the kids?'

About two weeks before he died he called me at home. He must have known that he didn't have long to live. Even so, he was helping to organise a testimonial match at Crystal Palace for Malcolm Allison. He wanted me to play but I couldn't because I was already committed to play in a charity match on the same night for the boxer Michael Watson. It was a shame because I never saw or spoke to Bobby again. He went to his last match as a commentator at Wembley on 17 February 1993 – England 6, San Marino 0. A week later he died. The sense of loss was felt throughout the world of football. It was felt most deeply by his family, of course, but also at West Ham, among the club's followers, and in the Hurst and Peters homes.

Life for Geoff and me would never feel quite the same again. Initially, I found it very difficult to accept that I'd never speak to Bobby again. Even now, when I see a photograph of the three of us together, I feel a little pang of emotion. Geoff feels the same. I suppose it's inevitable.

Originally, Geoff was competing with Bobby for the defensive left-half position, but he was never going to win that battle. Geoff was instinctively an attacking player. Bobby was a defender. Geoff, strong and powerfully built, enjoyed pushing forward and his unpredictable, eccentric approach to defending led Ron Greenwood to experiment with him as a central striker. Ron told him that he had no future in the game if he continued to believe he could play as a wing-half. I wasn't sure whether Geoff was totally convinced that football was his first sport. He was good at cricket and played for Essex – you could play both sports in those days – but decided eventually that he had more chance of making a living from football. His father, Charlie, had been a professional footballer with Oldham, Bristol Rovers and Rochdale before moving the family from Lancashire to Chelmsford in Essex.

Cricket played a big part in the lives of several West Ham players at that time. Goalkeeper Jim Standen, who played in the 1964 FA Cup final, was the best of us, topping the county bowling averages and winning a championship medal with Worcestershire. Bobby Moore, Eddie Presland, Ronnie Boyce, Alan Sealey and Geoff were all excellent cricketers.

Sadly, it was while playing a knockabout game of cricket during training that Sealey, two-goal hero of the Cup Winners' Cup triumph in May 1965, collided with a bench a couple of months later and broke a leg. He recovered but was never quite the same player again.

I enjoyed cricket and played at club level for Dagenham but I never let it get in the way of my football career. I was a bit of an all-rounder and played a lot for West Ham in charity matches. It was at one such match in East Ham that Kathy and I first met Geoff's fiancée Judith. She and Kathy became friends almost immediately.

When Ron gave Geoff the No. 10 shirt against Liverpool in the sixth match of the 1962–63 season and we won 1–0 with a goal from Tony Scott, it was the first time Bobby, Geoff and I played together in a winning side. After that, Geoff worked hard at his new role, listened and practised. He improved his running, his control, his sense of timing, his shooting and his heading. By the end of the season, he'd established a good working relationship with Johnny Byrne. He was dragging defenders all over the place and finished his first season as a striker as the club's top scorer with 13 goals from 27 First Division matches.

Geoff developed his all-round game rapidly and Ron stressed to him the value of attacking the ball at the near post when the crosses came in from the wings. At that time in the evolution of the game, no English coach had highlighted the near post as a fruitful option for strikers. They tended to challenge for the ball in the central areas of the penalty box, or at the back post, but Ron wanted Geoff to get in front of his marker and meet the ball before anyone else.

Ron had been enormously impressed by the great Hungarian side of the early fifties. The 1952 Olympic champions, the Mighty Magyars became the first foreign side to win at Wembley when they beat England 6–3 in November 1953. Ron had been in the crowd that day. He would talk glowingly of their vision, their technique with the ball and their movement off it. He had been particularly impressed by the early delivery of the ball from the wings to the near post. One day in training, he put some traffic cones on the pitch out on the wings. These, he said, were the marking full-backs. He instructed his wingers to run and cross the ball before they reached the cones. He wanted them to bend the ball so that it arrived in the space between the goalkeeper and the back line of defenders. It was Geoff's task to get into that space and attack the ball before any of the defending team could reach it.

We worked on that move diligently in training because Ron believed the near post was the soft underbelly of most English defences. Two very good wingers, Johnny Sissons and Harry

Redknapp, toiled away, week after week, until their crossing was perfection. Ron insisted that all his players should be able to cross the ball well so Bobby and I were involved, too, and Geoff was the main beneficiary.

In one game against Manchester City, when Bobby's mentor Malcolm Allison was the first-team coach, Malcolm apparently warned his players beforehand of the dangers of our near-post cross but it made little difference. I crossed one ball for Geoff to score at the near post and Geoff crossed one for me to score at the near post. West Ham won 2–1. When we got it right, there was not much the opposition could do.

Neither Geoff nor I thought we had any realistic chance of taking part in the World Cup in summer 1966. It was two years since either of us had played in the Under-23 side, which in those days was where you established your international credentials and made your bid for a place in the senior eleven. Over Christmas, we talked about where we would go with our families for our annual holiday when the season finished. We had no idea that the events of that summer would change both our lives so dramatically. As it turned out, we went down to Cornwall in a big group with Ronnie and Dawn Boyce and Peter and Doreen Brabrook and their families. That was our last holiday as an anonymous family.

Two things were memorable about those few days in the West Country. First, we all visited a zoo together. It was great fun, particularly for the children. Peter Brabrook and I teased one of the big gorillas. As we strolled away from the cage, Ronnie Boyce arrived. The gorilla took one look at him, picked up a bucket of something unmentionable and hurled it through the bars, all over him.

The other thing was watching the second great sporting event of that summer – Henry Cooper fighting Cassius Clay for the world heavyweight title. Henry was the local hero in London. Everyone loved him. He'd lost to Clay over five rounds three years earlier and, at thirty-two, time was running out for him. The build-up to Cooper–Clay II, staged at Highbury, was pure Vaudeville and competed with the World Cup preparations for space in the newspapers. We all wanted Henry to catch him with his famous left hook. He did well enough until Clay opened a cut above Henry's eye and Henry's cornermen couldn't stop the bleeding. The referee had little choice but to stop the fight in the sixth round.

Shortly after returning from that holiday, Geoff and I joined Bobby in the squad of twenty-seven selected by Alf Ramsey for eighteen days of intensive training. We reported to Alf at Lilleshall in Shropshire, where he laid his World Cup plans. Alf organised a rigorous, no-nonsense regime. No holiday camp, it was a bit of a contrast to the couple of weeks we'd just spent relaxing with the families in Cornwall. For Geoff and I, it was our first experience of this kind of thing.

The weeks that followed bound the three of us together in a way that few other players can have experienced. We were a unit within a unit. First in the Shropshire countryside, then in Helsinki, Oslo, Copenhagen and Chorzow where we played warm-up games, and finally at Wembley, the Upton Park trio gradually became an essential component in the England team.

Forty years later Geoff and I still enjoy recalling the old days together. He remains my best friend in football. Sometimes we wonder what would have happened if the three of us had stayed together at West Ham for longer.

I was the first to leave because I wanted the chance to win more trophies. I'd had a taste of success at club level with the Hammers and started each season genuinely believing we had a chance of winning the League Championship, but in truth the style of game we played wasn't suited to the nine-month marathon of the league programme, especially on the mid-winter pitches so common in those days.

I think Geoff accepted that we weren't good enough to win

the title, but any desire he had for the big time, was fully satisfied by his England call-ups. I loved playing for England, too, but it was a bonus. I felt league football was my bread and butter, my means of getting a better contract and a wage increase, and I wanted to test myself at the highest level. A time came when I felt that Tottenham would stretch me in a way that West Ham couldn't.

Some people thought I left because I was jealous of Bobby and Geoff and fed up with living in their shadow. It upset me to think that people felt that way. It was ludicrous. I had nothing but admiration for both of them. What I wanted was the chance to win medals. I wanted to play in Cup finals. Once I'd joined Spurs, I was delighted when we reached the League Cup semi-final in 1972. The reason for my joy? West Ham were in the other semi-final. The prospect of playing at Wembley against Bobby and Geoff really appealed to me but that scenario was too good to be true. Chelsea beat us in a titanic semi-final, Alan Hudson scoring the decisive goal direct from a free kick only seconds from the end of the second leg at White Hart Lane.

West Ham's semi-final against Stoke was even more thrilling. It took four games to decide the winner. In the second match Gordon Banks brilliantly saved a penalty from Geoff and in the fourth game at Old Trafford Bobby Moore had to go in goal when Bobby Ferguson was injured. Bobby saved Mickey Bernard's penalty but couldn't stop the follow-up and Stoke went through to meet Chelsea in the final.

Later that year, when Tony Waddington, the Stoke manager, was looking for an experienced striker he went to West Ham and asked if they would release Geoff. By then, the time was right for him to leave. West Ham agreed to sell for a fee of £80,000 so he and Judith packed up in Essex and moved to Stoke, where he played for three years and opened a pub. It was a bit of a wrench for the two girls after so many years together and Kathy would often go up to Stoke and stay with Judith for a few days.

Geoff later played a handful of games for West Bromwich Albion, Cork Celtic and Seattle Sounders before becoming player-manager of Telford in 1976. Three years later he was offered a coaching job at Chelsea and later became their manager, just failing to win promotion to the First Division in 1980. As I was to discover myself, failure in football management carries a high price – the sack. With typical fortitude Geoff bounced back. In a complete change of career he moved into insurance with a company called Motor-plan. In 1984 he persuaded me to join him as an insurance salesman and we were back on the same team again where we stayed for the next seventeen years.

7

THE BOYS OF '66

Love was in the air in the spring of 1966 and the newspapers were full of romantic speculation about two giant pandas. Would An-an and Chi-chi mate? As I recall, love failed to bloom, despite much human encouragement, and it was left to another of our four-legged friends to capture the hearts of the nation.

Pickles, a mongrel dog out walking with his owner – funnily enough, a Thames lighterman like my dad – discovered the solid gold Jules Rimet Trophy in a garden in Beulah Hill, South London. Overnight, Pickles was as famous as the giant pandas.

He'd spared the Football Association any further embarrassment following the theft of the trophy a week earlier from a stamp exhibition at Westminster Hall. This was the trophy that, a few weeks later, sixteen nations would be competing to win.

The 1965–66 season had been exciting, if ultimately frustrating. My own form had been good with 11 goals scored in 40 First Division matches, and I'd appeared in all our Cup ties. We'd reached the semi-finals in our defence of the European Cup Winners' Cup, and were keen to avoid Liverpool and Celtic. So when the draw was made, we were delighted to be paired with Borussia Dortmund of West Germany.

Unfortunately, the two legs of the semi-final coincided with a sudden period of dressing-room drama. Bobby Moore was unhappy and told the club that he wanted to leave, but Ron Greenwood refused to contemplate his departure. The two were at loggerheads and for the first leg Ron stripped Bobby of the captaincy and gave it to Johnny Byrne. We lost that match 2–1 at Upton Park. A week later we lost the second leg 3–1 in Dortmund. Bobby's heart wasn't in it but Borussia had a talented team that included three future World Cup players – goalkeeper Hans Tilkowski, Siggi Held and Lothar Emmerich. Of the five goals Borussia put past us, four were scored by Emmerich. Tall and strong, he possessed a wonderful left foot and was the Bundesliga's most prolific goalscorer at the time.

At least in the League Cup we reached the final but that, too, ended in disappointment. West Bromwich Albion beat us 5–3 on aggregate, which meant that we would not be competing on the European stage the following season.

While all this was going on, Alf Ramsey had, fortunately, been taking note of my progress since my Under-23 days. I remember Ron Greenwood once telling me that Alf had said to him, 'Your boy Peters can't play!' Well, he obviously changed his mind because one morning through the mail I received a letter from the Football Association telling me that I had been selected to make my senior debut for England against Yugoslavia at Wembley on 4 May. Strangely, a few days beforehand someone had told me that he'd heard from a friend of a printer that my name was among the players listed in the Wembley programme for that match. 'Just another rumour,' I thought at the time.

Elevation to the England squad was the ultimate accolade but for such a promotion to arrive just weeks before the World Cup began had special significance. On 7 April, the day before West Ham beat Tottenham 4–1 at White Hart Lane, Alf had announced a provisional party of forty players for the World Cup. I was one of those but, having never played for the senior team, I assumed I'd be one of the eighteen told, 'Sorry, not this time.' So you can imagine my excitement when I realised I'd be making my debut at Wembley on 4 May with the World Cup only weeks away. It suddenly dawned on me that perhaps I could actually nail down a place in Alf's squad for the finals.

This was the most exciting period of my entire career. I would be rubbing shoulders with one of the most famous players in the world, Bobby Charlton, the best goalkeeper in the world, Gordon Banks, and the best goalscorer, Jimmy Greaves. It was a big opportunity, expectations were high and I felt the pressure. I didn't want to let myself down.

Alf was still in the process of formulating his plans. A month before the Yugoslavia game, England had beaten Scotland 4–3 in the annual duel and Jimmy Johnstone, the little Celtic winger, had tortured England's left-back Keith Newton throughout the game. I suspect that his performance had reminded Alf just how destructive a world-class winger could be. Against Yugoslavia, he chose two wide men – Terry Paine of Southampton and Bobby Tambling of Chelsea. I was the only debutant, while Geoff Hurst, Norman Hunter and Tambling were international fledglings with just three caps apiece. In the previous couple of weeks, West Ham had beaten Arsenal, Tottenham and, just four days before my England debut, Manchester United. Seven members of the England squad were involved in that match at Upton Park, explaining Alf's presence in the stands.

England's 2–0 win over Yugoslavia, with goals from Greaves and Charlton, was greeted with impressive headlines the next day. I was pleased with my contribution. Alf told me before the game to play as I did for West Ham and that's what I tried to do. With sixty-five caps Bobby Charlton was unquestionably the star of the side. He provided much of the creative impetus in the team and always demanded the ball. As a youngster, keen not to make mistakes, I was more than happy to oblige while I found my feet. I would advise any youngster in that position to do the same – don't try too hard to impress, but do try hard not to make mistakes.

Shortly after this game Alf announced the party for Lilleshall. I survived the cut and so spent nearly three weeks closeted in a training camp where Alf and his two lieutenants, Les Cocker of Leeds and Harold Shepherdson of Middlesbrough, ran our lives with military precision, ably assisted by Wilf McGuinness, who later became manager of Manchester United. Before that, Wilf had played for United and England at wing-half. The facilities were fairly basic, although a team doctor had been appointed – the first time that had happened. Alan Bass, a Harley Street consultant, was Arsenal's club doctor and became a popular figure among the players. The Football Association had decided that round-the-clock specialist medical care was vital after Peter Swan became violently ill because local doctors gave him the wrong treatment for a stomach bug during the 1962 World Cup in Chile.

On arrival, Alf called the players together and spelled out a few rules. One in particular I've never forgotten. 'Anyone,' he said, 'who sneaks out for a drink will be finished with me, this squad and the World Cup.' The way that Les Cocker and Harold Shepherdson – better known as 'Shep' – came knocking on our doors in the evening to ask if we needed anything has become legendary. Alf wanted to be assured that his players were all tucked up in bed at night. No one betrayed Alf's trust. There were a few jokes about 'escape committees' – Jack Charlton used to walk down the long drive to shout at passing motorists, 'Help! Help! Get us out of here!' – but we all recognised the importance of what we were doing. After all, five of us were still to be cut out of the squad and none of us wanted to be among the five.

I was sharing a room with Gordon Banks, which was a bit daunting at first. I'd played with him once, but I didn't really know him. He was a superstar, a regular in the team, and I was one of the new recruits, but he was terrific, helping me feel a part of the squad. We became good friends.

The claustrophobic atmosphere at Lilleshall generated tensions among the players but over all of us loomed the considerable figure of Alf Ramsey. He wasn't big in stature but he was a leader of men, the unifying force. One day he had to intervene when a row between Jack Charlton and Nobby Stiles threatened to get out of hand on the training pitch. They were strong personalities and neither would back down – until Alf stepped in. The players never questioned his authority. I'm not sure that today's national coach could wield the same power in the dressing room or on the training pitch. For twelve hours a day Alf pushed us hard, organising defensive and attacking strategies and building team spirit while fostering a conviction that we were going to win the World Cup. To a man, we responded with energy and enthusiasm.

Eventually, the day came when Alf had to tell the unlucky five that they would not be in the squad. No hints or clues had been forthcoming. We had all been fitted for suits and overcoats and twenty-seven of each duly arrived. I'd already worked out that my chief rival for a place was wing-half Gordon Milne, who won a championship medal for the second time with Liverpool in 1966. He had fourteen caps and was vastly more experienced than I was, so I would not have been surprised had Alf selected him, but he didn't. He selected me. I remember running to the telephone to tell Kathy the news. I was thrilled but genuinely disappointed for Gordon, who was an outstanding player. The fortunate twenty-two commiserated with the unlucky five – Liverpool's Peter Thompson, probably the best natural winger in the squad, Chelsea's Bobby Tambling, Blackburn Rovers's full-back Keith Newton, who would return for the 1970 World Cup, my West Ham team-mate Johnny Byrne and Gordon. It was a sombre moment when Alf called them together as a group and told them they could go home. Johnny Byrne tried to lighten it by asking if they could keep the suits and coats.

With the squad, if not the team resolved, Alf took us on a four-match tour of Scandinavia and Poland. First, though, he sent us all home for a few days. It was great to spend the time with Kathy and our daughter Lee Ann, who was nine months old.

Alf had agreed a fixture schedule that involved playing four matches in four countries in ten days – Finland in Helsinki, Norway in Oslo, Denmark in Copenhagen and Poland in Chorzow. It was a formidable programme to undertake just days before the World Cup started.

He already had a very good idea of how he wanted his team to line up for the opening World Cup match on 11 July, and this tour was simply a matter of fine-tuning – or so I thought. I was surprised, for instance, when for the first game in Helsinki he chose the young Leeds United defender Norman Hunter ahead of Bobby Moore. Norman had played only three times before and Moore, after all, was the England captain. Alf gave the captaincy to Jimmy Armfield for that match.

An element in the media favoured Hunter, who was establishing a reputation as a formidable defender, and I know Bobby was concerned when his name didn't appear on the teamsheet that day. What few people realised at the time was that Bobby had a lot on his mind. His contract with West Ham was due to expire on 30 June and although Ron Greenwood had tried to keep negotiations quiet, the papers were beginning to run stories speculating about Bobby's future.

I was selected for my second cap and repaid Alf's faith by scoring in a 3–0 win. It wasn't a particularly inspiring performance but at least it gave Alf the chance to check my progress and that of Liverpool winger Ian Callaghan. I was left out for the next game, in Oslo three days later. Bobby was reinstated and Alf recalled Jimmy Greaves, who had missed much of the domestic season following an attack of jaundice. Alf also took the opportunity to have a look at his other wingers, John Connelly of Manchester United, and Terry Paine of Southampton.

Jimmy showed he had regained his appetite by scoring four goals in a convincing 6–1 win – the sixth occasion on which he had scored three or more goals for his country in one match. Perhaps feeling that he needed to make a lasting impression, Bobby Moore struck a rare and spectacular long-range goal.

With the World Cup less than a fortnight away it was an impressive statement of intent by the England team. Sadly, though, two days later the Football Association chairman Joe Mears suffered a fatal heart attack outside his hotel in the Norwegian capital. Just sixty-one, he was also the chairman of Chelsea and had played a big role in the preparations for the World Cup tournament.

A couple of days later in Denmark I was again omitted from an England team showing more changes. Chelsea goalkeeper Peter Bonetti was given his international debut and Arsenal's George Eastham celebrated his call-up by scoring in a comfortable 2–0 win.

The last match was the hardest and many questioned the wisdom of playing in Poland just six days before the World Cup opener against Uruguay. We had a long rail journey into the Silesian coalfields and then faced a truly hostile crowd and a team that had much to prove after failing to qualify for the finals.

No one realised it at the time – not even Alf – but the team he picked that day was the one that would later play in the World Cup final, with one exception. Jimmy Greaves started against Poland whereas Geoff Hurst started against West Germany in the final. Despite the close proximity of the World Cup, none of us could afford to hide or pull out of tackles. We were all playing for a place in the opening game. Bobby Moore, with his West Ham contract still unsigned, was magnificent in the heart of the England defence. I felt I played well and the fact that Roger Hunt scored the only goal in a really competitive match meant that we had won all four games on tour, scoring twelve goals and conceding just one. Alf had tried 4-3-3 and 4-2-4, he'd tried with wingers and without wingers, he'd tried three different goalkeepers – Banks, Bonetti and Ron Springett – and three different striking partnerships. He'd tried everything and now he was ready, or so we hoped.

When we got back to London Alf immediately summoned Ron Greenwood to the Hendon Hall Hotel. He wanted Bobby Moore's future sorted out before the World Cup kicked off. Moore and Greenwood had been playing brinkmanship but Alf was worried that the uncertainty might affect his captain's form. Spurs had expressed an interest in Bobby, who had been bitterly disappointed by West Ham's failure in the Cup Winners' Cup. I think he feared that West Ham's indifferent form might affect his England career. The face-to-face meeting seemed to focus their minds, though, and Ron left the Hendon Hall Hotel with Bobby's signature on a new contract. He would stay at West Ham for another eight years. Bobby was happy, Alf was happy and England were ready.

Alf had spent four years searching for the right tactics and the right personnel. The fine-tuning was over and, after all my doubts, I now felt that I had a real chance of a place in the starting line-up for the opening game against Uruguay, but I still had a lot to learn and, as we were to discover, so did Alf. Even at this stage, he wasn't entirely convinced about the make-up of his best eleven. The team that started the tournament against Uruguay was not the team that finished it against West Germany.

The one consistent element of the England team throughout the tournament was the defence – Gordon Banks in goal behind a back four of George Cohen, Jackie Charlton, Bobby Moore and Ray Wilson. It was probably the best defensive unit in the world at the time, well organised and resourceful. England conceded few goals and remained unbeaten in twelve consecutive away matches.

Banksie was certainly the finest goalkeeper on the planet. I can't recall a serious mistake by him in all the games we played together for England. He was the master of positioning and angles and, even in training, would treat any goal scored against him as a personal affront. Clinical rather than spectacular, he was a good shot stopper, as brave as a lion and particularly adept at punching away crosses. He had no serious rival between 1966 and 1972 when an eye injury sustained in a car accident ended his illustrious career. His diving save from Pele's header in the 1970 World Cup remains a classic example of the goalkeeper's art and is one of the most viewed pieces of goalkeeping film in history.

Gordon played for Chesterfield, Leicester City and Stoke City and very nearly joined West Ham in 1967. Leicester turned down West Ham's bid and Ron Greenwood agreed to buy Bobby Ferguson from Kilmarnock. Ron agreed to delay finalising the deal until after Kilmarnock were knocked out of the Intercities Fairs Cup, predecessor of the Uefa Cup. In the meantime, Leicester decided to cash in on Gordon's reputation and informed West Ham that he was now available for sale. It says much for Ron's integrity that he remained faithful to his agreement with the Scottish club.

Gordon was, and still is, a funny man and very good company. It was a privilege to play in the same team. In fact, I was lucky to play alongside two of the world's greatest goalkeepers – Gordon and, with Spurs, Northern Ireland's Pat Jennings. They were both quite brilliant but I think Gordon was marginally better.

George Cohen filled the right-back spot with distinction, winning thirty-seven caps between 1964 and 1967 before being forced to quit the game prematurely because of a knee injury. A strong, determined character, he used to make storming runs along the right flank for Fulham and England but even he admitted that crossing the ball wasn't one of his main assets.

More importantly, few wingers got past him because he was quick, alert, tackled well and was as strong as a bull, which I'm sure helped him in later life when he successfully fought off cancer. He's retired now from the property business he built up when his playing career ended. When we meet at a social event, he and his wife Daphne both look immaculate. They take pride in their appearance. Daphne can climb out of a swimming pool with hair and make-up intact!

Ray Wilson, on the left, provided the balance in Alf's full-back equation. No one who played with him would ever question his right to be described as a world-class defender. His tackling was crisp and his distribution accurate. Like George, he was small, neat and tough but, unlike George, he was a north-country man, from Derbyshire. George was a city boy from Kensington in the heart of west London. They played together for England on twenty-eight occasions and they had a great understanding on the pitch. When George ventured upfield, Ray stayed back and when Ray swept forward, George could be relied upon to hold his defensive position. It sounds easy but it doesn't always work that way with full-backs.

Ray was far more experienced than George, having made his debut in 1960. In all he won sixty-three caps and, at thirty-one, was one of England's most experienced players. A few weeks before the tournament started, he played in the Everton team that beat Sheffield Wednesday 3–2 in the FA Cup final. To begin with, Ray had been a forward but Huddersfield Town turned him into a left-back before selling him to Everton in 1964.

Ray had a very dry sense of humour, which probably helped him in his chosen career after he finished playing – the undertaking business. He and Jack Charlton, who filled the other centre-back position alongside Bobby Moore in the heart of the defence, were the old men in the side and they both loved taking the mickey out of the players from the south. Jack was a big, honest, hard-working, old-fashioned centre-half. Alf thought he and Bobby formed the perfect defensive partnership – Jack could win the ball, Bobby could distribute it. Jack was an uncompromising, no-nonsense stopper, Bobby was a skilled technician who read the game superbly. Alf once told Jack that he picked him because Jack fitted the pattern he had in mind. Jack was thirty when he made his international debut, and readily acknowledged that he'd never be in Bobby's class as a footballer, but he was awesomely effective when it came to preventing others from playing. He was a genuine tough guy who enjoyed a fabulous career at Leeds United and won thirty-five caps in a five-year international career, finishing on the losing side just twice, against Austria and Scotland.

I felt from the moment I joined the squad that Jack thought I wasn't good enough to be in the England side. He never said anything, but I sensed he had reservations about me. Why that should be I don't know. At Leeds, he played behind two great midfield men – Billy Bremner and Johnny Giles. Perhaps he felt I wasn't in their class or perhaps he felt I didn't tackle hard enough. It didn't bother me at the time, although I did think about it, and it doesn't bother me now. Kathy and I see Jack and his wife Pat two or three times a year and include them among our circle of long-standing friends.

Jack was very opinionated and often had rows with Alf, but what he learned on the training pitch served him well in later years in his successful managerial career with Middlesbrough, Sheffield Wednesday, Newcastle and the Republic of Ireland. By the time the England job became vacant in 2000, I think he'd lost his appetite for the cut and thrust of football, and preferred to spend his retirement fishing and shooting in the peace of the countryside – not that it's always peaceful. He tells the story of one fishing trip when he settled himself on a river bank at the side of a hump-backed bridge, with no one else around. A man leaned over the bridge to watch. Jack thought nothing of it, but within an hour he estimated more than a hundred people crowded the bridge, just watching him fish.

When he finished playing, his humour and northern bluntness made him a much sought-after celebrity. He never wanted to be famous, though. He and his younger brother Bobby came from the footballing Milburn family in the North East and all either of them wanted to do was kick a ball around.

Bobby was the superstar of the side, a fabulous player. No matter where you went in the world, people wanted to see Bobby Charlton. His recovery from the terrible Munich air crash in 1958 captured the imagination of the football public.

A brilliant schoolboy prodigy who began his career as a winger, he soon became famous for his shooting ability and by 1966 was firmly established as everyone's favourite player. I think the long-range goal he scored against Mexico was the launching pad for England's success. In fact, the power of his shooting was as much a trademark as his thin, flowing hair.

As a player he had everything – touch, pace, prodigious energy and the ability to score goals. A total of forty-nine goals in a twelve-year international career gave him a record he still holds as England's top marksman. He was the heart and soul of the team, dictating play from midfield and bursting forward to menace the opposition.

He was a carefree figure in 1966 and enjoyed a laugh and joke, but in recent years he has adopted a more cautious demeanour. Perhaps he feels that as a knight of the realm and a director of Manchester United he has responsibilities, although when he and his wife Norma are enjoying a break with the boys, it's just like the old days.

Bobby was the pivotal figure in Alf's strategy. He had the central midfield role that allowed him to create moves and push forward in support of Geoff Hurst and Roger Hunt. He was only able to do this as often as he did because of the support he received from his Manchester United team-mate Nobby Stiles.

Alf gave Nobby the holding role in midfield. Nobby protected the area in front of the back four, with me wide on the left and Alan Ball wide on the right. In many ways, Nobby and 'Ballie' epitomised the spirit and defiance of Alf's team. They chased every lost cause and ensured that everyone else did their share of the work. An angel off the pitch, Nobby had a reputation as one of football's hard men. Once he walked across that white line he was an aggressive little scoundrel who intimidated all those around him. Nobby put his heart and soul into every match he played and expected the same commitment from everyone else.

Nobby and his wife Kay – she's Johnny Giles' sister – are the most unpretentious couple and are always great fun at the 1966 reunions.

A few weeks after Nobby won the first of his twenty-eight caps, against Scotland in the spring of 1965, Alf introduced Alan Ball to the side for a game against Yugoslavia. That was the first time the two of them played together. By the time I became involved a year later, Stiles and Ball looked as though they had spent a lifetime playing in the same team. They were hugely influential, had a great understanding and were part of the balance that Alf was seeking.

At twenty-one, Alan was the youngest in the team. A chirpy, red-haired firebrand, he used to have the dressing room in stitches. Jack Charlton was usually the butt of his humour. Most people remember Alan for his work rate and the accuracy of his passing, and many consider that he was England's best player in the final. He ran the legs off Karl-Heinz Schnellinger and at the end Alf told him that he'd never play a better game. His energy in the thirty minutes of extra time gave us the edge.

Ballie played a total of seventy-two games in a ten-year inter-national career – not a bad record for a youngster who was told by Bolton that he wasn't big enough to become a professional. He learned the basics of the business from his dad – also a player and a manager – and became a big star with Everton, Arsenal and Southampton after he left Blackpool.

Geoff Hurst and Roger Hunt were the main beneficiaries of Alan's industry. Geoff captured the headlines with his goals but no one in the team of 1966 would diminish the role played by Roger. He had a fabulous goalscoring pedigree – 245 league goals in eleven years at Liverpool – and was vastly more experienced at international level than Geoff. They came together because of the injury to Jimmy Greaves but they made the perfect partnership. Once again, Alf got the balance right.

Both were strong runners who could force gaps in the opposing defences. The great thing about Roger was that he could be relied upon to give 100 per cent in every game. Even if he didn't score, you knew he would run his socks off for the team. Geoff acknowledges that he would never have scored the goals he did for England without Roger's support. Roger played in all six World Cup games, scoring three goals – one against Mexico and two against France. In 34 games for England he scored a total of 17 goals.

Roger's a very likeable guy with a lovely sense of humour. He attends our reunions with his partner Rowan and always looks well groomed and relaxed. When he retired from playing, he built up a successful haulage company with his brother. I often see 'Hunt' trucks on the motorways.

John Connelly, Terry Paine, Ian Callaghan and Jimmy Greaves played in some of the games, but not in the final, while Ron Springett, Peter Bonetti, Jimmy Armfield, Gerry Byrne, Ron Flowers, Norman Hunter and George Eastham didn't play at all. These were England's forgotten heroes but they were all as important as the eleven who took part in the last game. Alf had chosen his squad carefully. He wanted team players. He didn't want any disruptive elements. He wanted players who supported their team-mates. He stressed when it was all over that it had been a victory for the squad, and he was right.

8

THE WORLD CUP – AND HOW TO WIN IT

The preparations were over. The bonding process was complete. Physical conditioning had reached a peak. The games in Helsinki, Oslo, Copenhagen and Chorzow had sharpened appetites, honed match fitness and allowed Alf Ramsey to make any last-minute tactical adjustments he felt necessary. On 3 July, the day we beat Denmark, Alf had officially informed FIFA, the world governing body, of the names of his squad. The World Cup was due to start eight days later.

What was particularly interesting about the squad announcement that day in Copenhagen was Alf's allocation of shirt numbers – Nos 1–11 were Banks, Cohen, Wilson, Stiles, J. Charlton, Moore, Ball, Greaves, R. Charlton, Hurst, Connelly. The second and third-choice goalkeepers, Ron Springett and Peter Bonetti, were given 12 and 13. The replacement full-backs, Jimmy Armfield and Gerry Byrne, had 14 and 15.

You didn't need to be a genius to work out that the first eleven numbers went to Alf's proposed first-choice team, and I wasn't in it. I had No. 16. I hadn't been picked to play against Denmark that day so I thought, quite naturally, that I wouldn't be in the starting line-up for the World Cup opener – but then I was selected to play in our win against Poland. Perhaps I would start the World Cup after all, because this match was considered to be the final dress rehearsal.

I remember the great sense of optimism among the players as we flew home to London. I remember, too, Alf reiterating to the media his belief that England would win the World Cup.

Most of my one day at home with Kathy was spent in anxious speculation. I'd played three times, scoring one goal and I thought that maybe, just maybe, I'd done enough to earn a place in the team. At the time, I thought that Alf's intention was to play with a conventional winger and nothing has changed my mind on that score. He is remembered for his team of 'wingless wonders' but I'm convinced that his preference was for a team with at least one orthodox winger. So it was no real surprise to me when John Connelly was told on the morning of 11 July, after we had spent four days together in the Hendon Hall Hotel, that he would face Uruguay at Wembley a few hours later.

Alf picked the first eleven numbers with one exception – Geoff Hurst, who had been given No. 10. He was left out to make room for No. 21, Roger Hunt, who had scored England's goal against the Poles. Roger played upfront with the greatest goalscorer of that era – Jimmy Greaves. To leave him out would have provoked uproar. Connelly was chosen to play wide on the left. Nobby Stiles and Bobby Charlton were given the central midfield positions with Alan Ball wide on the right. It was disappointing not to be in the team, but it wasn't the end of my world. It was a thrill just to be involved and I think Geoff, equally disappointed, felt the same.

We all put on our new grey Football Association suits and gathered in the lobby for the coach journey to Wembley. Bobby Moore had warned us that Alf, who had been a Quartermaster Sergeant during the Second World War, expected his players to observe the squad dress code, right down to the tie and metal badge. He even had spare badges in case somebody lost one, as happened to Geoff. As relative newcomers to the squad, Geoff and I relied on our club-mate for guidance and advice.

That morning I'd read the newspapers over breakfast and they didn't give us much chance of reaching the latter stages, never mind winning the World Cup. Mooro's view was that, as the host nation, we had as good a chance as anyone of winning. Our preparation had been first class and I remember him saying, quite rightly as it turned out, that no team in the competition would be harder to beat than England.

The enthusiasm for England's cause was soon apparent out on the street as our motor coach with motorcycle escort nosed down the drive, out of the Hendon Hall Hotel, and began the short journey to the stadium. Wembley Way was heaving with fans and I think most of them slapped the sides of the bus as it approached the ground.

Inside, the stadium was decked out with the flags of the competing sixteen nations. The massed bands of the Brigade of Guards, Grenadier Guards and Coldstream Guards played as the opening ceremony unfolded in front of the Queen. Sir Stanley Rous, President of FIFA, invited Her Majesty to declare open the final series of the eighth World Championship. The whole ceremony took ninety minutes. We missed it all because Alf took the entire squad to the dressing rooms. Eventually, he asked the reserves to leave because he wanted to focus all his attention on the team before the kick-off at 7.30 p.m.

Uruguay were no pushovers. Although at the time they had a population of little more than two million – about one quarter the population of Greater London – they had won the World Cup twice and the Olympic title twice. Known as Los Celestes because of their sky blue shirts, their recent form had been unimpressive. The general opinion among the lads was that much of their reputation was based upon what had been achieved in the thirties. Nonetheless, Alf had highlighted the dangers of underestimating them and he identified the goal-scoring midfield player Pedro Rocha, of Penarol, as their most influential player.

It fell to Nobby Stiles to take care of Rocha. He did the job well in a game that was ultimately more about preventing goals than scoring them. Neither side wanted to lose the opening match. An early England goal would have forced Uruguay to come out of their defensive shell but, as the game developed, it became clear that their priority was to stop England scoring. So a match of indifferent quality ended goalless. It was the first time England had failed to score at Wembley for nearly thirty years. I thought Alf might have had a few harsh words to say afterwards, but he was surprisingly upbeat. 'We can win this without conceding a goal,' he said.

Inevitably, we got a bit of stick from the media the following day. I think we all realised that a win would have been invaluable from a psychological point of view, lifting much of the pressure from the team. The expectations were that much higher because we were playing at Wembley.

To help us relax, the next day Alf took us all to Pinewood Studios where we watched Sean Connery making *You Only Live Twice* and George Segal making *The Quiller Memorandum*. It was a good day out, the perfect therapy after the disappointment of the previous evening. We met Britt Ekland and Norman Wisdom and, as I recall, lots of young starlets wanted to be photographed with the England players. I guess it was too good a photo opportunity to miss. I enjoyed watching the actors working and remember George Segal turning to us after one scene and asking, 'Was that OK, boys?'

Alf allowed us to have a drink with lunch and one or two may have taken full advantage of the very unusual relaxation of the alcohol rule, but the following morning we were all back at work. Alf trained us hard and the emphasis was placed on attacking play. We could qualify from our group by drawing all three games, but it was unlikely. We needed to beat Mexico if we were to avoid a high-octane encounter with the French in our last qualifying match. Mexico and France had drawn their first match 1–1, which was perfect from an English point of view. We were buzzing again and I got a sense from training that the manager would make changes for the game against Mexico.

On the morning of the match my hunch was proved right when Alf announced the team. He dropped John Connelly and Alan Ball, and replaced him with Terry Paine and myself. This time Nobby Stiles, Bobby Charlton and I would fill the mid-field places.

Geoff Hurst was again overlooked but, like a good friend, he was as excited about my inclusion as I was. Like him, I considered it a privilege just to be in the twenty-two. To get a chance actually to play was a massive bonus as far as I was concerned.

The Mexicans had been based in Switzerland for six weeks before the tournament, playing local and Italian club sides. The import of foreign players, mostly Brazilians, into Mexico was holding back the development of home-bred youngsters and so their squad was one of the oldest in the tournament. Among these veterans was a famous World Cup figure – Antonio Carbajal, the thirty-seven-year-old goalkeeper and proud owner of an Errol Flynn-style moustache. He had played as an amateur for Mexico in the 1948 Olympic Games in London and now, as a professional, was in his fifth World Cup tournament.

Mexico chose a younger goalkeeper, Ignacio Calderon, to face England, which was probably just as well because we kept him busy that night. Like Uruguay, Mexico tried a blanket defence and were clearly hoping that another draw would enhance their chances of grabbing one of the two qualifying places. Their intentions were clear straight from the kick-off – they sent the ball deep into our half and made no attempt to retrieve it. They simply maintained their defensive positions, waiting for us to attack them.

In the thirty-fifth minute England scored. I got my head to a cross from Bobby Charlton and set up Roger Hunt, who

My father was a Thames lighterman, so I guess it was natural that I should be wearing a sailor suit.

My parents, William and Mary, on holiday together in Margate before I was born.

With a football on the grass outside our house in Raydons Road, Dagenham, aged about eight. I would be out there playing at every opportunity.

I'm the one on the left of the middle row in this photo of the Fanshawe School football team in 1958.

Kathy and me with my parents at Hemsby holiday camp around 1960.

Family times in the early 1970s: (above) Kathy, Lee Ann and Grant pose for the camera; while (below) I give them a push on the swings.

The London Schoolboys visit Manchester for a game against the Manchester Schoolboys in 1959. I am the one sixth from left.

I'm in the big time now! As captain of West Ham's youth side in 1961 I soon had to develop a good line in signing autographs.

Scoring West Ham's first goal in a 4–4 thriller against Spurs in December 1962.

The West Ham team lines up to play at Randall's Island, New York, during our summer tour in 1963.

The build-up to the 1964 FA Cup final: (above) some of the players were blowing bubbles, but I was to miss out on the final and perhaps my chance ever to play on the big stage; (left) me, Jackie Burkett, Ronnie Boyce and Geoff Hurst find the best form of transport we can to take our wives to Wembley. Times really have changed!

Joe Kirkup, me and Ronnie Boyce celebrate our 2–0 victory over Munich 1860 in the European Cup Winners' Cup final at Wembley in 1965.

I may have been adaptable and played in every position for the club, but this was surely taking it too far. (*Daily Express*)

One of my favourite goals: scoring West Ham's second against champions Manchester City in November 1968 from a cross from Geoff Hurst (who was returning the favour for one I'd made for him earlier in the match). (*Central Press*)

A statue of me, Geoff Hurst, Bobby Moore and Ray Wilson outside the grounds of West Ham United, 2003.

headed past Calderon. Our first goal? No such luck. The Italian referee Concetto Lo Bello disallowed it. I believe he thought I was offside.

Something special was needed to break the deadlock and it was provided by Bobby Charlton. Gathering the ball from Roger deep in midfield, Bobby began one of his majestic runs straight at the heart of the Mexican defence. He shot from about thirty yards, one of those thudding, bullet drives he specialised in. Calderon had no chance.

Late in the second half we put the matter beyond dispute. Calderon dived to save a shot from Jimmy Greaves, but pushed the ball out to Roger Hunt, who scored his thirteenth goal in fifteen matches for England.

We were little better than functional that day but the result set us on our way, and it was a significant moment in my career. From then on, I was part of the side, but for Terry Paine, it was his nineteenth and last game for England.

We were now in pole position in Group One. When Mexico and Uruguay drew 0–0 it meant that we could determine our own fate in the final qualifying game. If we beat or drew with France, we'd play Argentina at Wembley in the quarter-finals. If we lost to France, we'd play West Germany in Sheffield. Alf wanted to stay at Wembley.

Alf made it clear to us in the four-day build-up to the French match that he wanted a stylish win. The French could no longer qualify for the last eight, although they'd knocked England out of the European Nations Cup in one of Alf's first games in charge. That defeat still rankled with him and with Bobby Moore, Jimmy Greaves and Bobby Charlton, who had been in the team that suffered a 5–2 defeat in Paris.

Alf introduced his third orthodox winger for the match, recalling Ian Callaghan at outside-right. Ian replaced Terry Paine in the only change to the team that beat Mexico.

The French played with a lot of flair and optimism despite

Robert Herbin twisting his knee in the opening five minutes. No substitutes were allowed in those days, so he had to limp through the rest of the match, and the game was ultimately of questionable quality, briefly illuminated by Roger Hunt's two goals. At the end of it, England had secured a place in the last eight but at the cost of a couple of serious worries. Jimmy Greaves finished the match with a badly gashed leg that required six stitches, and Nobby Stiles was subject to widespread criticism for his tackle on Jacques Simon.

The consequences of Jimmy's injury were to hang over him like a black cloud for the rest of his career. At least in Nobby's case the fallout was brief, if intense. The injury cost Jimmy far more than a place in the quarter-final. He was to miss the rest of the tournament, and in fact played only three more games for his country. He made the mistake the following year of telling Alf that he didn't want to be selected for England squads if the manager had no intention of putting him in the team. That was it. Alf wouldn't be dictated to, not even by Jimmy Greaves, and never picked him again. Jim scored 44 goals in 57 matches, and it's a shame that he played his last game for England at the age of twenty-seven.

I wonder what he might have achieved had he remained in the England squad, because he had an unrivalled talent for scoring goals. Brian Glanville, the distinguished football writer, once observed: 'His instinct for being in the right place near the goal was almost psychic.' The game was changing, though. Jim had a relaxed attitude to training at a time when coaches were beginning to put more and more emphasis on athleticism, mobility and hard running. In the penalty box, however, there was no one to touch him. He lived off his wits and his sudden burst of speed, but he never wore shin pads. He felt they slowed him up. Well maybe, but shin pads might have reduced the risk of injury.

Some of the newspapers were saying that Jim's contribution to England's cause so far had been ineffectual, because he had played in England's opening three games without scoring. Some even suggested that Alf was looking for an excuse to leave him out. Well, he didn't really need an excuse. When we returned to the Hendon Hall Hotel that night, Jimmy showed me the gash on his shin. There was little chance that he would play in the quarter-finals.

That evening, we were also made aware of the storm gathering over Nobby Stiles. His tackle from behind on Simon, as he moved to collect a throw from his goalkeeper, had been gruesome, but Nobby insisted that it was simply a matter of bad timing. He hadn't intended to hurt the Frenchman. Nobby was aggressive but he wasn't vicious. Even so, he wouldn't get away with some of those old-time tackles in the modern game. Not many people realised at the time that he wore contact lenses and was extremely short-sighted. I can remember watching him in the dressing room, his eyes watering as he tried to put in his contact lenses before a match. In the years that followed I often played against him and sometimes I'd end up in a heap clutching my ankle. 'Sorry Mart!' he'd grin. 'Didn't see you.'

Many felt Nobby should have been sent off for his tackle on Simon. FIFA informed the Football Association that action would be taken if Stiles was reported again for violent conduct, and the FA took it very seriously. They actually suggested to Alf the day before the match that Nobby should be left out. It was, after all, likely to be a turbulent game. Argentina had already demonstrated their taste for rough-house football against Spain and West Germany.

Alf was horrified when asked to drop Nobby. He had accepted Nobby's version of events and refused to leave him out of the team. 'If he goes, I go,' he told the FA hierarchy.

Alf was angry that the Stiles affair had overshadowed the build-up to England's most important game for many years. He had difficult enough decisions to make without that, and showed that he was bold enough to make them. Wingers Paine,

Connelly and Callaghan had all had a chance. Each had played in one of the first three matches. I'm sure that Alf wanted to play with wingers because they provided an invaluable attacking option, but he knew something was not quite right about the shape of the team. So he took the radical option and abandoned wingers altogether.

For a nation raised on the exploits of Matthews and Finney this was hard to accept. Alf took the criticism on the chin and chose two midfield players in the wide positions – Alan Ball on the right and me on the left. With Jimmy still on the treatment table, he also called up Geoff Hurst for his first game in the tournament. We didn't know it then, but this was to be the team that played in the World Cup final a week later. The 4-3-3 formation was history. We were about to become Alf's 'wingless wonders'.

I can still recall the tension in the dressing room before kick-off. Shep and Les Cocker pinned Nobby to the wall. 'Alf's stuck his neck out for you,' they said. 'Don't let him down.'

He didn't. Nobby was outstanding against Argentina. Composed, disciplined, he ignored the provocation, the spitting and the cursing and did a great man-marking job on Ermindo Onega. Alf stressed before the match, and particularly to Nobby, that we shouldn't rise to the bait. Although they were enormously talented, Argentina possessed a repertoire of annoying tricks. It was just as well we were ready for them because it was clear from the kick-off that they had no intention of taking any prisoners.

One name looms over this match – Antonio Rattin. The imperious Argentine captain stood 6ft 3in and seemed to be permanently at war with the short, balding West German referee, Rudolf Kreitlein. Whenever the referee blew his whistle, Rattin protested. When Roberto Perfumo was booked, Rattin protested. When Rattin himself was booked, for trying to trip Bobby Charlton, he protested. When Luis Artime was booked ten minutes before half-time, Rattin protested, jabbing his finger at the referee. No one could understand what he was saying but the referee knew by his tone that it wasn't pleasant. Finally, he'd had enough. He glared at the leering Rattin and pointed to the dressing room. Rattin had just become the first player to be sent off at Wembley but he refused to go. He gestured to the Argentine bench for help, he shrugged his shoulders, held his head in his hands, a picture of injured innocence.

Rattin's ten team-mates walked off. Ken Aston, the lofty former schoolmaster who was head of the World Cup referees, walked on to support Kreitlein. Harry Cavan, the FIFA match commissioner from Ireland, also came on to adjudicate.

Ray Wilson sat on the match ball in the sunshine, seemingly quite unconcerned. We'd talked about Rattin before the match and he kept referring to him as 'The Rat'.

Finally, after eight minutes, Rattin accepted his fate and walked round the edge of the pitch towards the tunnel like a man heading to the gallows. It was a pity because he was a fine footballer.

The Argentines were no easier to break down with ten men. They kept the ball well and, to be honest, we were struggling to make any real impression. For a long period, I feared we were heading for extra time. They held out until twelve minutes from time when Ray Wilson broke up an Argentine attack and sent a short pass upfield to me. I remember gathering the ball and carrying it forward a few paces before curling a cross to the near post with my weaker left foot. I didn't know precisely where Geoff Hurst was at the time but I suspected that he'd be waiting for me to deliver the ball into his path at the near post because we'd done the same thing so many times on Saturday afternoons up and down the country. Geoff, who had been able to exploit some of the spaces vacated by Rattin, met the ball with a glancing header, directing it into the net just inside the back post. The goalkeeper Antonio Roma didn't know much about it, but the 90,000 crowd did, leaping to their feet in relief and jubilation. It was a moment of classic football in what was otherwise a torrid, hard-fought game that did little for the long-term relationship between England and Argentina.

As we trooped off the field at the end, George Cohen tried to complete the ritual shirt exchange with Alberto Gonzalez but Alf rushed up and stopped him. It was bedlam in the tunnel leading to the dressing rooms. The police had to protect the referee from angry Argentine players. They were in a foul mood and threw a chair into our dressing room. We shut the door and they began hammering on it. Jack Charlton wanted to fight them all. 'Let them in,' he shouted.

Much of the black humour that rose to the surface after what had happened on the pitch survives to this day in the fund of stories each of us calls upon in our after-dinner speaking routines. One of my favourites involves Nobby, slumped in a corner at the end of the match.

'Shep, come and take a look at this leg,' he called to our physiotherapist.

'Why? What's wrong with it?'

'I don't know whose it is!'

Alf, surveying a dressing room that looked like a battlefield dressing station, saw nothing to laugh about at the time. He was so angered by the Argentine tactics that in a television interview after the match he described them as 'animals'. That unfortunate comment reverberated around the football world and was to haunt him for years.

The game had other profound consequences. The South American nations threatened to pull out of FIFA because of, they claimed, a European conspiracy. It was a fact that the four semi-finalists were all European. It was also a fact that at Hillsborough, the English referee Jim Finney had sent off two Uruguayans – Hector Silver and Horacio Troche – in their quarter-final with West Germany.

Pele also got in on the act, complaining that lenient refereeing had allowed Bulgaria and Portugal to kick him out of the competition. It was indeed true that one of the most cynical fouls of the entire tournament had been committed on Pele by Portugal's Joao Morais in their 3–1 win over defending champions Brazil. Another English referee, George McCabe, had been in charge of this game.

Now it was our turn to face Portugal. The nation was rejoicing at our progress but we all knew, deep down, that we had not played to our potential, although there had been some encouraging signs in our performance against Argentina.

Despite being a great fan of Jimmy Greaves, I had to admit we hadn't missed him. Jim could turn a match with a flash of brilliance but he was a bit of a lone wolf. I thought we looked a better-balanced unit with Geoff in the team. The other thing I felt was that the absence of wingers actually gave Bobby Charlton more scope in the midfield areas.

Bobby was our finest creative player but when we had a winger in the team he had to share some of the defensive duties. With two workers, such as Alan Ball and me, on the flanks, Bob was able to jettison some of the defensive donkey-work and focus more on his attacking play. Ballie and I were both young and superfit. We could run all day.

We might not have played especially well, but beating Argentina, the South American champions at the time, was psychologically important for us. The final was just one match away. We had three days to prepare to meet Portugal.

I remember talking to Geoff about it in our room one evening. It seemed like a dream to both of us. Had you suggested to either of us a few months earlier that we might be playing in the World Cup final, we'd have both fallen over with laughter.

The Portuguese were one of Europe's most creative football nations, although England had won six of the nine previous encounters. Portugal had beaten us just once. Their defensive flaws were fairly obvious in their quarter-final at Goodison Park, where the heroic North Koreans raced into a three-goal lead before eventually collapsing. Eusebio, one of the world's great players, was the man who brought about their downfall. He scored four goals as Portugal won 5–3 in one of the most memorable matches of the entire tournament.

With Pele out, Eusebio was dubbed the World Cup's most exotic personality in 1966. An awesome player known as the 'Black Panther', he combined muscular pace with the kind of ball control we used to drool over in England. His fabulous international career had begun against England at Wembley five years earlier. Alf's game plan had special provision for him. Nobby was once again given the man-marking job.

They knew each other – Nobby had twice successfully marked Eusebio when Manchester United played Benfica in the European Cup – but Eusebio was the European Footballer of the Year and, quite fittingly, the tournament's top marksman with seven goals. It would take something special to stop him.

Alf told us that he planned to retain the same team. Jimmy's cut leg was healing but he wasn't quite ready. Would Alf have risked him anyway, if he wouldn't wear shin guards?

At our team hotel, Alf stressed the dangers of complacency. Portugal, he assured us, were one of the world's great attacking teams and players such as Eusebio, the huge Jose Torres and the winger Antonio Simoes could destroy us if we allowed them the time and space their game needed.

The night before our match we watched West Germany beat Russia 2–1 on TV in the other semi-final at Goodison Park. It was a bad-tempered game, illuminated only by the performance of Russia's legendary goalkeeper, Lev Yashin. In contrast, our semi-final was a wonderful game of football without a trace of malice. In fact, the match was twenty-three minutes old before Pierre Schwinte, the French referee, blew for a foul. I was the culprit, having obstructed Eusebio.

On the half hour, the Portugal goalkeeper Jose Pereira threw himself at a shot from Roger Hunt. He couldn't hold the ball and it flew out to the edge of the penalty area from where Bobby sweetly drove it into the net. Twelve minutes from the end, Geoff pulled a cross back from the by-line into Bobby's path. Without breaking his stride Bobby hit a thudding shot into the back of the net from the edge of the penalty area.

We thought it was all over then, but there was still a twist and some late drama. Jack Charlton handled a header from Torres on the goal-line. In the modern game he would have been sent off and ruled out of the final but Jack wasn't even booked. He just watched as Eusebio scored from the penalty spot, some consolation for a wonderful player whose influence on the match had been severely curtailed by Nobby's diligent marking.

Driven on by their midfield inspiration, Mario Coluna, Portugal swept forward in search of an equaliser but we survived the last few desperate minutes, with Nobby's critical intervention denying Simoes a certain equaliser in the last moments of an enthralling match.

Eusebio, with tears in his eyes, congratulated all the England players as we left the field. When we got back to our dressing room Alf, who didn't often praise individuals, asked for a round of applause for Nobby Stiles.

'Yes, well done Nob!' enthused Jack. 'We can have a drink tonight, Alf, can't we?'

'No,' said Alf, 'we can't. We have another match in four days. It's the World Cup final and I expect you to win it.'

9

'SORRY, MUM!'

Before 30 July 1966, I was just another of the 2000 or so professionals in the Football League. By the end of that day, I'd become one of only eleven Englishmen to win the World Cup. From then on, life would never be quite the same for me, or for many others. It was, for instance, the day that made Sir Geoff Hurst and the day that broke his friend Jimmy Greaves.

It goes without saying that, professionally, no other day before or since has provided the same sense of achievement. Even now, I feel inordinately proud of our unique success at Wembley. It wasn't all laughter and triumph, though. I learned a lot about myself, and a mistake I made then still gnaws at me. I was just twenty-two, a gullible youngster swept along by the excitement and expectation that embraced the entire nation throughout that summer. I was earning less than £100 per week at West Ham, which was considerably more than the national average for a working man but nothing like the equivalent of the wage of a modern Premier League player. To supplement income, it was quite common for players to sell their complimentary match tickets on the black market and I was no different from anyone else. As a married man with a baby daughter, and having just bought a new house, I felt under some financial pressure.

In the euphoria following the semi-final win over Portugal, most of the players were approached by touts and asked if they wanted to sell their complimentary tickets for the final. As you can imagine, tickets for the final were like gold dust. They ranged in price from ten shillings (50p) to £5. The players were each given two £5 seats. It might not sound much today, but a tenner represented more than half a week's wages for many working men.

'Fat' Stan Flashman, one of the most famous of the London ticket touts, asked if I would sell my two complimentaries, and without considering the consequences I said, 'Yes.' I don't remember what he gave me for the tickets but whatever it was it was no compensation for the shame I've felt since that day. I still regret the consequences of my decision to sell those tickets because it meant that my mum and dad were unable to go to Wembley to watch the match. It didn't occur to me at the time that I was denying my parents the opportunity to watch their son play in the World Cup final. They sat at home instead and watched on their black and white television set.

They never complained. It was simply not spoken about within the family, but over the years it became clear that everyone outside the immediate family assumed that William and Mary had been at Wembley for the big day. If asked what it was like watching her son win the World Cup at Wembley, my mother would always reply, 'I don't know. We weren't invited.'

You can't rewind history. I was naive and immature and, with hindsight, wish I had avoided the temptation to cash in. My mum and dad had watched me play for West Ham in the European Cup Winners' Cup final the previous year and must have hoped to return to Wembley for the World Cup final. I wonder sometimes how I could have been so stupid but I just didn't think about what I was doing. I simply took advantage of a system that most of the other players also used to their financial benefit.

Occasionally, in the years that followed, there were one or two uncomfortable moments when 1966 came into the conversation, but my parents never tried to make me feel guilty. That, I think, illustrates how close we were – a typical London working-class family I suppose.

My parents reacted like the rest of their generation when they realised that our opponents in the final would be the Germans. It's perhaps difficult for younger generations to appreciate, but in 1966 the aftermath of the Second World War still hung over many families. Wartime austerity had extended well into my youth. Recovery was slow. I remember the rationing of meat, butter and coal in the fifties, and London bombsites were still used as car parks in the sixties. Others still counted the human loss. Kathy's family, for instance, suffered an appalling tragedy one night at the height of the Blitz on the capital.

A bomb fell on her granddad's house in East Ham. Her father Wally was the sole survivor. He lost both parents that night, plus his three married sisters and their husbands, who were all home on leave. Everyone was together in the same house. The three sisters were Kathleen, who was pregnant, Doris and Winifred. They were the three names given to Kathy when she was born two months after the end of the war.

Although the war had been over for twenty-one years by 1966, many Londoners still felt animosity towards the Germans. References to the war might have been considered tasteless in some quarters but the fact is that they were inevitable in some homes. To many of those who'd lived through the war, defeat by the Germans in a football match would have been a devastating humiliation. As players, we didn't talk about it in those terms, but I think we were all aware of an added responsibility that wouldn't have been present had the opposition been Portugal or the USSR.

West Germany – the result of the division of the nation at the end of the war – had established an impressive international pedigree in football in a short time. They'd won the World Cup at their first attempt in 1954, beating the Mighty Magyars of Hungary, and had finished as semi-finalists in 1958 and quarter-finalists in 1962 – but they had never beaten England. They had lost four times, conceding eight goals and scoring just two in the process. As a united country before the war, they had lost to England twice and drawn once, 3–3 in Berlin in 1930. East Germany had lost once in Leipzig in 1963.

The record books and home advantage clearly favoured England. Many in the rest of the world were not so sure if that was the result they wanted. I think most neutrals wanted West Germany to win. The French, the Portuguese, all the Latin Americans and the Scots – we'd won 4–3 at Hampden Park three months earlier – seemed to be hoping for a German victory.

Why was this? Well, I think our style of play had not endeared us to everyone. I also believe that many felt the tournament had been loaded in England's favour. The old Empire Stadium at Wembley was England's stronghold and it was an enormous advantage to play all our games there. I remember the rumblings of a controversy when a Football Association brochure mistakenly suggested that an England semi-final might be played at Everton's Goodison Park ground. Under FIFA rules at the time, the World Cup organising committee chose the respective venues and when they decided that England's semi-final would not be played in Liverpool but at Wembley, the conspiracy theorists accused Sir Stanley Rous, the English president of FIFA, of favouritism.

As I understand it, the truth was that the World Cup organisers believed an England–Portugal semi-final at Wembley would attract a full house of 90,000 while a West Germany–Russia semi-final might attract only half that figure. The crowd for Germany's semi-final at Goodison Park was 38,273.

I still have a newspaper cutting at home in which the *Daily Mirror*'s famous sports columnist of the time, Peter Wilson, wrote that England's semi-final victory over Portugal answered 'those who have enviously, maliciously and malevolently tried to say that the World Cup tournament was rigged for us'.

As far as style of play was concerned, some found this irksome and tedious but it's beyond dispute that we improved as the tournament progressed. We were not Brazil, I agree, but we did the simple things well. That was at the heart of our game.

We'd been careful not to allow the opposing teams time and space. As soon as we lost possession it was a matter of pride to us that we got all our players behind the ball. It may not have been pretty to watch but it was all part of the development of the team. No one was going to beat us easily. Our confidence grew with each clean sheet and it was this self-belief that was to be so important at critical stages in the World Cup final.

In five matches, against Uruguay, Mexico, France, Argentina and Portugal, we'd conceded just one goal – Eusebio's penalty in the semi-final. We were easily the best defensive side in the tournament and we had the benefit of the world's best defender in Bobby Moore. We also had one of the world's best strikers in Jimmy Greaves. Poor Jim! Now fully fit, he was expecting a recall to the team for the final.

Four years earlier, Spurs had paid a record fee of £99,999 to bring Jim home from AC Milan. Manager Bill Nicholson had refused to pay the extra pound because he didn't want to saddle Jim with the burden of being football's first £100,000 player. Jim's stay in Italy had been short and sweet. He scored goals but, typically, resented the authoritarian style of management, the disciplined training regimes and the negative tactics of Italian football. He was his own man and I've always felt that his stubborn refusal to wear shin guards weighed against him when Alf was pondering the make-up of the final team. With no substitutes, if we lost a player in the final through injury, we would have to finish the match with ten men. Alf knew that if the cut reopened on Jimmy's shin, England might be reduced to ten players.

On top of that, there was little doubt that Geoff Hurst's inclusion for the matches against Argentina and Portugal coincided with an improvement in our team play. We were better as a unit with him in the side. Jim could win a match for you in a flash, but with Geoff you got a guaranteed ninety minutes of non-stop endeavour. Alf liked that.

In the build-up to the final, the Greaves question dominated the headlines. Should he be risked? Had Hurst done enough to retain his place? Geoff and I trawled through the newspapers. We were room-mates and, as we were both junior members of the team, we spent a lot of time together speculating about the line-up. He was anxious. He'd played well against Argentina and Portugal but he knew that he would almost certainly be dropped if Alf decided to recall Jimmy.

Just as in the long days at Lilleshall, when we studied every move in every training session in the hope that we'd find some clue to the make-up of the squad, now we studied training again, hoping for a clue to the team for the final. Alf had already told the media that he would not make his team selection public until a couple of hours before kick-off.

There were no clues in training. Alf gave little away, although it was apparent to everyone that Jimmy was training again and expecting to play. He was rooming with Bobby Moore, and although we were club-mates, we knew that Bob considered Jimmy to be an integral part of the England team.

Some newspapers believed that the return of Greaves would be a great psychological boost to England while others claimed that no manager, not even Ramsey, would break up a winning team.

Although Bobby and Jim were close, Geoff and I both knew him, too. I liked him as an individual and recognised him as a unique talent among footballers at the time. After all, at that stage of his career he was the most prolific marksman in England's history with 43 goals in 54 matches. Geoff had scored just two goals in his first seven England matches. A couple of weeks earlier, no one – not me, not Geoff, not Alf, not the man in the street – would have given England the faintest hope of winning the World Cup without Jimmy Greaves in the team.

That Friday morning, twenty-four hours before the match, we trained as normal at Roehampton. In the afternoon, Geoff and I left the hotel and took a bus to Golders Green High Road where we sat in a little delicatessen we'd visited a few times. One or two of the other lads were in there. We all looked at each other with enquiring eyes, but no one actually asked the question, 'Are you in?' In all probability, no one knew for sure whom Alf would pick, although a few individuals had been told by then. The same team had played against Argentina and Portugal and we, or at least most of us, felt that Alf was unlikely to change it.

At various stages during the day, Alf had told several of us separately that we were playing, and sworn us to secrecy, but he hadn't told everyone. One man he didn't tell was Jimmy's room-mate Bobby Moore. I suppose the England captain didn't need to be told he was playing. He would have known automatically.

Alan Ball wasn't told, either. He was the youngest player in the team and he had a theory that he might have been left out to accommodate Jimmy in a 4-3-3 formation. I don't give any credence to that. I can't imagine Alf thinking for a second of playing three front strikers – Hurst, Hunt and Greaves – against West Germany. Alan heard that he was playing the following morning. The first thing he did was telephone his dad, Alan senior. 'Dad said he'd come to Wembley only if I was playing,' Alan explained to us.

Ballie's reaction on hearing that he was in the team was one of jubilation mixed with relief, but when the news that he had not been selected finally reached Jimmy, he was broken-hearted. He had feared the worst and confirmation of it must have been the worst moment of his illustrious career. That morning, while we were preparing to play in the World Cup final, he was packing his bags, talking to his wife and making last-minute plans to go on holiday.

Jimmy's disillusionment with football began that day. For him, the game would never be quite the same again. I can understand how he must have felt. He was such a consistent goal-scorer, he was always confident of selection. He'd become an iconic figure in English football and I believe he felt he deserved a place in the team that day. Playing for England was the pinnacle of a professional's career and playing in the World Cup final was a once-in-a-lifetime experience. Jimmy knew that he was unlikely to get another chance.

Alf's decision hurt him and I think, forty years later, he still resents the fact that he was denied a role on the biggest stage in English football history. His decision to quit international football at the age of twenty-seven illustrates just how disenchanted he became with the game. Geoff Hurst, for whom Jimmy's dark cloud had a silver lining, is still a friend of his and will tell anyone who wants to listen that, as a goalscorer, Jimmy Greaves was on another planet!

We will never know what would have happened at Wembley that day had Jimmy played but I suspect the Germans were pleased that he was on the sidelines. That, I'm sure, would have been their attitude before kick-off. They had their own worries, not least about young Franz Beckenbauer, who was emerging as one of the world's great footballers. Just twenty, he was almost as important to the German team as Bobby Charlton was to the England team.

Beckenbauer had received his second caution of the tournament in the semi-final win over the USSR and then, as now, two bookings meant an automatic one-match suspension, but only if FIFA's disciplinary committee ratified each booking. Some they ratified, which meant the disciplinary process followed its due course, and some they didn't. Beckenbauer's second caution was never ratified, which meant that Franz was free to play against England.

This was very good news for the Germans. Although still a student of the game, Franz was a superb player and he spent ten years in the heart of the West German team. He played 103 times for his country and captained Bayern Munich to domestic domination plus three consecutive European Cup triumphs in the mid-seventies. He lifted the World Cup as captain (1974) and manager (1990) and is considered by many to be the most influential German footballer of all time.

Beckenbauer could play in any midfield or defensive position but against us in 1966, he was used to do a marking job in midfield. His task was to mark Bobby Charlton, vastly more experienced and eight years older. They share the same birthday – 11 October. It was an onerous responsibility for a youngster but the diligence with which he pursued the great Charlton marked him out as a player with special qualities. He had a wonderful touch, a good passing range, could be aggressive when required and had organisational skills that he would later use as the German captain.

He introduced the concept of the attacking sweeper, frequently striding forward from deep defensive positions to reinforce his attack and outnumber the opposition. He was a bit like Bobby Moore in the way that he could read the game and anticipate dangerous situations. The cool, regal way he brought order to chaos earned him the nickname 'The Kaiser'.

Franz and Bobby became good friends in the years that followed and, after Bobby's death, he became a regular contributor to The Bobby Moore Fund for Cancer Research. He's an affable, charming guy whom I see occasionally. It was no surprise when the Germans used him to promote their bid to host the 2006 World Cup.

Alf reminded Bobby Charlton of the threat posed by Beckenbauer in our dressing room before kick-off. At much the same time I guess, Helmut Schoen, the West German manager, was having a similar conversation with Beckenbauer about Charlton. I've often thought that the natural consequence of this man-marking policy by the coaches was that the two best players on the field that day cancelled each other out. Neither played to anything like their full potential because they were more interested in the negative aspects of their jobs. The losers were the spectators.

In the couple of hours immediately before kick-off, our dressing room was a scene of chaos. Uncharacteristically, Alf had invited TV crews, photographers and FA officials into our sanctuary. I can't recall another England match when he allowed this invasion of our privacy.

Several players, myself included, spent a few minutes painting the three white adidas stripes on our boots. Some, like me, were wearing genuine adidas boots and were simply enhancing the stripes for the benefit of television. Others were doctoring old boots made by different manufacturers, because no one wanted to wear brand new boots. In fact, I don't think Alf would have allowed it.

The lucrative boot contracts offered to modern stars did not exist, and the opportunity to help bootmakers exploit the TV exposure merely provided a little bit of extra cash. A couple of days before the final, an adidas representative had approached us offering each player £300 to wear their boots – or appear to be wearing their boots. We all agreed, except Gordon Banks who was lured by Puma with a better offer.

About thirty minutes before kick-off, Mooro, usually a picture of serenity before a game, shouted above the racket in the dressing room, 'Aren't we supposed to be getting ready for a big match?'

I wasn't too bothered. I was tense and excited but I didn't suffer from nerves. I'd slept well the previous night and was probably more concerned about Kathy. After moving house the day before, she was so exhausted that she missed the players' wives trip to see The Black and White Minstrel Show on the evening before the final. She was there at Wembley, though, in all her finery, sitting with the other girls in a block especially reserved for the wives. I was thinking of her as we walked up the tunnel into the sunlight of the stadium.

We could hear the chants of 'England, England' as we left our dressing room but the noise as we emerged on to the running track around the pitch took your breath away. As we warmed up on the pitch, I remember testing my studs in the turf. When we walked about the pitch an hour earlier, it had been raining and the pitch was damp. I always preferred screw-in studs to the moulded rubber boots, which were only suitable for hard, dry pitches. The screw-in studs gave you a better grip on a soft surface and, I felt, made more of an impact when you tackled. I'd decided that afternoon to wear short screw-in studs and, after a few sprints and a bit of twisting and turning during the warm-up, I was sure I'd made the right decision.

This was not a day for making mistakes, however small. It was typical of me that I kept telling myself that the most important thing in the next ninety minutes was to do the simple things well, take no unnecessary risks and make no mistakes. The prospect of scoring a goal didn't enter into the equation as far as I was concerned. That was such an outrageous possibility that it wasn't worth thinking about. At my age, with just seven caps to my name, it would have been very presumptuous of me even to consider that I might end up on the scoresheet.

It was a privilege simply to pull on the England shirt and be involved on such a great day. Many far better players, before and since, never had the opportunity to play in the World Cup final – Jimmy Greaves, sitting up there in the stand somewhere, was one.

As the newest member of the team – my debut had been just ten weeks earlier – I tended to keep my thoughts to myself. I was quietly confident that we would win, and so was Geoff. We had each played seven games for England, though not the same ones, and had both finished on the winning side in all of them. Neither of us had known disappointment in an England shirt and, after weeks and weeks of training and rooming together, we had convinced each other that we played in a team good enough to win the World Cup.

Alf had also convinced us that we were good enough to win. He'd spoken to us all individually as we left the dressing room, reminding us of specifics that he felt would be important during the match. He had a word or two with me about Wolfgang Overath. I would be playing directly against him on my side of the pitch, and Alf reminded me that I would be attacking the ball at the near post every time we had a corner. He also asked me to make sure I was in the right position for set pieces. One of my responsibilities was to line up our defensive wall if the Germans had a free kick near our goal, a role that took on special significance in the final seconds of normal time. He said with some certainty that he could practically guarantee the Germans would contest every ball, every tackle and every header until the final whistle. He was right.

My last thought as Gottfried Dienst, the Swiss referee, blew the whistle was that I did not want to let down Alf Ramsey. He had given me this big chance and I wanted to repay him with a victory.

That began to look unlikely as early as the thirteenth minute. There was little remarkable about the opening skirmishes until Siggy Held, in possession out on the left, drove a deep, aimless pass to the far side of England's penalty area. With no German challenging for the ball, Ray Wilson, a solitary figure in yards of space, rose easily to head it clear. He had time to head the ball to the side but instead headed it back down the middle of the field. This was compounded by the fact that his header lacked power. The ball barely reached the edge of the penalty area where an astonished Helmut Haller suddenly realised that he had been presented with a goalscoring opportunity. He controlled the ball quickly and drove it past the advancing Bobby Moore, the lunging Jack Charlton and the unsighted Gordon Banks into the England goal. For the first time in the tournament England were behind.

The roots of the German goal could be traced back to Ray Wilson, but there was no finger-pointing, not then nor later. The strength of our team lay in the fact that we sank or swam together. In six matches in that tournament Ray made just one mistake. His rare miscalculation had given the Germans an enormous boost at that early stage in the match. It was a test for us and we overcame it. Confidence was high and morale was strong. Six minutes after their goal we equalised.

Bobby Moore was the critical figure in our first goal. People don't realise just how often he would start attacking moves with a good pass from the back, or pick up the ball and move forward with it into an attacking position. If you watch video footage of him in action, you'll see that he loved nothing better than getting hold of the ball and carrying it forward. What gave him an advantage was the speed with which he could assess all the available options. On this occasion, having just received a pass from Bobby Charlton, he was tripped by Overath. As the referee whistled for the foul, Bobby picked up the ball and within a fraction of a second had placed it ready for the free kick.

Forty-five yards from the German goal, Mooro addressed the ball and was about to strike it when he suddenly checked himself. As the Germans jostled for position in their penalty area Bobby looked up, saw Geoff Hurst begin his run, and drove the ball with inch-perfect accuracy into his path.

We'd used that free-kick ploy dozens of times at West Ham. Bobby knew where Geoff was going. He simply had to check when Geoff started his run and then Geoff would know where Bobby was sending the ball and, sure enough, he met it at the appointed time and place with a clinical header that beat Hans Tilkowski in the German goal.

The German defence simply didn't have the high-ball special-ists needed to counter both Geoff and Roger Hunt in the air. They played with a sweeper, Willi Schulz, and three markers – Wolfgang Weber, Karl-Heinz Schnellinger and Horst Hottges. Weber was the only orthodox central defender and he marked Roger Hunt. Hottges, a full-back, was given the job of marking Geoff and, as we know, there was only one winner in that clash.

Alf thought Tilkowski might be vulnerable in the air and I remember Geoff testing that theory early in the match with a thunderous challenge on the anxious German goalkeeper. They collided in mid-air and Tilkowski required treatment. He was a bit wary of Geoff after that.

Geoff's run and unchallenged header had caught the Germans unaware and had, to all intents and purposes, swung the balance of the game. We were in the driving seat once more.

Just before half-time, Ray Wilson made one of his surging runs down the left and sent over a well-judged cross that Geoff, outjumping the German defence again, steered into the path of Roger Hunt. He drove his shot straight at Tilkowski and I won-dered if I was the only player thinking, 'What would Jimmy have done with a chance like that?'

Alf had a few words of reassurance at half-time. Remember, he said, the Germans won't throw in the towel. They will fight until the last kick of the match. How true!

When we emerged for the second half it was raining. I was glad I was wearing my studs. The pitch was a little slicker and the ball moved a little quicker. Alan Ball, a bundle of energy out on the right, skipped past Schnellinger a couple of times in one of the more intriguing personal duels of an absorbing match. The battle in midfield between Beckenbauer and Charlton was equally engrossing although, ultimately, unsatisfactory for both teams. Neither player really posed a threat.

I thought we looked the fitter side but there was no sign of either of us breaking the deadlock until thirteen minutes from the end. Ballie won a corner on the right, took it himself and surprised me by driving it deep to the back post. Geoff latched on to it and drove the ball at the goal. Hottges, slipping on the wet surface, stuck out a leg and the ball cannoned off him and rose into the air. I watched the ball hang for a second and then begin to fall. I was still standing in my designated position for corners and I remember thinking 'Hell, it's coming to me!'

Jack Charlton was a yard or so away from me. He always says, 'Thank God it fell to Martin and not me!'

As the ball fell I had time to think and my thought was, 'Hit the target! Hit the target!' I could see the goal in front of me and suddenly the ball was in the same frame. I'd always been a pretty good volleyer and I knew that timing was critical. I got my knee over the ball and from about six yards volleyed it sweetly towards the goal with my right foot. Tilkowski and Schnellinger, both under the crossbar, lunged at the ball as it flew between them and hit the net.

For a second I couldn't take it all in. I'd just scored a goal in the World Cup final. Suddenly, the roar from the crowd was rolling down the terraces. I'd scored – in the World Cup final! I wheeled away, running back up the field, Geoff and Roger sprinting towards me. I saw Banksie running towards me from the other end of the field. It was the most extraordinary moment, like being struck by lightning. My fingers were tingling with the excitement. My head was spinning.

As we lined up to restart, I must confess that the thought crossed my mind that we had won the World Cup and we had won it with a Martin Peters goal. Then I remembered what Alf had been telling us. The Germans had a reputation for durability and in the last thirteen minutes of that match, I discovered the reasons why. They powered forward looking for the equaliser. We tried to keep possession, tried to stay calm and tried to hit them on the counter-attack.

One superb pass from Alan Ball to Roger Hunt produced a

wonderful chance for Bobby Charlton. Sadly, he sliced at the ball and hit it wide. It was to prove a costly miss. Less than a minute remained when Jack jumped above Held to head clear. Jack insists that Held was backing into him but Held claimed he had been fouled. Herr Dienst sided with the German and awarded a free kick just outside the penalty area to the left of the England goal. It was my job, remember, to line up the wall when we were defending at free kicks.

I was on the end of the line trying to communicate with Gordon Banks and get the wall in position. The opening sequence of the film *Goal* shows me doing this, with the players pulling and tugging each other when, suddenly, Lothar Emmerich smashes the free kick. The wall was lined up OK but the England players positioned behind it could have pushed up a little closer and then we might not have conceded the late equaliser. Emmerich's low drive caused disarray behind the wall, hitting Schnellinger and George Cohen before Held turned it across the face of our goal. Wolfgang Weber slid in to steer the ball home from close range past the lunging Ray Wilson.

As many have pointed out since, but for that moment I would have been credited with scoring the winning goal in the World Cup final. Instead – devastation! That served me right, I thought, for thinking it was all over. This is just what Alf had warned us about. The sense of triumph was quickly replaced by the realisation that we now faced thirty minutes of extra time. As soon as Bobby Charlton kicked off again, the referee blew for the end of normal time.

We were gutted. Having got out of jail so dramatically we all knew that the psychological pendulum had now swung in favour of the Germans. Physically, I didn't feel too bad. I didn't have an ounce of spare flesh. I wasn't quick but I was a good long-distance runner. I wasn't suffering, for instance, in the way that George was. Nobby had his socks rolled down and Bobby Moore was slumped on the pitch.

Alf and Shep came on with drinks. Those moments when we stood, exhausted, on the pitch listening to Alf deliver his rousing team-talk are now ingrained in the folklore of the game. The first thing he did was ask Bobby Moore to stand up. 'Look at the Germans,' he said. 'They're finished. They're flat on their backs.' I half expected him to launch into us because of the way we'd let it slip but he didn't. There wasn't a word of admonishment, just encouragement. 'You're the better team, you're the fitter team,' he said. 'You won it once. Now go and win it again.'

It was what we needed to hear. Within a minute or two of the restart I was involved in a move that gave Bobby Charlton a scoring opportunity. Alas, he drove his shot against the foot of a post. I remember the ball bouncing off the post into the chest of a relieved Tilkowski, and thinking, 'Perhaps it's not going to be our day.'

Then, ten minutes into extra time, Nobby hit one of the best passes of his career. People said he couldn't play but he drove a fantastic ball over Schnellinger and into space for Alan Ball on the right. Ballie scampered after it and, without looking, drove his pass to the near post.

Geoff ran to meet it and, if anything, arrived just a fraction too soon. This meant that instead of moving on to the ball, it was falling short, so he had to adjust his body and take a couple of touches to get into a shooting position. He hit the ball powerfully, toppling over as he did so. His shot hit the underside of the bar and bounced down on the line.

The Laws of the Game state that the whole of the ball must be over the line for a goal to be awarded. Was it all over the line? No one knows for sure. I always say in my after-dinner speeches that it was at least three yards over, but it wasn't.

I was close to the penalty spot at the time and I honestly thought it was over. Honestly! Roger Hunt turned away, acclaiming the goal, and some people think that is significant. They insist that if Roger had any doubt he would have continued his run and applied the finishing touch as the ball came off the bar. I don't think he could have done that. By the time he reached the ball, the scoring opportunity would probably have gone. As the ball bounced off the line, Wolfgang Weber headed it away and he was closer to it than Roger. I don't think Roger could have got there first but, if he had, it might have avoided a great controversy. I think he honestly believed it was over the line.

The Germans didn't. They were waving their arms and shouting, 'Nein, nein, nein!' The Swiss referee, besieged by protesting players, consulted his Russian linesman, Tofik Bakhramov, who thought the ball had crossed the line. Herr Dienst pointed to the centre circle. We were back in front with twenty minutes left to play.

Once more the Germans launched a series of attacks and Uwe Seeler almost equalised again, but as they grew increasingly desperate they took risks at the back. In the final seconds of the match Bobby Moore, a picture of composure, cut out a cross from Willi Schulz, played a short pass to Roger Hunt, received the return and then looked upfield, wondering what to do next. At this point I remember the referee, whistle in mouth, looking at his watch and waving 'play on'.

The German defence looked thin and Bobby knew that if he picked out Geoff with a good pass it would ease the pressure and buy us time. He finally made his selection and hit a superb, long pass upfield. It was the perfect ball forward. Geoff ran on to it, carrying the ball deep into the German half. Schnellinger was moving across to challenge him when Geoff released a terrific shot, half hoping that it would fly over the goal and bury itself deep in the stadium, wasting a few moments while it was retrieved.

The match was all but over. The late Kenneth Wolstenholme was telling a nation glued to their TV sets, 'Some people are on the pitch – they think it's all over.' As Geoff's shot flew into the net Ken added the last few words of the most famous piece of football commentary in the English language: '… it is now.'

There was no time to restart. The match was over. England had won the World Cup, 4–2 after extra time, and Geoff Hurst had become the first man in history to score a hat-trick in the final. I'd scored the other one. Not a bad day's work, I thought. Was it going to be like this every year?

The controversy over England's third goal raged for weeks, and still rumbles on whenever England play Germany, but there was no unpleasantness on the pitch, in the tunnel or in the dressing rooms afterwards. I'm not sure you would be able to guarantee the same behaviour these days if such an incident occurred again in such a big match.

If you take that one incident out, I thought the referee's handling of the match was OK – not brilliant, but OK. The controversy over Geoff's goal eclipsed everything else but a small mystery remains concerning my being cautioned by Herr Dienst. He did pull me up for one crude challenge, awarded a foul against me and ordered me to turn round so that he could check my shirt number. I saw him at a 1966 reunion in Germany years later and reminded him of the incident. He couldn't remember it but assured me that he had not taken my name.

Perhaps, on reflection, the World Cup organisers should have appointed match officials from outside Europe. Few countries in Europe had been untouched by the war years. Herr Dienst, the referee chosen to officiate, came from neutral Switzerland, but the Germans claimed for decades afterwards that the Second World War experiences of Bakhramov, the linesman from the Soviet Union, had coloured his judgement.

A stocky, silver-haired figure with a moustache and baggy shorts, his nod of assent when approached by Dienst has become one of the enduring images of the 1966 World Cup. That moment changed his life, much as the hat-trick changed Geoff's life. He became a personality back home in Azerbaijan, the former Soviet Republic. They named the airport in the capital city, Baku, after him and later made him president of the Azerbaijan FA. They have also renamed the national stadium, built in Stalin's honour seventy-five years earlier, the Bakhramov Stadium.

When England played in Baku in a World Cup qualifying tie in October 2004, Geoff Hurst and the chairman of the English Football Association, Geoff Thompson, were part of a UEFA delegation that unveiled a statue in Bakhramov's honour.

When he died, aged sixty-six, a month after Bobby Moore's death in 1993, he took several secrets to the grave. Did he really know whether the ball had crossed the line? Was it true that he had given two jars of caviar to the Malaysian on the FIFA referees committee, Koe Ewe Teik, to secure his appointment as a linesman for the final? When the Germans scored their equaliser in the dying moments of normal time, did he raise his flag because he thought Schnellinger had handled the ball. He certainly did raise his flag but he lowered it immediately. Had he seen a handball offence and had the referee blown his whistle and awarded England a free kick, extra time would not have been necessary and the match would have finished 2–1. Bakhramov would have remained as anonymous as the linesman on the other side of the pitch. Few remember his name. It was Doctor Karoi Galba, and he was from Czechoslovakia.

Twenty-one of the thirty-one referees selected for World Cup duty in 1966 were European. Just six came from the Latin American countries – Argentina, Brazil, Mexico, Chile, Uruguay and Peru. West Germany provided one, Rudolf Kreitlein, and Italy provided one, Concetto Lo Bello. Wales, Scotland and Northern Ireland supplied one referee each and England provided seven: Kevin Howley, William Clements, Ken Dagnall, John Taylor, Jim Finney, Ernie Crawford and George McCabe.

Ken Aston, an Ilford schoolmaster who had officiated at the Chile World Cup in 1962, was head of FIFA's referees committee, and he answered to another Englishman – Sir Stanley Rous, the President of FIFA. He was also a former schoolmaster and, as secretary of the Football Association, he had rewritten the rules of the game, revolutionising the way linesmen and referees controlled matches.

It's no surprise really that the Germans felt a bit hard done by!

However, the World Cup was ours and of that there was no doubt. We had won it fair and square and, forty years later, the scoreline remains indelible in the record books. Before we left the stadium in the team coach, Geoff went back on the pitch just to check the electronic scoreboard.

In the jubilation at the end of the match we had tried to coax Alf from the substitutes' bench. We wanted to carry him shoulder high around the pitch but he was having none of it. He was very unemotional. As we lined up to climb the thirty-nine steps to the royal box to receive the Jules Rimet Trophy, he made a point of shaking each of us by the hand. 'Thank you, thank you,' he said to all his players.

Bobby Moore led the team up the steps to meet the Queen. She was wearing white gloves. Typical of Bob, he tried to dry his muddy hands on his shorts. Not satisfied with that, he discreetly wiped them on the velvet front of the royal box before receiving the trophy. Turning to face the crowd, he lifted the trophy into the air and the place erupted. It was one of those moments you just don't forget.

As we drove away from the stadium, the area around Wembley was still thronged with jubilant fans. That evening we were taken to the West End where we attended the World Cup official banquet in the Royal Garden Hotel. The police had closed Kensington High Street to traffic and crowds were building outside the hotel.

The great and the good were at the banquet, including the Prime Minister Harold Wilson and all the top FIFA officials. Sadly, the players' wives and girlfriends were not invited. They dined separately that night.

There was one other significant absentee – Jimmy Greaves. He'd already disappeared and at the time no one knew where. Fearing that he would have found the celebrations hard to take, Jim had gone off on holiday. We all felt for him, but it was such a momentous occasion that I think we were more interested in enjoying the moment. I certainly was, and so was Geoff. He was the hero, the man of the moment, but the person I most wanted to be with was Kathy. I had hardly seen her, or my baby daughter Lee Ann, in the previous eight weeks.

After a long dinner, we appeared with Alf on the balcony of the hotel and waved to the cheering crowds in Kensington High Street. The wives were still waiting patiently to see their husbands.

Geoff and Judith had decided to go to Danny La Rue's club in Hanover Square, which was one of the most popular night-spots at the time. Some of the others were going, too, and Geoff asked if I would like to join them.

'Thanks – but no,' I said.

I wanted to spend the rest of the evening with Kathy, which is exactly what I did.

'That goal of yours,' she said. 'I couldn't believe it!'

I found it difficult to believe, too. The day had raced by and there had been so little time to savour it, but over the years, as others have tried and failed to emulate our success, I've come to appreciate the full significance of our achievement.

It was the start of a new era in football, the first World Cup final to be beamed around the globe. An estimated 600 million people watched the game and, in Britain, it's reckoned that 75 per cent of the nation heard Kenneth Wolstenholme's famous commentary. Mum and dad were among them. I wish they'd been at Wembley instead. Sorry, Mum!

10

FAME!

In the long summer days that followed I quickly came to realise that nothing would be quite the same again. Like it or not, I was now a World Cup hero and everything I did in the future would be judged in that context.

On the morning of Sunday, 31 July 1966, my new life started in our hotel room in Kensington with a lie-in and a cup of tea as Kathy and I scoured the newspapers. Naturally, they were full of our victory the previous day with plenty of speculation about whether Geoff Hurst's second goal had crossed the line.

In mid-morning the whole squad, with wives, gathered in the hotel lobby. We were to be ferried to the ATV studios for a televised celebratory lunch, to be hosted by Eamonn Andrews. In a quiet moment before lunch, Alf Ramsey told us about the bonus payment that had been awarded to us. Until that moment I knew absolutely nothing about any bonus payment from the Football Association. So it came as a bit of a surprise when Alf told us that we had £22,000 to share. He thought it would be best to divide the money between us according to the number of games we'd played in the final series. He said this system had been proposed by the FA. This meant that players who had appeared in all six games, such as Bobby Moore and Bobby Charlton, would receive considerably more than Geoff Hurst, who'd played in three, or Peter Bonetti and Jimmy Armfield, who'd played in none at all. I'd played in five and was still working out what this might be worth to me when a delegation of senior players said that they were going to tell Alf they disagreed with the system of sharing out the bonus money. They felt that it should be shared equally between all twenty-two players.

On reflection, it was the right thing to do and spoke volumes for the team spirit and sense of togetherness that had played such an integral part in England's success. Twenty-two of us were involved and those who hadn't played were as important as those who had. Years later, when I had a stab at management, I realised that the players left on the sidelines are often the ones who determine the mood of a squad.

So the twenty-two players in Alf's squad each received a bonus of £1000 – not a fortune but still a significant sum in those days. We had to pay tax on it, as we did on the £60 appearance fee we received for each match we played in the tournament. Kathy and I had stretched ourselves a bit to meet the price of £7400 for our new house, so the bonus was very welcome. We planned to use it to buy some new furniture. Kathy was delighted.

You can appreciate, then, that Kathy and I were feeling quite pleased with life when we climbed into the taxi, supplied by the FA, to take us home from lunch. We'd said our farewells. For the players, who'd been together for eight weeks, it was the end of a great adventure. Alf, typically, remained unmoved by the emotion of the occasion. We left at the same time as Geoff and Judith, and I recall Geoff saying goodbye to Alf. Geoff, remember, was in the foothills of superstardom after his three goals.

'See you soon, Alf,' he smiled.

'Perhaps, Geoffrey, perhaps,' was the manager's reply.

The inference was obvious – don't take anything for granted.

My first example of how life was about to change came during the drive back to our house. We were halfway home when another car drove into the back of us. No one was hurt but the accident happened outside a block of flats and attracted some attention. We'd barely got inside our front door when the telephone started ringing. It was the press wanting to know if I'd been hurt. Next morning the headlines read: 'World Cup hero in car smash!'

West Ham had told Bobby, Geoff and me to take a couple of weeks off, so Kathy and I spent a few days looking in furniture stores, where I quickly became aware of my new status. To be honest, I wasn't comfortable with it.

At first, I found it difficult to cope with fame. I was used to the fans at West Ham asking for my autograph but nothing had prepared me for the level of adulation that followed England's World Cup victory. Strangers stopped me in the street, on the train, in shops and restaurants. I found it embarrassing. It wasn't what I wanted. Being a professional footballer was simply a job I enjoyed doing. I didn't feel like a star or a celebrity. I just wanted to be left alone to lead my life the way I had been doing.

I tried to hold on to my old life as much as possible but it became increasingly difficult. People wanted me to open shops, attend prize-givings and make guest appearances. I could understand it with Bobby Moore. He was, after all, the England captain, the golden boy of football and he'd lifted the Jules Rimet Trophy. I could understand it with Geoff Hurst, who had become the first man in history to score a hat-trick in the World Cup final. But why me? I wanted to lead my life in peace and quiet but it soon became clear that this wasn't going to happen. I gradually accepted the fact that I had a higher profile but I didn't want to use my fame in any positive sense. I didn't try to capitalise on, or exploit, my new status.

I don't suppose that would be possible today. If I was a twenty-two-year-old World Cup winner in the modern game, I don't think I'd be happy with all the fuss such an achievement would inevitably generate. Today, you can make two forty-five-minute appearances for England and, almost overnight, you're a celebrity superstar. Times are different. I'm not criticising modern players. I wish them luck. What I'm saying is that the level of adulation they now attract would not have appealed to me at all.

I tried to explain the way I felt to the Chelsea captain John Terry a year or two ago. I met him when I took Kathy to see *We Will Rock You!* in London. Someone must have spotted us as we arrived because, just as we took our seats, one of the theatre staff asked if we would like to go to the VIP room. I wasn't bothered but Kathy looked eager. So we went along for a drink and were told that John Terry would be at the show that evening. When he turned up he, too, was ushered into the VIP room where we were introduced. His girlfriend, I soon discovered, came from Dagenham.

John was casually dressed in blue jeans, the attire of choice for most professional footballers these days. I was in my usual suit and tie, the customary dress for a footballer on a night out in my time. We chatted for a while. He was quiet, demure and polite. He asked a lot of questions about football in the sixties. Kathy and I both thought he was a really nice boy. Then a few days later we read in the tabloids about some controversy or other they claimed he'd been involved in. It seemed totally at odds with the bloke we'd met in the theatre that evening.

It seems to me that every aspect of a top footballer's life is exposed to scrutiny these days. I wouldn't have liked that, even though I had very little to hide. We weren't all angels in the sixties and seventies but, in general terms, professional footballers were more aware of their responsibilities and took greater care of their reputations.

What 1966 gave me was my own identity and I was grateful for that. I had been simply a midfield player at West Ham, noted for versatility. I could play literally anywhere. Some would say this was a blessing, but it certainly didn't help when Ron Greenwood came to pick the FA Cup final side for 1964, for instance. On that occasion I thought my versatility was a curse. I'd been used as a dogsbody during the season to fill in when someone was injured and, even though I played a lot of games, it didn't secure me a place in the team when it mattered most. I felt the World Cup final changed that. It gave me a status within my profession that I hadn't enjoyed until that moment.

This became obvious as soon as the new season started – exactly three weeks after the World Cup final. Season 1966–67 opened on 20 August and West Ham's first opponents were Chelsea at Upton Park.

Ron Greenwood had spared Bobby, Geoff and me the rigours of pre-season training, figuring that rest was better than more work on the football pitch. All three of us had been to the Chadwell Heath training ground since the final to chat with our club-mates and get weighed, but none of us had done any serious pre-season work.

All three of us were selected for the opening game and the manager decided that we should go out on to the pitch ahead of the rest of the players. That was one of the most memorable moments of the summer for me. These fans were our people, local East Enders. They'd watched us all grow up in the team. I'm sure they felt proud of what their club had been able to give to England's cause. A wall-to-wall crowd of 36,126 gave us a tumultuous standing ovation as the three of us ran out on to the pitch. It was a really good moment – perhaps the only good moment of the afternoon. We lost 2–1. Chelsea goalkeeper Peter Bonetti, who'd been in the England squad with us that summer, was outstanding. There were rumours at the time that West Ham were trying to buy him.

We were given a similar reception a week later when the three of us walked out at Filbert Street to play Leicester City. On this occasion, Leicester's World Cup goalkeeper Gordon Banks walked out with us to receive the acclaim of the locals.

That game was a thriller, but we lost 5–4. In fact, we didn't win a game until we played Manchester City at Maine Road in our sixth match of the season. Nowadays, such a set of circumstances would probably provoke debate about whether the clubs were demanding too much of their players. Should World Cup heroes be thrown back into action just three weeks after the final? Surely, according to today's theory, we were playing too much football.

Well, I don't think so. We played three weeks after the final without even thinking about it. I can't remember feeling exhausted and Ron Greenwood must have been happy with the three of us because we remained in the team. There was no question of anyone being rested and no debate about overplaying. It simply wasn't an issue. Everyone accepted that the new season would follow three weeks after the World Cup final.

By today's standards, though, the schedule for the England players during that period in the game's history was remarkable. I don't think the authorities now would expect the Beckhams and Rooneys, or their clubs, to adhere to such a programme of matches. Just consider this. From the start of the 1965–66 season to the end of the World Cup, Bobby Moore played a total of 72 first-class matches – 56 for West Ham and 16 for England. Geoff Hurst played 67, 59 for West Ham and 8 for England, and I played 68, 60 for West Ham and 8 for England.

Few Premiership stars would play as many games these days. Young Frank Lampard played 67 for Chelsea and England and has been a record-breaking model of consistency, but he is a very notable exception. It's worth noting, too, that in the modern game clubs are able to share the workload among their players because of the substitution rules. Substitutes were not introduced in the Football League until 1965–66 and not in the World Cup until 1970.

In 1966–67, Bobby played 54 first-class matches, 48 for West Ham and 6 for England, Geoff played 55, 49 for West Ham and 6 for England, and I played 54, 49 for West Ham and 6 for England. So, over two seasons, separated by a break of only three weeks, Bobby Moore played 126 games and Geoff Hurst and I each played 122. Today's Premiership coaches wouldn't allow their players to undertake such intensive schedules.

I agree that the pace of the game is faster today, but otherwise the modern player has all the advantages. The pitches are superb compared to the conditions we played in – mud heaps in the winter and hard, bare wastelands in the summer. The balls are lighter, the boots are lighter, and you'd hardly know you were wearing modern-day shin guards. Diet, medical treatment and the general care of players are far superior to my day.

On the field, players are protected by referees to a degree that was unheard of thirty years ago. The tackle from behind, for instance, has been eradicated, nor is any goalkeeper challenged in the way that Banks or Bonetti were.

So I think the fixture schedule that we followed without complaint makes a complete mockery of the whining you hear from coaches such as Sven Goran Eriksson and Arsene Wenger. I understand the financial importance of the Champions League and the need to rotate players and rest the best before critical games, but that applies to a mere handful of clubs. Some Premiership clubs might play just forty to forty-five games if they get knocked out of the domestic cup competitions in the early stages. Those are not the clubs complaining about playing too much football. In fact, they want more matches. It's the élite clubs that complain loudest, which I find difficult to understand. They have the biggest squads and this allows some of their best players to appear in perhaps half the number of games per season that we would have played.

I'm not envious. I'm glad I played when I did. We may not have earned the money they get now, but I was paid well to do a job I enjoyed – and, of course, I was one of the lucky few Englishmen to have played in a World Cup winning team. The lack of any significant achievement at international level since 1966 means that our success remains at the forefront of the English game. I'd love England to win the World Cup again but I must be honest. I think that I speak for all the 1966 team when I say that we're quite content to retain World Cup gloating rights in England for a little bit longer!

I had a spring in my step that summer. Although I had no desire to change my profile or lifestyle, I have to concede that much of what I've achieved since, both on and off the football field, has been as a direct result of winning the World Cup. Wages are a case in point. Before the World Cup I was earning £45 per week. Then Ron Greenwood asked me to step into his office at Upton Park one day in the autumn of 1966 to tell me that, at his recommendation, the board of directors had agreed to increase my salary to £100 per week. Geoff and Bobby were given similar pay rises. Two years later, they improved my terms again and when I left to join Tottenham in 1970, I was earning £147 a week.

11

TEN YEARS AHEAD OF MY TIME

Alf Ramsey was a diamond and, like the rest of the 1966 team, I had great respect and affection for him, but he did me no favours when he described me as a player 'ten years ahead of his time'.

This phrase stuck and I've lived with it for the last forty years. It confused me at the time but I understand now that it was meant as a compliment. I think he was identifying me as a player with qualities that would not be common in the game for another decade. At least, that's what I think he meant. How he could know that I can't imagine.

Anyway, being ten years ahead of your time had a downside. As any professional will tell you, football dressing rooms are notorious breeding grounds for derision, ridicule and mickey taking. Having been so publicly elevated by Alf, I was clearly a target for the jokers. Prominent among them was Jack Charlton, who was one of the first to realise the wind-up potential in Alf's remarks. Eventually, I got used to the gags about living in a parallel universe or in a different time zone!

Alf announced my new futuristic status to the media in the aftermath of a 1–1 draw with Scotland at Hampden Park in February 1968. It was an important game, watched by a crowd of 134,000. Part of the Home International Championship, this match also served as a European Championship qualifier.

The Scots had beaten us 3–2 at Wembley in April 1967 and they needed to beat us again at Hampden Park to qualify for the quarter-final stage of the European Championship, but a draw was good enough for England. I played well – I usually did against Scotland – and scored our goal with a crisp volley from the edge of the penalty area. I could have scored a couple more. I was so pleased with myself at the end of the match that I picked up the match ball, sneaked it into the dressing room and kept it. We had won the Home International title and finished top of the qualifying group. The Scots were distraught. Geoff and I couldn't stop chuckling. We loved teasing the Scots.

Afterwards, in answer to a question from the media, Alf spoke glowingly about me, saying, 'He's a player who is ten years ahead of his time.'

Later in the day, as we travelled back to London, I was told what he'd said and was puzzled. What did he mean? Did he mean that my time was still ten years away? Did he mean that I wouldn't be at my best until I was thirty-five?

For much of my early career I'd had the feeling that I didn't quite fit. I didn't slip into any easily recognisable category. I wasn't a striker. I wasn't a midfield player. I wasn't a full-back. I could play in all those positions, and did, quite successfully, but a lot of people didn't have a clue about my role. Whenever there was a suggestion for an England team in a magazine or newspaper I was never in it. I remember Kathy saying one day, 'The only person who ever picks you for England is Alf Ramsey.'

Well meant as I'm sure it was, Alf's statement nonetheless initially resurrected feelings of insecurity. I lay awake that night thinking about it, telling myself that it had to be a compliment because he never said anything critical about his players in public. I consoled myself with two thoughts, neither of which made any sense. The first was that Alf was a visionary who could see into the future. The second was that I was so good, so far ahead of everyone else, that I hadn't even been invented!

Some years later, I began to wonder whether Alf had indeed had some idea of how the professional game would develop. When the great Dutch coach Rinus Michels came up with the Ajax team of the early seventies, I realised I'd at last found a category into which I could slip quite comfortably. Michels, who died in 2005, created the concept of 'total football'. He was the architect of a coaching framework and style of football that encouraged outfield players to switch positions during the match. Good individual technique was the key to this strategy and it worked for the Dutch, producing some of Europe's finest footballers.

He also urged his players to 'press' the ball, another idea that was widely copied and modified. This meant that he wanted his team to close down quickly on the opponent in possession of the ball. Three or four players 'press' the man with the ball, blocking all his avenues, forcing an error and then attacking from an advanced position. Dennis Bergkamp and Arjen Robben are good modern examples of what Michels believed in. His coaching doctrine helped develop a stream of great players, including Johann Cruyff, Ruud Krol, Johan Neeskens, Ruud Gullit, Marco Van Basten and Frank Rijkaard.

I felt at home watching Ajax in the early seventies. They had versatile players who were given the freedom of the pitch. In a sport that was becoming increasingly negative, he encouraged his teams to play an attacking game. Ajax dominated European football in the early seventies, winning the Champions Cup in three consecutive seasons. They also provided the hard core of the Dutch side that reached the 1974 World Cup final.

When Alf made his statement about me, he can't have known what was to develop in Holland a few years later, but I certainly had a better grasp of what he was alluding to when I watched Cruyff and Neeskens in action. Yes, it was indeed a big compliment. Thanks, Alf!

Looking back now, I realise that I was a different type of player in a sport that, for decades, had pigeon-holed its participants. No one was quite sure what compartment I should be in. Only the purists, it seemed, really appreciated what I had to contribute. I was flattered, for instance, by what Ron Greenwood said about me in his book, *Yours Sincerely*.

> Martin Peters was not a typical English player and the terraces didn't relate to him. In a way, his ability went above their heads. But I had no reservations about him. He was the answer to a manager's prayer. He was a connoisseur's dream. His understanding of time and space was delightful. He knew when to move and where to move. He had a nice, easy relationship with the ball, which made him look as if he was never in a hurry. But he had a steely temperament. He did everything so perfectly he made it look too easy. He brought refinement to whatever job he did and some people mistook that for softness.

He was absolutely right about the softness. Some opponents, especially in the early part of my career, made the mistake of thinking I was a soft touch. I was never a dirty or violent player but I would not be intimidated or bullied at a time when the professional game was full of so-called hard men. I never made a fuss when a tackle hurt me, but I could hand it out when necessary.

Football was a more aggressive sport in those days and opponents often considered West Ham to be a team that would buckle under intense physical pressure. Consequently, many would try rough-house tactics in the opening skirmishes in the hope of frightening us. I still remember the first time an opponent flew into me with an over the top tackle. My assailant caught me with his boot, cutting my left ankle down to the bone. It may have been an accident, but I didn't think so at the time. It was a part of the learning curve and helped prepare me for what was to come.

Although it could be physically aggressive, I didn't consider football to be a violent sport. It was just the way it was played in those days. Compared to the present day, there is little doubt that the Laws of the Game provided much greater potential for the type of challenge that has since been outlawed.

At club level, lesser teams – Mansfield, Rotherham, Swindon, Huddersfield and Blackpool are just a few that spring to mind – knocked West Ham out of Cup competitions because their game plan was to stop us playing. Ron encouraged us to play a passing game. Our one-touch football was pure and simple, glorious to watch, and our movement off the ball ensured there was always space to move in to. The trouble was, when we lost possession, the opposition exploited the space we had created. This was our Achilles heel and why we were often muscled out of games by teams whose values were totally different from ours.

At one point, Ron decided that we needed a tougher presence alongside Bobby Moore in the heart of the defence. He signed an uncompromising Scottish centre-half, John Cushley, from Celtic for £25,000. 'Cush' was as tough as old boots and a formidable tackler, but he wasn't really Ron's type of player. 'We don't do that sort of thing here,' Ron told him at the end of one match. After a couple of such reprimands, and a total of forty-six games, he was sent back to Scotland where he joined Dunfermline.

Winning was as important then as it is today, but the spirit in which the game was played was important, too. Ron felt that some coaches belittled the spirit of the game. He believed that there were finer values in football than winning simply for the sake of winning. Not everyone agreed. Almost every team employed one, if not two, players who were noted tough guys. Their principal function was to stop the opposition from playing. Today's defensive midfield players are angels alongside some of the hard men I faced, including Tommy Smith, Ron Yeats,

Maurice Setters, Gerry Byrne, Ronnie Harris, Dave Mackay, Norman Hunter, Johnny Giles, Billy Bremner, Vic Mobley, John McGrath, George Curtis and Peter Storey. They could all play, but they all had a hard streak and were acknowledged experts in a tough battle. Rule changes, better refereeing and the fact that there is no hiding place on a pitch covered by fourteen TV cameras means that much of what they got away with thirty years ago would not be tolerated today.

One or two players took it as a personal affront if you got the better of them and I think this was probably at the root of my annual duel with Billy Bremner. Small, Scottish and ginger-haired, Bremner was a truly great competitor and did much to create the reputation that made Leeds United one of the most feared teams in Europe. He and I locked horns on a regular basis at both club and international level.

Billy took great exception to what happened on a chilly autumn evening at Upton Park in 1967. Leeds, under Don Revie, were one of the most powerful First Division teams of the time and that season they reached the final of the old Intercities Fairs Cup, but they came spectacularly unstuck against West Ham in the League Cup. We'd already beaten Tottenham and Arsenal when Bremner jauntily led his team out at Upton Park, clearly believing that a Leeds United victory was a formality. When we'd met previously, they'd beaten us 5–0 with Norman Hunter scoring two and the Elland Road crowd chanting 'easy, easy'.

This time, our crowd was chanting 'easy'. We beat Leeds 7–0. Johnny Byrne was outstanding that night, Geoff Hurst and Johnny Sissons scored three each and I got the other one, dribbling past two defenders before hitting a good shot beyond the disconsolate David Harvey late in the game.

Revie's Leeds squad read like a Who's Who of international footballers – Gary Sprake, Billy Bremner, Peter Lorimer, Johnny Giles, Eddie Gray, Jack Charlton, Terry Cooper, Paul Madeley, Paul Reaney and Norman Hunter. They were one of the most talented teams in Europe, although they were not averse to resorting to cynical tactics when necessary. Losing, especially by seven goals, was a rare and unwelcome experience and the ill-feeling that took root that night lingered for years.

The two managers, Greenwood and Revie, had different ideas about the game and their relationship could best be described as frosty. There was no love lost. At the end of the match, Revie came to our dressing room to congratulate Ron. He told Ron that we had been world-beaters. Ron, who could be a bit pompous when he wanted, simply said, 'Thanks.' Revie went back to the Leeds dressing room and told his players, 'You will never lose to that man's team again!'

You had to be smart and composed when playing against Bremner because he would try to provoke you. Harry Redknapp once lashed out at his shins in retaliation during a 2–0 defeat at Elland Road and was sent off, only the second player to be dismissed during Ron's time as manager. Bremner later dived in our box to earn Leeds a penalty.

Leeds were always difficult opposition and made few friends. I remember two of my England team-mates, Norman Hunter and Francis Lee, having a terrific punch-up at Derby. The referee, Derek Nippard, sent them off for fighting and, as they left the field, they started again and had to be separated by their colleagues.

A similarly infamous incident took place at the start of the 1974–75 season when Leeds, the champions, met Liverpool, the FA Cup winners, in the annual Charity Shield match at Wembley. The acrimony between the two sets of players reached an ugly climax after an hour when Bremner and Kevin Keegan swapped punches. They were sent off by referee Bob Matthewson and as they left the pitch both petulantly tore off their shirts and threw them aside.

The match was shown live on TV for the first time and the public outcry prompted the Football Association to take unprecedented action. Both players were fined £500 and banned until the end of September, which meant that they each missed eleven games.

Ted Croker, the FA secretary at the time, said, 'We are trying to make football more acceptable to a wider range of people. Players must realise that they cannot throw punches.'

It wasn't often that fists flew. Subtler methods were usually employed. Johnny Giles, for instance, was a master at niggling the opposition. Standing just 5ft 5in, he nonetheless tried to intimidate you. Even late in our careers, when I was at Norwich and he was at West Bromwich Albion, he was still trying to provoke me. He was perhaps my most difficult opponent – tough but creative, cool and calculating, whereas Bremner was fiery and spontaneous. There wasn't much of either of them but they made a fearsome midfield partnership.

Bremner and I chipped away at each other for another ten years. I particularly remember the rough and tumble we had at Hampden Park a few months before that 1974 Charity Shield match. It has stuck in my mind because that was my sixty-seventh and last England cap, and just a fortnight after the Football Association's disgraceful sacking of Sir Alf Ramsey. I was the only member of the 1966 team in that side and we lost 2–0 in front of a delirious Scottish crowd of 93,271. They didn't beat us often, but when they did, they made the most of it.

In fact, that was the first time they'd beaten us since 1967 when we brought with us the proud record of being undefeated in the previous nineteen games. Alf kept faith with the same team for the three matches immediately after the World Cup triumph but recalled Jimmy Greaves for that Home International Championship match at Wembley. His return, the Scots claimed, made England an even stronger team.

The English victory in the World Cup final had irritated the Scots, especially as they hadn't even qualified for the finals. So you can imagine their sense of pride and achievement when they beat us 3–2. We were disappointed to lose our unbeaten record but we all knew that, had we been at full strength, we'd probably have won the match. I'm not making excuses, but Jack Charlton broke a toe after fifteen minutes, challenging Bobby Lennox. He returned to the field after treatment but spent the rest of the match hobbling about as the spearhead of England's attack. Further injuries to Ray Wilson and Greaves made matters worse for us and we finished the game with Bobby Charlton playing at left-back.

Scotland had a very talented team. Jim Baxter was at his mercurial best, the great Denis Law opened the scoring and the competitive Bremner held it all together in midfield, but it was a narrow victory. Jack Charlton scored a rare goal, in off a post, and Geoff Hurst notched the second with a late looping header that caught Ronnie Simpson out of position.

That victory gave the Scots the Home Championship title and the distinction of being the first team to beat Alf's World Cup winners – the Scots claimed that their victory meant they were the new champions of the world. They deserved the win but, in the days before substitutes, I have always thought that it was something of a hollow victory.

At the time, Law was one of my favourite players. He had grace, flair and magnetism – and he played for Manchester United, who were among the most glamorous names in world football. Pale and thin when he first played for Huddersfield, Denis developed into one of the most dangerous and athletic strikers in the world. He had a distinctive style – shirt hanging outside his shorts with the cuffs bunched in his fists. A goal was invariably marked with one arm raised in salute. He scored 30 goals in 55 games for Scotland and nothing motivated him quite like a match against England. It is part of sixties football legend that, while England were winning the World Cup, he was playing golf. On hearing the result, he was supposed to have said, 'That's really spoiled my day!'

There must have been a good deal of mickey taking in the Old Trafford dressing room in the sixties and seventies because of the mix of English, Scots and Irish players, including a mega star from each country – Bobby Charlton, Denis Law, and a skinny young kid called George Best. Many genuinely believed George to be the greatest player of the era, but I'm not so sure. He had wonderful dribbling ability, scored goals and was a thrilling player to watch but he quit Manchester United at the age of twenty-seven when, arguably, his best years were still in front of him. Rather like Jimmy Greaves and Paul Gascoigne, George never quite fulfilled his enormous potential. We will never know how good he could have been. He may have attained Pele's status had he not been sidetracked by the social whirl of the sixties. Nonetheless, he remained a folk hero, hugely popular despite his battles with alcohol, until his death at the age of fifty-nine in November 2005. The crowds at his funeral in Belfast demonstrated the enduring affection he generated.

In a way, he was a flag-bearer for youth, along with the Beatles, the Rolling Stones, Twiggy and Mary Quant, and he seemed to take that duty almost as seriously as his football commitments. This was the era of *Ready, Steady, Go*, mini skirts and Carnaby Street. The maximum wage for footballers had been lifted in 1961 and George was one of a growing number of famous young players who had money to spend and wanted to enjoy life. I was quite content to view the 'swinging sixties' from the back seats but George wanted to be in the thick of it.

There were temptations but I was reluctant to get too involved in the party scene in London. Bobby and Geoff were big stars who were more comfortable with that sort of thing. Football's personality cult developed further in the seventies and embraced more people, including Malcolm Allison, Terry Venables, Rodney Marsh and the boys from Chelsea, David Webb, Alan Hudson and Peter Osgood, who died so tragically at the age of fifty-nine in February 2006. Somewhere in my house is a photograph of me in an England shirt with five beautiful models draped around me. I kept the picture purely for its rarity value! I didn't do things like that very often.

Law, Charlton and Best gave Manchester United the finest attacking team of that period and their success culminated with an epic European Cup final win over Benfica at Wembley in 1968. Bobby (two) and George both scored in a 4–1 win after extra time but Denis missed the match because of injury.

However, despite United's success, the greatest club team of the sixties in my opinion was Bill Nicholson's Tottenham Hotspur. They were the first team in the twentieth century to win both the League Championship and FA Cup in the same season, and the first English club to win a European title – the Cup Winners' Cup in 1963.

Tottenham won the double in 1961 playing glorious football, setting new records for consistency and demonstrating a degree of sportsmanship that has disappeared from the game. It's astonishing by today's standards, but in 1960–61, Spurs had no players sent off, only one booked and conceded just one penalty.

Although I was just a kid at West Ham, I knew enough to appreciate that Tottenham had two truly outstanding players in their team – Danny Blanchflower and Dave Mackay. Danny was a thoughtful, elegant midfield player, one of those who always seemed to have time on the ball. An experienced Northern Ireland international, he was the Tottenham captain and provided the creative momentum in their assault on the double that year.

If Danny provided the guile, Dave Mackay supplied the guts and sweat. They were the ideal partnership. Talk to anyone who played for Spurs and they will tell you that their hero is Dave Mackay. A tough, barrel-chested Scot, Dave didn't know the meaning of the word defeat. He had ten great years at White Hart Lane, recovered from two broken legs and then provided the foundations for Brian Clough's championship-winning team at Derby County. He later rejoined Derby as manager and steered them to the First Division title in 1975. He was, by any yardstick, a remarkable football man.

I was fortunate enough to play against both him and Danny in 1962–63. I'd played only a handful of games in the West Ham first team when Nicholson's mighty Spurs came to Upton Park for the third game of the season. We'd lost the first two, to Aston Villa and Wolves, conceding seven goals, so our confidence wasn't high. It was even lower when John Lyall scored an own goal after just ten minutes.

Most of the Tottenham double team played that day, and they had been strengthened by the arrival of Jimmy Greaves. He scored twice as they beat us 6–1. The quality of their football made a big impression on me.

Four months later, by which time our form had improved a little, we had a chance to exact some revenge at White Hart Lane. At least it was an enthralling game this time. I scored a great goal as we turned a 2–0 deficit into a 4–3 lead. Then, in the last minute, Spurs equalised, making it 4–4, with a goal from, yes, Dave Mackay. That goal gave him a hat-trick.

If Tottenham are my personal choice as the team of the sixties, I suspect that most people would plump for Liverpool as the team of the seventies, although you could make a case for several other clubs. Derby County, for instance, won the championship in 1972 under Brian Clough, and in 1975 under Dave Mackay, who had the benefit of Francis Lee, one of the great strikers of that time. Some might argue for Arsenal, who followed Spurs by winning the double in 1971, or Clough's Nottingham Forest, who followed their championship victory in 1978 with two consecutive European Cups.

Leeds, too, are worth considering, but theirs is a story of near misses rather than achievement, and I sometimes wonder whether it was resentment that generated some of their questionable tactics. Leeds, under Revie, won the title twice but finished runners-up five times. They won the FA Cup once and finished runners-up three times. They were also European Cup runners-up in 1975, by which time Revie had moved on to succeed Alf as England manager.

Liverpool, on the other hand, won the championship five times between 1971 and 1980 and finished runners-up three times. On top of that, they won the European Cup in 1977 and 1978 and the UEFA Cup in 1973 and 1976.

Bob Paisley was the manager from 1974–83 and, until Sir Alex Ferguson came along, enjoyed an unrivalled record of success among managers. He inherited a very good team from Bill Shankly, who in a sense laid the foundations for the modern Liverpool.

One of Shankly's best signings was a little fellow from Scunthorpe called Kevin Keegan. Just as he began to make an impact at Anfield, George Best was going off the rails at Manchester United. The football world was looking for a new superstar and Kevin fitted the bill beautifully.

He was a wonderful player but very different from Best. His ambition, dedication and love of hard work enabled him to achieve his potential. When he left Liverpool, with a sackful of medals, he moved to Hamburg where he won the European Footballer of the Year award in consecutive seasons.

Kevin was given the first of his sixty-three England caps by Alf Ramsey in 1972 but although our international careers overlapped, we never played in the same team together. He established a long and successful playing relationship with my former West Ham team-mate Trevor Brooking. Both would have graced the 1982 World Cup in Spain had it not been for injury. They each played for less than thirty minutes in a goalless draw with the host nation in Madrid. A win by two goals would have put England into the semi-finals for the first time since 1966.

I think the international careers of both suffered because of England's failure to qualify for the 1978 World Cup. They would have both been key members of an England squad in

Argentina. The seventies are still remembered for England's failure to qualify for the finals in Germany in 1974 and in Argentina four years later. This period is a big black hole in England's international football history.

At club level, though, the First Division began to dominate in Europe. In 1977 Liverpool kicked off England's six-year reign in the European Cup. They also won the UEFA Cup twice in the seventies, along with Spurs. The big English clubs were to enjoy an astonishing period of success on the European stage for almost a decade and I've often wondered why their players, good enough to bring silverware to Liverpool, Nottingham Forest, Aston Villa and the others, couldn't do it for England.

12

SOUTH OF THE BORDER

The beginning of the end of my career at West Ham came on the day Ron Greenwood accused me of saving my best performances for England. It was an affront to my professionalism and something I never forgot.

His half-time outburst occurred in front of my team-mates in the away dressing room at Nottingham Forest in April 1968. West Ham were fifteenth in the First Division and trailing to a thirty-second minute goal from Joe Baker.

As I sat on the bench, sipping water, he stood in front of me and announced that I didn't play as well for West Ham as I did for England. 'Why is that, Martin?' he asked.

I couldn't answer him. I didn't agree with his assessment and told him so. It didn't develop into a blazing row but, even so, it was most unlike him to pick out a player for criticism in front of the others. Occasionally, he'd have a quiet word, but I'd never known him set upon one of his players in this way.

Perhaps he felt under a bit of pressure himself. West Ham had not been playing well. We'd won two of the previous eight games and, once again, the season was petering out lamely. As a club, we'd won nothing since 1965.

I'd missed a couple of first-half chances against Forest but I wasn't playing badly. In fact, I scored our equaliser in the second half and Geoff Hurst hit the crossbar. We could have won it in the end.

I always gave 100 per cent effort to my club. I didn't differentiate between West Ham and England. Both deserved, and got, all I had to give. That was the only way I knew how to play. So his suggestion that I was saving myself for my country hurt. I felt it was very unfair and can only assume that he'd watched me play for England three days earlier – when we'd beaten Spain 1–0 at Wembley – and then come to the wrong conclusion.

I think in his heart of hearts Ron knew, much as Bobby, Geoff and I knew, that the way West Ham played wasn't conducive to winning the big prize in English football. I genuinely believed at the start of every season that we had a chance of winning the League Championship but I also believed that at least half a dozen other clubs were better equipped for the task. Why? Because they played a different kind of football.

Our one-touch, passing game was based on flair and freedom of expression. Ron encouraged his players to attack. The crowd at Upton Park loved us for it because the football we played was entertaining and exciting. On our good days, we were brilliant, there was no better team, but we couldn't sustain that style of play throughout a forty-two-match programme.

Our game was not designed to close space and grind out 1–0 victories. We could put together a run of good performances that would win one of the cup competitions, but over the nine months of the league programme, we were, well, consistently inconsistent. It was one of our endearing qualities!

Initially, I started each new season bursting with optimism but after a few seasons I grew to accept that we weren't going to win the championship. In my time at the club, the highest we finished was eighth and the lowest was seventeenth. For a while, I don't think Bobby, Geoff or I felt any need to play at a higher level in club football because we played in a fantastic

England side that included the best footballers in the country. That is probably why the three of us stayed at Upton Park for so long after the World Cup win in 1966. I didn't consider myself to be world class, by any means, but I did want to win some domestic medals and I came to realise that I wasn't going to do that at West Ham.

By this time, Jimmy had played his last game for England but several others from the 1966 squad were still very much part of Sir Alf Ramsey's plans. Our win against Spain – Bobby Charlton scored the goal – was the first leg of the European Championship quarter-finals. A few weeks later, we went to Madrid for the second leg and I scored, along with Norman Hunter, in a 2–1 win. This meant that for the first time England had reached the last four of the European Championship, an achievement repeated by Terry Venables and his team at Wembley in 1996. As a result of beating Spain, we were drawn to meet Yugoslavia in Florence while Italy met the USSR in the other semi-final.

Four days before the game with Yugoslavia we faced West Germany in Hanover in a warm-up match. I wasn't in the starting line-up. From the 1966 team, Banks, Moore, Hurst and Ball played. It was a hot day on a hard pitch and adidas had persuaded us to wear their new boots. That didn't help our cause. A Franz Beckenbauer shot bounced off Brian Labone and flew past Banks to give the Germans a 1–0 victory. They were jubilant. It was the first time they'd beaten us in thirty-eight years of trying. How the balance of power has changed in European football! Alf was disappointed because it was his first defeat on the Continent since losing his debut match as England manager in France in 1963.

The game against Yugoslavia did nothing to ease his disappointment. As world champions, we were the team that everyone wanted to beat and, as far as the Yugoslavs were concerned, it didn't matter how they beat us. At least, that's how it appeared in the opening minute when Alan Mullery was hacked down. That was just a taste of what was to come. The game degenerated into a series of skirmishes, and 'Mullers', who'd replaced Nobby Stiles as our midfield anchorman, took more than his fair share of buffeting.

The Italian crowd loved every minute of it, screaming with delight every time an English player was fouled. You can imagine how they reacted when Mullers became the first England player to be sent off in an international match.

When Miljan Trivic caught him with his studs, Mullers retaliated, lashing out instinctively with his right boot and catching the Yugoslav across the legs. Trivic rolled about in mock agony and Mullery was sent off. As he left the field, shepherded towards the tunnel by Nobby, the jubilant Trivic jumped to his feet and started running around in circles waving his arms in triumph.

To make matters worse, four minutes from time Bobby Moore missed a dipping cross, allowing Yugoslavia's outstanding winger Dragan Dzajic to score the goal that denied us a place in the final. After the match we were taken to a reception that was so shambolic that Alf ordered us back to the hotel. There was a lot of ill-feeling at official level. The following day we all went to the Vatican and looked around Rome and although it was interesting it was little compensation.

Italy, who had drawn 0–0 with the USSR, progressed to the final on the toss of a coin. So, we then played the USSR in Rome, with Nobby back in the team to replace the suspended Mullery. We won 2–0, thus becoming officially the third best team in Europe.

The Yugoslavia defeat was England's third since winning the World Cup two years earlier and the inevitable sour media reaction included calls for the reinstatement of Greaves. The campaign gathered momentum and seemed to affect Roger Hunt's confidence, although Jim was never recalled.

A prodigious goalscorer with Liverpool, Roger had been one

of England's most loyal retainers and, although widely appreciated by Alf and the rest of the team, I don't think he received the public acclaim he deserved for his dedicated and unselfish work. A few months later, after a 1–1 draw with Romania, he asked Alf not to pick him again.

The following season, 1968–69, started with a flourish and for once my optimism survived into the autumn. We lost just one of our opening twelve games and, briefly, led the First Division after a 5–0 win over Burnley. What I remember most about that match is that the referee, having been knocked out by the ball, had to be replaced by a linesman who, in turn, was replaced by a spectator from the crowd.

By November, normal service had been resumed. Our results were inconsistent once again and the lowest crowd of the season, 24,718, turned up for our match against Sunderland. Those who decided to stay away have regretted it from that day to this because we beat Sunderland 8–0. Geoff Hurst scored six goals – a hat-trick in each half. He admitted afterwards that he'd punched in the first goal but that didn't detract from the fact that he'd given a supreme masterclass in goalscoring. At the time, he was one of the world's best strikers. Sir Matt Busby, the manager of Manchester United who'd won the European Cup the previous season, obviously thought so because he offered a world record fee of £200,000 to sign him. Ron Greenwood quickly said, 'No.'

By the New Year our season was almost over once again. A run of seven First Division matches without a win preceded one of our most humiliating defeats – 3–0 at Mansfield in the FA Cup third round. The giant-killers were from the Third Division and that win remains one of the greatest nights in their history.

What a contrast that was to our 7–2 win over Bolton in the League Cup. Nat Lofthouse, the former England centre-forward who was Bolton's caretaker-manager, described us as 'magnificent'.

It was all depressingly predictable. We failed to secure a single win in our final nine First Division matches and, having been jostling with the leaders in the first half of the season, we ended up eighth, 23 points behind the champions, Leeds. Despite this, it had been my most productive season from a goalscoring point of view. I scored in our final game, a 1–1 draw with Manchester City at Maine Road, to take my tally to 24 goals in 48 first-team matches. Only Geoff scored more (31). We applauded the City players on to the pitch before the match because they'd beaten Leicester City 1–0 in the FA Cup final four days earlier.

After the game, Geoff, Bobby and I chatted to our England team-mates Francis 'Franny' Lee, Colin Bell and Mike Summerbee. We had a busy summer ahead of us in South America, preparing for England's defence of the World Cup the following year. First, though, we had the Home International Championship series, which, for the first time, was to be played over eight days in May. I was looking forward to these games because I was enjoying some good form. I scored in a 3–1 win over Northern Ireland in Belfast and hit two more in a 4–1 win against Scotland at Wembley. We also beat Wales 2–1, and retained the title.

More important, perhaps, was Franny's emergence as a striker of international class. He'd scored on his debut in a 5–0 win over France and a goal against the Irish and another against the Welsh more or less guaranteed his role in England's World Cup dress rehearsal in South America.

Geoff, Bobby and I were travelling to South America via the United States, where we joined West Ham's close-season tour. Ron Greenwood quite rightly believed that his team benefited from playing foreign opposition and during that trip we played Kilmarnock, Dundee United, Cologne, Karlsruhe, Bayern Munich and Slovan Bratislava and finished runners-up in the North American International Tournament.

The three of us didn't play in every match but we did play in an exhibition game against Tottenham, who were also touring. The game took place in a baseball stadium in Baltimore and the pitcher's mound in one corner of the pitch troubled our full-back John Charles. Spurs beat us 4–3. Jimmy Greaves skipped past Bobby Moore to score twice but Bobby scored one of our goals, so that was some consolation for the England captain.

Shortly after that game, the three amigos bid farewell to our West Ham mates and flew to Mexico City where Alf Ramsey and the England squad had arrived a few days earlier to acclimatise to the altitude. The first of the tour games was arranged for the Aztec Stadium on 1 June.

In the four weeks since the domestic season ended we had been involved in three Home International matches and travelled around America with each of us playing in a handful of friendly games. Now we were about to spend another fortnight touring South America with England. The tour made perfect sense to us. Mexico were hosting the 1970 World Cup and, as the defending champions, we wanted to prepare properly. This meant we had to learn about playing in heat, humidity and at altitude.

For us, high-altitude football was uncharted territory. The British Olympic Association had researched the subject before the Olympic Games in Mexico City in 1968 and I knew that Alf and the Football Association were grateful for the advice they received, but there's nothing like trying it for yourself. Mexico City is 7200 feet above sea level. The air is thinner than at sea level and this can be a problem if you spend ninety minutes running around a football pitch. You can lessen the impact of the thin air by acclimatising to it.

More than 100,000 fans crowded into the spectacular Aztec Stadium for our first match. It was hot and humid, but breathing wasn't as difficult as I had feared. We drew 0–0 and I remember sitting in the cool of the dressing room afterwards, confident that I'd be able to cope when the real business began the following summer. I'd lost a couple of pounds in weight but otherwise I was fine.

I also remember returning for the second half and noticing that a television cable ran right across the middle of the pitch. At the far end of the cable, holding a microphone was Jimmy Hill, interviewing Alf Ramsey. In the middle of the pitch a Mexican band played. All the players stood looking at each other until Jim finished his interview and the cable was wound up and the bandsmen ran off in different directions!

Four days later we played again, but it wasn't a full international. An England XI faced a Mexico XI in Guadalajara, a provincial city about an hour's flight from the capital. Alf picked nineteen-year-old goalkeeper Peter Shilton. He hadn't made his England debut at that time but was called up to replace Gordon Banks, who had flown home to attend his father's funeral.

Before the match, Alf gestured Alan Ball and me to one side. 'I want you to run as much as you can in the first half,' he said. 'I want you to burn yourselves out because I'm going to take you both off at half-time.'

We kicked off late in the evening and although the sun had gone down it was still very humid. After forty-five minutes we were leading 3–0. My legs ached and my feet hurt, but I was far from exhausted. Alf took us both off as planned and sent on Alan Mullery and Bobby Charlton for the second half.

We won 4–0 with goals from Allan Clarke (2) and Jeff Astle (2), but Mullers was sent off again a few minutes from the end. I was sitting on the touchline by this time and suddenly the air was filled with coloured cushions as the Mexican crowd of 45,000 expressed their displeasure.

Those two games taught us the value of retaining possession, of playing in bursts and the futility of chasing lost causes. Peter Shilton and our other goalkeeper, Gordon West, also learned that the ball moved differently in the thin air.

The pitch in Guadalajara's Jalisco Stadium was excellent and

I remember feeling as we left the ground that I couldn't wait for the World Cup to start again. Alf spoke to us that night and was clearly pleased.

'It will be difficult for us to retain the World Cup,' he said. 'But it will be even more difficult to take it away from us.'

The following morning we began a twenty-four-hour journey, via Peru, to Montevideo in Uruguay. The city was full of old American Buicks and Packards and had a feel of the Roaring Twenties about it. The day after we arrived, Gordon Banks returned and was selected to play. The climate in the Uruguayan capital at the mouth of the River Plate was far less gruelling than it had been in Mexico, but we didn't play very well. Nevertheless, we overcame the referee and a poor pitch to win 2–1 with goals from Geoff Hurst and Franny Lee. The real fun came a few hours later when we attended a barbecue at a golf club.

We were told that we had misbehaved, insulted our hosts, drunk too much and upset the waitresses – all the usual complaints. As I recall, when the president of the Uruguayan FA was addressing the party, a flagpole collapsed and fell on the head of the young lady who was interpreting for him. She wasn't hurt and it was difficult not to laugh. That was the extent of the horseplay. In fact, when we returned to Gatwick a week later, the FA councillor who travelled with us, Major Wilson Keys, called the players together and said, 'This has been a very good tour. You have all been gentlemen as well as good players.'

We finally flew home on 14 June, having narrowly lost 2–1 to Brazil before a 160,000 crowd in the Maracana Stadium in Rio de Janiero. As you might imagine, it was an enthralling experience playing against Pele, Gerson, Tostao and Carlos Alberto.

Alf had played for England in Rio in the 1950 World Cup and had some idea of what to expect. When we arrived at the ground a couple of hours before kick-off, we assumed we would go out on the pitch and test the turf before deciding what boots to wear.

'Senor Ramsey, sorry, ees not possible,' Alf was told. All entrances to the pitch were barred for our protection. Alf didn't mess about.

'If we don't see the pitch,' he said, 'you won't see us play. We'll go home.'

The Brazilians relented. Then they asked Alf for his team line-up.

'You can have my team when you give me your team,' he said.

They tested him just once more. A few minutes before kick-off, a knock came on the dressing-room door and Alf was told that the referee was on the pitch waiting for us to come out. He thanked the messenger and ordered us to stay where we were. Then he went to check for himself to make sure the Brazilians were out. They were.

The match itself was a disappointment for us. We took the lead through Colin Bell and held it until the eightieth minute. Gordon Banks saved a penalty from Carlos Alberto but then, right at the end, we succumbed to heat and collective exhaustion. A right-wing cross from Jairzinho was fired past Banks by Tostao – what a clever player – and two minutes later Tostao returned the favour, setting up Jairzinho for the winning goal.

The result was a pity because we'd played well and didn't deserve to lose. If nothing else, it gave me first-hand experience of playing against the legendary Pele. He was a wonderful player all right but, as I often found with other great players with huge reputations, the man didn't quite justify the myth. The mystique was gradually stripped away as that match unfolded and much credit for that has to go to Alan Mullery, who did a superb job marking him.

Bobby Moore, too, had demonstrated why he was widely regarded as the best defender in the world. He had played in all four games and was at his best against the Brazilians. He was exhausted in the dressing room at the end and I suspect a long season had finally caught up with him. I think he might have had a stomach bug, too, because he was sick all over me as we took our boots off.

Alf wasn't too despondent about the Brazil defeat. The tour had been a worthwhile exercise for him, although his curt behaviour, particularly towards the media, would rebound on him later. He complained in Mexico about the lack of a motor-cycle escort, the intrusion of the local media and the fact that a band played outside our hotel all night. He finally relaxed with his players on Copacabana beach the day after the Brazil game. Spending time on that beach was an unforgettable experience for a bunch of young men.

After a reception at the British Embassy, we were taken to the airport but the flight home was delayed for several hours. So we sat around in the airport lounge and Jeff Astle sang songs from the shows. I particularly remember his version of 'Catch a Falling Star'. Perry Como he wasn't! Jeff and Alan Ball, who acted as the master of ceremonies, kept most of the passengers in the terminal entertained for hours. The fact that we'd been invited to take advantage of the free drinks service obviously enhanced the ambience. We made a fair bit of noise and I kept one eye on Alf. It was clear he didn't approve but eventually he smiled, if somewhat grudgingly.

He knew we were tired and needed to relax. It was mid-June. We'd been playing for ten months. We'd just finished a four-match tour with England and, because of West Ham's commitments in the US, Bobby, Geoff and I had travelled thousands of miles. In four weeks we were due to resume training to prepare for the new season at the beginning of August.

It was no surprise then that most of us slept during the long flight home. Bobby Charlton, who was awarded the OBE a few days later in the Queen's birthday honours, happened to mention to Alf how exhausted he felt after a long, hard season.

I can be seen dancing with delight after providing the cross for Geoff Hurst to score the winning goal in our controversial World Cup quarter-final against Argentina. (*Daily Mirror*)

Scoring England's second goal in the World Cup final against West Germany. (*Topix*)

Celebrating with Geoff Hurst after he scored his controversial second goal in the final. Of course it crossed the line.

The final whistle blows, and Geoff and I embrace, while the emotion of the occasion has clearly over-whelmed Jack Charlton.

Hat-trick hero Geoff Hurst raises the Jules Rimet trophy, flanked by his two West Ham team-mates. (*Topix*)

The perks of the job: Denis Follows looks on as I am presented with a pair of shoes after winning the World Cup. I believe the bonus scheme these days is somewhat better.

More perks: Bobby and Tina Moore and I look on during an advert 'looking at your local' that was filmed at the Valentine pub in Gants Hill. Only the biggest events would do for us in those days.

Tina Moore, Judith Hurst and Kathy check out the back page news ahead of England's European Championship game against Spain in 1968.

A tough assignment in 1971: don't smile! (*Daily Express*)

Scoring against Northern Ireland in 1969 – any goal past Pat Jennings had to be a good one. (*Daily Mirror*)

'Back home!' Undoubtedly one of the great football anthems of all time. Perhaps.

Willie Morgan acts as peacemaker between me and Billy Bremner in one of our regular tussles against the Scots. (*Daily Mirror*)

No wonder it felt so good to score! (*Daily Mirror*)

A proud moment: leading England out at Wembley for the first time, against Wales in 1971.

Bobby Moore and me together in our last season playing for England in 1973–74. (*Daily Mirror*)

'I'll be glad to get home and put my feet up,' he said.

'Had I known you felt like that, Bobby, I wouldn't have selected you,' Alf replied.

13

FADING BUBBLES

I knew that my time at West Ham was drawing to a close when Ron Greenwood decided to leave me out of the team in October 1969. It's true that I was becoming increasingly frustrated with West Ham's lack of success, but the manager believed I thought I would only flourish if I escaped from the shadow of Bobby Moore and Geoff Hurst.

I know he shared this opinion with other people and, over a period of time, it became the popular theory in the game. It was not true. I did not feel I was in the shadow of Geoff and Bobby. I was not jealous in any sense. They were both good friends and Geoff, in fact, was godfather to our daughter Lee Ann.

But as much as I loved West Ham I have to be honest and say that I was beginning to feel that if I wanted to enjoy further success at club level I would have to leave Upton Park.

My usual early season optimism quickly disappeared at the start of 1969–70. We won only two of the opening nine games and when we lost 5–2 to Manchester United at Old Trafford, we slumped to seventeenth position. Ron Greenwood left me out of the next game, the first time I'd been dropped since the World Cup final.

He didn't tell me until the day before we were due to play

Burnley at Upton Park. Ironically, the evening before, Sir Alf Ramsey had appeared on BBC TV and described me as 'not just a good player, but a great one'. He then named four men who would definitely be in Mexico to defend the World Cup the following summer – Bobby Moore, Alan Ball, Francis Lee and me.

As it was the start of the World Cup season, the media made a big deal of my axing. My England place, according to the tabloids, was now under threat. The fact that Kathy was pregnant simply added to the pressure I felt at the time. I was an established international player. England's defence of the World Cup was just nine months away and I wanted to be part of it but that meant I had to be playing regular first-team football in the First Division.

I realised it was a big story for the newspapers. We had to take the telephone off the hook. Then the reporters started knocking on the front door. I took Kathy and Lee Ann to my mum's home in Dagenham to escape the press.

Instead of going to Upton Park to watch the Burnley game, I played golf with my good friend Dave Readings. When we moved from Barkingside back to Hornchurch, Dave was our new next-door neighbour. Jimmy Greaves had previously lived in his house. Dave and I and another long-time friend, Ricky Jupp, still play golf regularly, although Ricky now lives on the Isle of Man. Since 1973 we've played annually for the same silver cup – the Big Three International Trophy. We play all over Europe and the UK. They have been good friends to me and, over the years, I've learned from them that it helps sometimes to get an independent view from people you trust. In return, I taught them both to putt!

While I was playing golf that day, West Ham beat Burnley 3–1 with two goals from Clyde Best and another from the man who took my place, Trevor Brooking. Unfortunately, Geoff Hurst went off with back trouble after seventy-four minutes, having set up both Clyde's goals. It was the first time since 1966 that both Geoff and I had been missing from the team at the same time.

Losing my place in the team hurt me. I didn't know what the future held. I remember agreeing to be interviewed by Sam Leitch of the BBC. He came to the house with a film crew, but halfway through the interview I had to ask them to stop filming because I found it very emotional talking about West Ham. I was still only twenty-five and felt the world crowding in on me.

I was left out of the side again for the next game, against Stoke at Upton Park. Bobby Moore was injured, too, so all three of the World Cup players missed a West Ham game together for the first time since 1966. Initially, it didn't seem to worry the rest of them. They were three goals up within twenty minutes – then they collapsed and conceded three in the last twenty minutes. It ended 3–3. Typical West Ham!

I was left out for a total of four matches. One day, at the end of training at Chadwell Heath, I was told the manager wanted to talk to me. When all the other players had left, Ron strolled out of his office and asked me to walk out on to the training ground with him.

It was a damp, misty day and the place was deserted except for a groundsman working on one of the pitches in the distance. We sat in a little wooden shelter that the coaches used beside one of the training pitches and talked around the subject at first. Ron was clearly worried about West Ham's position. We were sixteenth in the table and had won only four of the previous sixteen matches. A few weeks earlier we'd been knocked out of the League Cup by Nottingham Forest. Ron made it clear that he considered me a valuable asset – either in the claret and blue of West Ham or as a bargaining tool should they decide to sell me.

He said that he didn't want to sell me but suspected that both parties would benefit if I moved to another club. I hadn't asked for a transfer and didn't on this occasion, but I did tell him that it was my honest opinion that West Ham were not good enough to challenge for the major honours. He disagreed. We struck a deal. He agreed that he would recommend to the board of directors that they should sell me if West Ham didn't make significant progress in the FA Cup that season. He then said that he realised an England game was approaching and he knew that I would want to be selected. So he said he was going to recall me to the side. We shook hands and walked back to the dressing rooms.

When I got home that afternoon I discussed the situation with Kathy. I didn't talk to anyone else about it. I trusted Ron totally. I had no agent or adviser. I didn't know whether he would tell the board about the deal he'd struck with me.

A couple of days later, I was back in the team. We played Sunderland at Upton Park and in the nineteenth minute I controlled a high pass from Bobby Moore and slid the ball beyond goalkeeper Jim Montgomery's dive. We couldn't hold on to the lead, though, and drew 1–1. Again, typical West Ham! At least I felt reassured by my goal and hoped that Ron felt I was pulling my weight.

A few days later I flew to Amsterdam with Alf and the England squad. Although I wanted to retain my place in the England side, I was in something of a quandary because Kathy was about to give birth. The baby arrived at six in the morning of the day before the match. Kathy rang me at the hotel. I was in bed asleep.

'D'you know what bloody time it is?' I said when I picked up the phone in my hotel room.

'Yes, I bloody do,' she replied. 'I've been up all bloody night having your baby!'

With that she slammed the phone down. I sensed that I could have handled the situation a little better! I called back but the damage was done.

Anyway, I was thrilled that Lee Ann had a brother, Grant. One of the newspapers in London took a photograph of Kathy with the new baby and wired it to Amsterdam where I was then photographed, surrounded by my England team-mates, holding a copy of the picture.

Alf picked me in the starting line-up to face a Dutch side that included such talented youngsters as Johann Cruyff, Ruud Krol, Rob Resenbrink and Wim Van Hanegem.

England's team included the late Emlyn Hughes, making his debut. The Liverpool defender went on to play sixty-two games for his country, many of them as captain. Peter 'the Cat' Bonetti, the Chelsea goalkeeper, also won a rare cap that day. It was a match of indifferent quality but the Cat played a big part in denying Holland a goal. England won 1–0 with a late goal from Colin Bell.

That match was the start of an encouraging run of results that helped our confidence in the build-up to the 1970 World Cup. We were unbeaten in nine games before beginning our defence of the trophy against Romania in Guadalajara the following June.

Alf's fine-tuning of his squad during this period suggested that there would be at least five changes to the 1966 team by the time the tournament started. Keith Newton, Tommy Wright and Terry Cooper were rivals for the full-back positions. Brian Labone appeared to have ousted Jack Charlton as the first-choice centre-half. Alan Mullery had taken over in midfield from Nobby Stiles. Franny Lee had succeeded Roger Hunt in attack and Colin Bell was also staging a serious challenge for a midfield place.

My place looked reasonably safe but I realised much would depend on what happened at West Ham in the following months. When England played Portugal at Wembley, Alf relegated me to the substitutes' bench, sending me on to replace Bell.

I was recalled to the starting line-up for a 3–1 win over Belgium in Brussels, and I set up one of Geoff's goals – a header at the near post. I played well and was relieved at the end of that game because, according to the media, my place in the England side was under serious threat.

It was important to me to play for England because the reality of life at West Ham was becoming harsher. England trips were a bit of light relief. A 4–1 defeat against First Division pacemakers Leeds, for instance, sent us plunging back down to seventeenth in the table. It was our fourth consecutive defeat.

On the first weekend of 1970, we travelled to Middlesbrough for the third round of the FA Cup – the North East in January, against a team from the Second Division. The omens couldn't have been worse. Middlesbrough were notoriously difficult to beat and they used all their spoiling tactics to stop us finding any rhythm. We were trailing 2–0 when Alan Stephenson scored a late consolation goal. Three hairline offside decisions went against us and at the end some of our players sarcastically applauded the officials off the pitch. That gesture changed nothing. West Ham were out of the FA Cup once again in the early stages. We hadn't progressed beyond the fifth round since winning it in 1964.

In the light of what Ron Greenwood had said to me at the training ground two months earlier, I wasn't sure what would happen. I didn't automatically assume I'd be sold the next day. Ron smiled, but said nothing.

A week later, when we travelled to Hillsborough to play Sheffield Wednesday, my name was on the teamsheet. We won 3–1 and I scored twice, but the inclusion of Peter Eustace, signed from Wednesday for £90,000 a few days earlier, made me wonder whether Ron had earmarked him to replace me.

I played another nine games for West Ham, without scoring, but we won only one of them. I could sense the growing unease at the club. Ron dropped our goalkeeper Bobby Ferguson, our long-serving midfield player Ronnie Boyce and Geoff's striking partner Clyde Best, but nothing seemed to help. We were just seven points clear of the relegation zone and the fans were unfurling banners at Upton Park proclaiming: 'Greenwood Out!'

My last match for West Ham was also my 364th in the first team – a goalless draw against Ipswich at Upton Park. I didn't realise at the time that I would never again pull on the claret and blue shirt. Although the March transfer deadline was only a few days away, I assumed that I would be staying at West Ham at least until the end of the season.

Then, a couple of days after the Ipswich match, Ron Greenwood called me at home. I was playing with Lee Ann, who had a temperature and a heavy cold. Kathy was out.

'I've got someone who wants to talk to you,' Ron said down the phone.

'Who?' I asked.

'Bill Nicholson,' he replied.

Unknown to me, Ron had already set in motion the wheels of a record-breaking transfer deal. The previous day he had called the Tottenham Hotspur manager and asked to meet him. They met outside Walthamstow Greyhound Stadium and sat in Bill's car. Apparently, at this point, Bill still didn't know what it was all about. When Ron told him that I wanted to leave West Ham Bill's face lit up. Within thirty minutes they'd agreed the details of my transfer.

I was valued by West Ham at £200,000. Bill Nicholson agreed to give West Ham Jimmy Greaves in part exchange and pay a cash adjustment, which I believe was about £140,000. It was a huge deal. The record transfer fee at the time was the £165,000 Leeds United had paid Leicester City for Allan Clarke.

In those days, a player was entitled to 5 per cent of the fee, providing he had not asked for a transfer. Although there was a lot of newspaper speculation suggesting that I'd demanded to go, I hadn't, so the deal was worth £10,000 to me personally.

This was a large sum of money, far more than a year's salary.

When Kathy returned to the house, I told her that Bill Nicholson wanted to talk to me about a transfer. She wasn't as excited as I was but, in theory, it was a great move for us. We wouldn't even have to move house. Kathy was a real home-lover and I knew the prospect of a move to Manchester or Liverpool would not appeal to her.

It was a Monday afternoon and that evening I was due to join the Football League squad that was preparing for a match against The Scottish League at Coventry. Sir Alf Ramsey was selecting the Football League team. I called him from home to tell him that I might be late because I was going to talk to Bill Nicholson. I asked him whether he thought a move to Tottenham would be good for me. A Dagenham boy, he had played for Spurs himself, winning a League Championship medal in 1951.

'A great club and a great manager,' he said. He stressed that it would be a big challenge for me. 'They've got a lot of outstanding players,' he said. 'You won't be an automatic first choice.'

Thus warned, I left Kathy and drove over to Tottenham where I found Bill Nicholson waiting for me in his office at White Hart Lane. I'd not met him before. We shook hands. I was in awe of him, I must admit. He was one of the great football managers of the time. A strait-laced Yorkshireman, Bill was from the old school – firm, friendly and very correct. He seemed to share the same kind of values as Alf Ramsey. That was good enough for me.

Bill explained what was happening. He told me that he had seen Ron Greenwood and they'd agreed a deal. Jimmy Greaves, he said, was at West Ham talking with Ron as we spoke.

'Do you want to join Spurs? he asked.

'Yes,' I replied.

'Good,' he said, 'because I want you in my team. What about salary? How much do you want?'

I told him that I'd be happy to receive exactly what I was getting at West Ham – £147 a week.

'What kind of contract d'you want, Martin?' he asked.

'I don't mind,' I replied. 'I'll leave it to you.'

'What about a three and three?' he said. This meant committing myself to the club for three years and allowing them an option on me for a further three years.

'That sounds fine,' I said.

There was no haggling at any stage. I later wondered whether I should have asked for more, but I wasn't leaving West Ham for more money. That wasn't the point at all. Even so, no player in my position in the modern game would go into such talks without teams of agents, lawyers and accountants present. Our negotiations took about an hour. These days big transfer negotiations drag on for days, if not weeks.

When we'd agreed everything, Bill said that he would have to call Ron Greenwood to ensure that his end of the deal with Jimmy Greaves was going through. When he was satisfied that Jim had joined West Ham, he put the contract in front of me and I signed it. There was no fuss, no photograph, no television cameras. It was just the two of us in his little office with a secretary running in and out occasionally.

I called Kathy to tell her that I'd signed. Then I called Ronnie Boyce, who lived near us in Hornchurch. I told him I'd just joined Tottenham and asked him to pick up a few bits and pieces of mine from the training ground the next day. After that, I picked up my bag, with my boots and toiletries, thanked my new boss and headed to Coventry.

It was Monday, 16 March 1970. I'd just become the most expensive player in British football history. I couldn't believe that it had all gone through so smoothly. Newspaper stories had appeared during the last year saying that I was unhappy at West Ham and suggesting that Tottenham might be interested in signing me but I'd not taken much notice. As a professional footballer, you get used to that sort of speculation in the newspapers. It's part of the game and, even today, the big stars are constantly being linked to other clubs.

Over some months the newspapers had run a catalogue of different 'exclusive' reasons for my unhappiness at West Ham. Most popular was the assumption that I was jealous of the status enjoyed by Geoff and Bobby, which was rubbish, as was the suggestion that I wasn't popular with the Hammers' fans, and that I'd lost my form because I was worried about Kathy. I just wanted to make the most of whatever talent God had given me.

Even so, I had mixed emotions that evening. I was relieved to be making a new start – it would be a big challenge for me – but I was sorry to be leaving West Ham. I'd been there for eleven years. They were my friends, not just Bobby and Geoff, but all of them. I knew I could stay but would I be able to fulfil my potential? I wanted to experience more success at club level and I seriously doubted whether I could do that with West Ham. As it turned out, they didn't win another trophy until 1975.

I thought then, and still do, that a First Division club with three World Cup winners and West Ham's resources should have been good enough to challenge regularly for the major prizes in the English game, but we weren't. In the time that Geoff, Bobby and I were together, the club won the European Cup Winners' Cup, the FA Cup and finished runners-up in the League Cup. What I must say, though, is that as a teaching academy West Ham were one of the finest in the land. The calibre of player developed by the club in the sixties was outstandingly high. Everything I learned from ages fifteen to twenty-five I owed to West Ham in general and Ron Greenwood in particular. They taught me 'good habits' that served me well throughout my career, both on and off the field. I shall be eternally grateful to Ron and all the coaches at West Ham who helped shape me as both a player and a person.

As I bade farewell to Bill Nicholson late that afternoon, he asked me to take particular care when playing for the Football League.

'Don't get injured,' he said. 'I want you fit for your debut on Saturday.'

I made my way to Paddington and caught a train to Leamington, where I was to join the Football League squad. By this time, the press were aware of what had happened and, according to poor Kathy, the telephone at home was ringing non-stop. When I arrived at the hotel at Leamington, the other players already knew that I'd joined Spurs but were unaware of all the details. I couldn't bring myself to tell them the fee. That would have been presumptuous and arrogant. At least, that's what I thought.

Anyway, they were full of congratulations and all agreed that it was a great move for me. West Ham had a wonderful reputation for the quality of football played, but there was no doubt that Tottenham were considered a bigger and more successful club. Ten years earlier they'd won the double and the general opinion was that Bill Nicholson had assembled a squad capable of recapturing past glories. Most of his players were internationals or were to become internationals – Pat Jennings, Alan Mullery, Mike England, Cyril Knowles, Joe Kinnear, Martin Chivers and Alan Gilzean. They also had two of the outstanding youngsters of the day – Steve Perryman and Graeme Souness.

What had become obvious during my conversation with Bill earlier in the day was a growing feeling at White Hart Lane that it was about time they started winning trophies again. They had a great squad, some of whom had cost a lot of money, but they'd won nothing since the FA Cup triumph over Chelsea in 1967. Also, Arsenal were on the move. Spurs' great north London rivals won the Fairs Cup in 1970 and, a year later, would emulate Tottenham by winning the League and FA Cup double.

Two days after signing for Spurs, I sat on the substitutes' bench at Highfield Road, Coventry, watching the Football League XI beat their Scottish counterparts. Sir Alf used the match to look at some new faces but, in the second half, put me on in place of Manchester United's twenty-year-old Brian Kidd. We won 3–2 with goals from Jeff Astle (two) and Don Rogers, the Swindon striker who had destroyed the mighty Arsenal in the League Cup final at Wembley the previous year.

I travelled home the following day and, on the Friday, had my one and only training session with Spurs before my debut against Coventry. It was good to get involved with my new colleagues. I must confess, I was a little anxious about the reception I might receive from the crowd at White Hart Lane. I'd heard they were hard to please and I knew that neither Terry Venables nor Alan Mullery had found it easy to win them over. It would help if I could score a goal on my debut and, as luck would have it, in the thirteenth minute Ray Evans crossed from the right and I headed the ball past the Coventry goalkeeper Bill Glazier. It was a relief for me and, I'm told, a relief for Bill Nicholson, too. He was the man, after all, who had jettisoned local legend Jimmy Greaves and replaced him with me. Bill stood and applauded, along with a crowd of 34,942.

The goal was some consolation for the fact that Coventry beat us 2–1. It was disappointing to lose my first game but I'd trained only once with my new team and it would take considerably longer than that for me to familiarise myself with their style of play.

In our dressing room after the match, as the other Saturday afternoon results filtered through on the radio, we heard that West Ham had beaten Manchester City 5–1 at Maine Road. Jimmy Greaves, also making his debut, scored just the two! He'd made a habit of scoring on his debut – England, England Under-23, Chelsea, Milan, Spurs and now West Ham.

Geoff had also scored two and Ronnie Boyce had supplied a spectacular goal that passed into West Ham legend – a volleyed shot that beat England goalkeeper Joe Corrigan from the centre circle. After four matches without a win, West Ham would have been in party mood on the train back to London.

It already looked like a dream move for Jimmy and I was delighted for him, but I could sense some resentment from the terraces at Tottenham. They'd loved Greaves. He was their greatest goalscorer and he still holds the Tottenham record – 220 goals scored between 1961 and 1970. Spurs had swapped their goalscoring genius for Martin Peters, but the fans were not sure what they were getting. I felt I'd been down this path before and suspected that, with the best will in the world, I was unlikely to replace Jimmy in their affections. My biggest problem in adapting to life at Tottenham, I realised, was not going to be me, but Jimmy Greaves.

14

RECORD BREAKER

These were anxious days for me. As well as all the fuss about becoming Britain's most expensive footballer and making my debut for Tottenham, I was very conscious that the World Cup in Mexico was just nine weeks away. The pressure was greater than it had been in 1966. Now we were preparing for the defence of the Jules Rimet Trophy – we had something to lose. We were the world champions and everyone wanted to beat us.

I played in the last seven games of the season for Spurs, scoring two goals. Jimmy Greaves played in West Ham's last six games, scoring four goals. The media compared us, as did the fans on the terraces. Which club was getting better value for money? I could sense the suspicion at White Hart Lane. Reporters asked me whether I found the record fee a burden. Did it weigh on my shoulders? Was the price tag a handicap? The answer to those questions was no. The fee didn't worry me. The pitch did, and so did Jim's fabulous reputation. I knew I was never going to match his scoring rate. I would just have to impress the fans in some other way.

The pitch was sandy and cut up easily. On wet days it was heavy and drained the energy from my legs. My game was based on running and anticipation. I could make nine fruitless runs into the penalty area but the tenth might produce something. The fans would have to be patient.

My new team-mates were a source of great support. Some of them I already knew. Alan Mullery, Martin Chivers and Cyril Knowles, for instance, had all been with me in the England squad at various times. It was easy slipping into the dressing-room culture and, just as at West Ham, Spurs had their share of clowns, although no one messed about in the presence of Bill Nicholson. It was clear that he was a manager of authority who enjoyed the respect of his players.

The training routines were different. The playing style was also different. On the field, there were times when I'd do something instinctively but the rest of the lads were simply not on the same wavelength, and the same thing happened in reverse. I felt that the demands for success were greater at Spurs than they had been at West Ham but Bill Nicholson didn't put any pressure on me. He realised better than anyone just how difficult it could be to win the support of the fans at his club.

Happily, we finished the domestic season on a high note, beating Arsenal 1–0 at White Hart Lane with a goal from Alan Gilzean. That victory ensured we finished midway in the table, one point ahead of Arsenal and that, I soon learned, was important in the north London gloating stakes. West Ham finished sixth from bottom.

I'd left West Ham so suddenly that I'd not had a chance to say goodbye properly to the players or the fans. The opportunity just didn't arise. I regret that now. I cross-examined Geoff Hurst for all the gossip when the England squad gathered at the end of April for the Home Championship matches. Once again, we played three games in eight days, drawing 1–1 with Wales in Cardiff, beating Northern Ireland 3–1 at Wembley and drawing 0–0 with Scotland in front of 137,438 at Hampden Park. It was an undistinguished tournament, notable chiefly for Bobby Charlton's hundredth England cap in the win over the

Irish. It was reassuring for me to score that day – my first England goal since joining Spurs.

The Scotland result meant that England had been unbeaten throughout the season and Alf Ramsey's optimism was clearly matched by that of the football-loving public. Within a few days of the squad recording 'Back Home' it had shot to number one in the charts. In many ways, 'Back Home', written by a Scotsman Bill Martin and an Irishman Phil Coulter, was the original England football song. It set the standard for all that followed! What do you mean, you don't remember it? In pop music terms it was a classic – 'Back home, they'll be thinking about us when we are far awaaaay ...' Well, I thought it was a classic.

When Bill Martin first met the players, he needed all his persuasiveness to talk us into going to a Pye recording studio to make the LP he was suggesting. Alf actually liked the idea and told us that we should do it, but he said, 'Either you all go, or none of you go.'

Bill Martin was convinced it would be a success. He had been responsible for some big hits, including 'Puppet on a String' and 'Congratulations'. His judgement proved to be right. 'Back Home' was taken from the album and zoomed up the singles chart. We all appeared on *Top of the Pops* in dinner jackets to promote it. Whatever the musical quality, the public loved it. That spring it outsold the Moody Blues, Tom Jones, Roger Whittaker and the Hollies and sailed to the top on a tide of hope and anticipation. All the members of the squad were given a silver disc and I still have mine in my loft at home.

I think the record was still at number one when we left for Mexico. Typically, Alf took no risks. We left London for acclimatisation and warm-up matches twenty-nine days before the tournament was due to start. Kathy, who hated being left alone at home, wasn't happy, and neither were many of the other wives, but that's what Alf wanted. He left nothing to chance. Knighted in the New Year's honours list a few months after winning the trophy in 1966, he was acutely aware that he had established a high benchmark against which all his future achievements would be judged. In short, he knew that he had to win it again or he would be branded a failure.

With Mexico City more than 7000 feet above sea level, Alf realised that it would be at least a fortnight before we could train properly. That's why the twenty-eight players who met at White's Hotel, near the old FA offices in Lancaster Gate, flew out on 4 May for a tournament that wouldn't start until 2 June, when we were due to face Romania in our opening match.

Debate had raged about the effects of heat and altitude on the players since FIFA awarded the 1970 World Cup to Mexico. Alf had taken advice from the London School of Tropical Medicine and the Medical Research Council as well as the British Olympic Association. He had also visited Mexico City twice. The 1968 Olympics had demonstrated quite clearly that teams from low-altitude countries could adapt to the conditions. The three medal-winning nations in the soccer tournament were Hungary, Bulgaria and Japan.

Alf worked hard to ensure that we were the best prepared of the sixteen competing nations. Not everyone shared his opinions on acclimatisation. The West Germans, for instance, arrived just a week before kick-off.

We spent our first fortnight in a hotel we shared, first, with the Mexican squad and then with the Italians. The Italians were even noisier than the Mexicans. Each day we trained at the Reforma Club, a leafy British institution on the outskirts of the city. Here, rich Brits got away from the chaos of one of the world's largest cities. We played the locals at football and cricket and spent our leisure time playing darts, cribbage and the occasional game of golf.

Alf restricted our sun bathing to thirty minutes – fifteen minutes each side. Every morning we were weighed and had heart, lung and blood tests. They also checked to make sure we hadn't been laying in the sun. One day, Jeff Astle, one of the squad jokers, crept up on to the roof of the Reforma Club for a little illicit sunbathing.

'Don't worry, I'm going to wear a vest,' he said. 'They'll never know.'

Next morning, stripped to his vest and shorts for weighing, his red face aroused some suspicion. The doctor asked him to remove his vest, which was of the aerated, string variety, and his chest and back were covered in red diamonds.

You couldn't fault the FA's preparations. They had looked after every detail right down to food and the team bus. We shipped our own bus, and driver, to Mexico and brought in most of our own food, although the Mexicans refused to allow the import of British meat. Unfortunately, bringing our own food offended local sensibilities. Alf could be heavy handed and he did little to help matters with some of his curt remarks to the press. It was obvious from glancing at the local newspapers that England were not popular.

Alf had upset the local press during our tour the previous summer. Diplomacy was not one of his qualities and the legacies of that trip came back to haunt him in 1970. The Mexican media were waiting for him, which was unfortunate because it created an unpleasant, hostile atmosphere in which we had to live and work. I always supported Alf 100 per cent but, with hindsight, I think that we could have done a bit better on the public-relations front in Mexico.

Alf was from the old school. A private, taciturn man, he had little time for the personality cult that was developing in football. In 1966, he had kept us locked away in a remote part of Shropshire for nearly three weeks before the tournament and there is no doubt that this had helped to transform us into a unified team with a shared belief in our own ability. He tried to do something similar in the build-up to the 1970 finals by shielding us from outside influences. It was obviously going to be harder in a foreign country, but that didn't stop him trying.

He wanted us together as a unit at all times. Strangers were not encouraged. Even wives were forbidden access. Kathy came over from London with Judith Hurst, Tina Moore and Frances Bonetti and they all had to stay in a hotel some distance away. We rarely saw them.

Some thought that Alf was developing a siege mentality within the squad. I don't think he thought about it in those terms but the protective shield he tried to wrap around us undoubtedly lead some people to believe that we considered ourselves untouchable. We were accused of being arrogant and aloof and the local media seemed to interpret almost every move we made as an insult to the Mexican nation. When Alf, quite rightly, criticised the pitch in Guadalajara, it caused uproar.

Other nations, on the other hand, ensured they curried favour with the locals. Brazil were the best at it. The Brazilian players were photographed visiting sick children in hospital and handing out gifts to the poor in shanty towns. They even threw in some free seats at their matches for the Mexican kids, which was a brilliant publicity coup that helped win them a new generation of fans. The locals obviously wanted Mexico to win but the Brazilians were not far behind in their affections. Pele, Rivelino, Tostao, Gerson – these were giants of the game, symbolising the World Cup among the Latin nations. We were simply the champions, and everyone wanted to beat us.

As part of our preparations, Alf had persuaded the FA to organise two full international friendly matches. The first was against Colombia in Bogota, 8500 feet above sea level, and the second against Ecuador in Quito, 9300 feet above sea level. I remember how good it was to have a change of scenery when we flew to Bogota, high in the Andes. After a fortnight of training and acclimatisation in Mexico, the boys were itching to play.

Bogota was a bustling city, full of noise, colour and street vendors. We were advised not to buy anything on the street –

in fact, not to leave the hotel alone in the unlikely event that Alf should give us permission to go out at any stage during our four-day stay. Alf was our father figure and, to be honest, we were quite happy to live and travel in our own little world. It was as though we were together in a capsule protected from everything outside. He took all the decisions. We just did as we were told. It was an orderly arrangement that worked well — most of the time.

We checked into the Tequendama Hotel in Colombia's capital city around midday and Alf told us we could have a leisurely afternoon, which was a rare break in the routine for us. Ironically, it was during this free time that the world suddenly caved in on our bid to retain the Cup.

To kill time, the two Bobbys, Moore and Charlton, strolled down to the hotel lobby and looked into the Green Fire jewellery store. Bobby Charlton thought he might see something to buy for his wife, Norma. They looked into one or two showcases then drifted out of the shop and sat in armchairs in the hotel lobby about ten yards from the shop window. While sitting there, they were approached and asked to return to the shop. 'Some jewellery is missing,' they were told.

Thus began a squalid little episode from which Bobby Moore, ludicrously accused of stealing a bracelet, eventually emerged with great dignity. No one with half a brain could have doubted that it was a shabby little fit-up but, as a result of the accusation made against him, 'Mooro' was engulfed in lurid headlines for days and placed under house arrest.

Initially, the two Bobbys, in the presence of Alf Ramsey and FA officials, made formal statements to the police. Everyone in our party knew about it but not a word of the incident was whispered to any outsiders, which tells you something about the strong sense of loyalty within Alf's squad. I don't think you'd have much chance of keeping such an incident a secret today.

With the World Cup only days away, we all hoped the matter was behind us but Alf was fearful of a foreign conspiracy, and in our hushed deliberations, we all suspected that sooner rather than later one of us would find a bracelet planted in his room.

Two days later, as Alf told us who would be playing against Colombia, the secret remained safe within the confines of the squad. Mooro seemed completely untroubled by it. Such was his casual demeanour that Alf had no hesitation in naming him in the England team that day and he was a figure of authority in our 4–0 win over a talented Colombian side. The game demonstrated the value of Alf's training regime because we were better than our opponents in every department.

I was particularly pleased with my own performance. I scored twice, each time drifting unmarked into the danger zone, and created another goal for Bobby Charlton. Alan Ball scored our other goal with a rare header right on the final whistle.

It was hot and humid, but we passed the ball well and kept possession, realising the importance of not wasting energy by chasing lost causes. I left the field knowing that I could cope with ninety minutes of football at 8500 feet. At the end of the match the Colombia manager Lopez Frettes described England as 'a superb unit'.

On the same day, an England B team played Colombia B, winning 1–0 with a goal from Jeff Astle. Other significant figures in that team included Peter Bonetti, Jack Charlton, Nobby Stiles, Norman Hunter and Peter Osgood. We all knew that within a few days Alf would have to trim his squad of players from twenty-eight to twenty-two. Six of us would be bitterly disappointed – which six we still didn't know.

Four days after the Colombia match we played Ecuador in Quito, an ancient Aztec capital at the foot of the Pichincha volcano. Quito is on the equator, higher than Bogota. Breathing is more difficult and the speed and movement of the ball in the air is noticeably different. These conditions made it the hardest place I've played in, but we overcame these difficulties, some questionable, rough-house football from Ecuador and the disturbance caused by two airforce jets as they screamed over the pitch just a couple of hundred feet above us.

England won 2–0 with goals from Francis Lee and Brian Kidd, the young Manchester United striker. 'Kiddo' replaced Franny in the second half, heading home my cross eight minutes from time, while a hat-trick from Astle helped the B team beat the champions of Ecuador, Liga University, 4–1.

It was Brian Kidd's twenty-first birthday a couple of days later but it was not to be a happy occasion for him. He was one of the six unlucky players pruned from the squad.

Alf had wanted to tell all six individually but he'd been badgered into revealing the names to Sunday newspaper journalists, who had difficult deadlines to meet. It was unlike him to confide such delicate information to newspapermen but he swore the press corps to secrecy. Had things gone to plan, he would have told the unlucky six players before the Sunday papers arrived on the breakfast tables back home in the UK.

Unfortunately, he was let down by a journalist in Manchester, who, having been informed of Ramsey's decision by the paper's correspondent in Mexico, immediately pursued family reaction to the news that Manchester United's David Sadler was one of the six left out. David learned his fate not from the manager but from his wife, telephoning from home.

For Alf, it was the final straw in a deteriorating relationship with journalists. He never much liked them, but he trusted no one in the press after that incident. He felt he'd been badly let down and for him this was further justification for keeping strangers at arm's length.

The other four left out with Kidd and Sadler were Peter Thompson, Ralph Coates, Peter Shilton and Bob McNab. I felt sorriest for Peter Thompson, the Liverpool winger who had also been omitted from the 1966 squad. Kiddo and Shilton were youngsters and I thought they'd both be back in the future. I was only half right. Peter went on to become a goalkeeping legend with 125 caps for England, but Kidd, with just two caps to his name, never played for England again.

Alf told all six that they could stay with the squad in Mexico if they wanted to. Sadler and Thompson took up the offer while the others went home over the following few days. Bob McNab, the Arsenal full-back, was the first to leave because he'd been offered a role by ITV on one of the first television panels.

Speculation about who would and who wouldn't survive the cut had dominated our thinking to such a degree that when we boarded the plane at Quito to fly back to Mexico, no one gave a second thought to the fact that we had a five-hour stopover in Bogota. Alf had arranged for us to spend that time back at the Tequendama Hotel, where he had arranged for a screening of the film *Shenandoah*. The England manager always enjoyed a good western.

There was something uncomfortable about the scene at Bogota airport on our arrival. The British Charges d'Affaires, Keith Morris, met Alf and they had a long conversation as the party's baggage was checked through transit. Alf took Mooro to one side and told him that Mr Morris would be accompanying him to the police station to make a statement about the alleged missing bracelet.

The media were still unaware of what was supposed to have happened a few days earlier. It wasn't until we were back in the air, *en route* to Mexico, that the pressmen travelling with the squad realised the captain was missing. I knew he hadn't made the flight because I carried his hand luggage on to the plane.

By the time we stopped to refuel at Panama City, Alf and FA officials had explained to the press that Clara Padilla, a shop assistant, was claiming that Bobby had pocketed a gold bracelet studded with emeralds and worth about £625. These were the days before mobile phones and the media frenzy we witnessed during that hour at Panama City was hilarious as all the reporters tried to send this sensational story to London all at the same time.

When we finally got back to Mexico City on a hot, humid evening, we were greeted by an electric storm of flash bulbs. Jeff Astle, a very nervous air traveller, was photographed arriving in a state of some disarray. 'Drunks and thieves' more or less covered the headlines in the papers the next day.

While we had been in the air the world had learned that the captain of England had been accused of theft, was under house arrest in Bogota and unlikely to take any part in the tournament. To lose Bobby Moore from the squad would have been a disaster for us but no one ever seriously thought we would kick off against Romania without him. We all knew it was a farce, a complete fabrication, and we gradually learned of other cases where famous personalities had faced similar allegations in Bogota. It was a bit of a cottage industry there at the time it seemed to me.

Diplomatic pressure, the hardening suspicion that he'd been framed and Bobby's face-to-face confrontation with Clara Padilla in front of a judge produced the inevitable result and on 29 May he was released. Bobby had spent four days under house arrest, accompanied by FA chairman Dr Andrew Stephen and secretary Denis Follows. He had also had a surprise visit from Jimmy Greaves, who was competing in the World Cup motor rally.

By the time Bobby was released, four days before we began the defence of the World Cup, the squad was in Guadalajara, preparing for the opening game. Mobbed by well-wishers at Bogota airport, he finally joined us with a smile on his face. He'd lost a couple of pounds but was otherwise unaffected by his ordeal. He'd retained his calm and dignity throughout an extraordinary chapter in his illustrious career. We were all jubilant when he sauntered on to the training pitch.

'Have I missed much?' he asked.

15

SIMPLY THE BEST!

Could we win it again? We had a good chance. Our team was considered by some to be even better than the champions of 1966. We'd played well in the warm-up matches and had proved to ourselves that we could cope with the heat and altitude.

Our preparations had been thorough. The medical team had examined all of us individually and identified potential problems. Salt deficiency was my worry. This was something I could cope with easily at home but it was going to be a much bigger problem in the heat of Mexico.

I was unaware of it until my late teens. I remember playing in a pre-season match for West Ham's reserves against the first team on a really hot July afternoon and feeling completely drained at the end. When I got back home I sat with my mum in the scullery and complained of serious pains in my stomach. Then my sight suddenly went. For some minutes I was curled up in agony unable to see anything until the pain gradually subsided and my sight returned. After a series of hospital tests, it was discovered that my body wasn't replacing lost salts as it should. Although I was never much more than skin and bone, I sweated profusely during a game and was losing all the salts in my body. The doctors decided that, from then on, I would have to take salt tablets before each match, which I did for the rest of my career.

The exceptional conditions in Mexico dictated that I follow a particularly strict regime on match days – four tablets before each game, two at half-time and two at the end. The England tour the previous summer had given me an idea of what to expect. We knew that on some match days temperatures would be hovering around 100°F. What didn't help anyone was the fact that the World Cup organising committee had agreed with the big TV companies to kick-off many of the games, including the final, at midday. You'd think that before making a decision like that they'd consult the players.

To his credit, Alf had done all he could to ensure that we were ready for the heat of a Mexican summer and the breathing problems associated with playing at high altitude. As well as the attention paid to acclimatisation, he'd had special lightweight kit designed and provided us with an American energy drink. He'd also brought gallons of bottled water from England – a further source of annoyance to our hosts. In short, the manager had removed all the hurdles. Footballers like an excuse if it starts to go wrong but, for us, there could be no excuses. Alf had spotted all potential excuses and wiped them from the agenda.

We had world-class players with big reputations, we had vastly more experience than we had four years earlier, and although we had good individual skill, we were essentially a team with a sound work ethic. We had prepared properly and no one shirked his responsibilities. Nevertheless, deep inside every England player a little voice was saying, 'It's going to be very difficult to play your natural game in these conditions.'

We worked bloody hard for each other. In our warm-up games we were each losing 10–14lbs. We would run until we dropped but we all knew that our high-intensity pressing game wasn't suited to high summer in Mexico. We had to conserve energy and to do that we had to keep possession of the ball.

Despite the oppressive conditions, I think many people at

home thought we had a good chance of retaining the trophy. New stars had emerged to replace old favourites George Cohen, Ray Wilson and Roger Hunt. These were the only three from 1966 not included in Alf's squad in Mexico. Although Jack Charlton, the oldest man in the squad at thirty-four, and Nobby Stiles played limited roles, they were still with us, and their experience in the dressing room and on the training pitch remained invaluable.

Alf's team for the opening game included six of the World Cup winning side – Gordon Banks, Bobby Moore, Alan Ball, Geoff Hurst, Bobby Charlton and me. Everton's Keith Newton had replaced George at right-back and Terry Cooper, a whippet-like twenty-four-year-old from Leeds, had made the left-back spot his own. In fact, for a while he was considered to be the best left-back in the world. He replaced Ray, who had been unquestionably the best left-back, while Brian Labone, from Everton, had been given Jack's centre-half role alongside Bobby Moore. Alf gave Nobby's defensive midfield job to Alan Mullery and Francis Lee came in to replace Roger at the front.

Others who later got a chance to shine in the sun included most notably Colin Bell, the Manchester City midfield player with the prodigious reserves of energy. He was nicknamed 'Nijinsky', after the racehorse, not the Russian ballet dancer! Jeff Astle, Peter Osgood, Allan Clarke and Tommy Wright also figured in England's defence of the World Cup.

The average age of the team was now twenty-seven and some, such as Bobby Moore, Gordon Banks and Geoff Hurst, were perhaps at the very peak of their playing powers. Other teams certainly had greater flair and artistry but none could better our strength, experience and team spirit. Gordon Banks had 59 caps, Bobby Moore had 80 and Geoff Hurst had 38. Bobby Charlton had amassed 102 caps, Alan Ball had 41 and before our first game I had 38.

The opening match of the tournament – a midday kick-off

in the vast Aztec Stadium in Mexico City – produced a dull goal-less draw between the hosts Mexico and Russia. Three days later, we began our defence in the Jalisco Stadium in Guadalajara. I felt so proud, standing in line listening to the anthems before the match. Sweat was already pouring off me as our names were announced over the public-address system. Each England name was greeted with a barrage of jeers. The Romanian names were indecipherable but each was greeted with cheering.

The Romanian players, clearly loving it, responded by waving and throwing kisses to the crowd. A friend of mine, who was sitting next to an English-speaking Mexican in the crowd, told me later that the locals jeered us because we wouldn't eat their food.

I think the Romanians thought that, with the crowd behind them, they were going to pull off a big shock. They stormed all over us in the opening five minutes and had one outstanding opportunity to score that was headed wide by Florea Dumitrache. Gordon Banks, oozing calm and experience, quickly had a word with his defenders and once the back four had settled we were in business. The Romanians didn't really threaten our goal again until late in the game.

By then Franny Lee had smacked a shot against the crossbar and Bobby Charlton had seen two shots blocked. We'd also lost Keith Newton, hacked down shamelessly after beating his opponent with a brilliant change of direction. He was replaced by Tommy Wright, who received the same treatment moments after arriving on the pitch.

The match turned out to be a test of our temperament as much as anything else. The Romanians were preoccupied with defending and had nothing against a few knee-high tackles. So it was particularly sweet when Geoff Hurst scored the only goal in the sixty-fifth minute. Franny's back header from Alan Ball's centre set up Geoff, who just squeezed his shot home between the goalkeeper and a post. I was unmarked in the centre of the goal and had half expected a pass from him but he clearly thought a shot was the better option, and he was right. Perhaps Alf thought he should have passed to me, too, because after the match when he was being interviewed by David Coleman on BBC TV, he described how I had scored the goal.

'But Alf,' Coleman interrupted, 'we've said it was Hurst.'

Alf thought for a few seconds and then corrected himself.

We played a bit after that goal but, crucially, Gordon had to make a save late in the game when he turned a shot on to the bar from Radu Nunweiler, one of seven brothers who all played for Dinamo Bucharest. Near the end, Alf felt confident enough to take off Franny and send on Chelsea's Peter Osgood for his second cap. 'Ossie' was one of the great attacking players of his generation but he never quite made it at the highest level, which was a pity and may have been more to do with his attitude than his skill.

Alf was very pleased with us at the end. I remember cooling down in the dressing room afterwards, completely relaxed and confident that I could cope with whatever lay ahead. However, that evening, when Alf gave me permission to take a taxi across the city to visit Kathy, I felt light headed. It passed, but I was a bit concerned until I was given a clean bill of health the following day.

Kath hadn't been impressed with our performance but understood that the result was far more important than how we played because it put pressure on our main group rivals, Brazil. They were due to meet Czechoslovakia the following day.

Alf allowed us to go to the top floor of the Hilton Hotel in Guadalajara, where we had a few beers with some well-heeled England fans and a group of Texans in cowboy hats. They were cattlemen and we got talking to them about a rodeo show we'd watched a few days earlier in Mexico City. One of the bulls we'd seen was the size of Moby Dick and someone asked Jeff Astle, 'Would you ride that for £1000?'

Quick as a flash Jeff replied, 'For £1000 I'd milk it!'

The following day we trained as usual and then went as a group to watch Brazil's first match. The stadium was a mass of green and yellow flags with the locals making it quite clear that they and the Brazilians were spiritual brothers, committed to defeating the Europeans, who had filled the last four places in the 1966 finals.

The Czechs treated Pele with so much respect they almost gave him the freedom of the pitch. On the two occasions when he fell and was slow rising they kicked the ball into touch. The crowd loved that but it seemed to me to be an example of how to win friends and lose matches.

We left the stadium just before the end, by which time Pele, Rivelino and Jairzinho (2) had won the match 4–1. Brazil were brilliant and innovative. I particularly remember Pele's outrageous sixty-yard shot that drifted just wide. It was also the first time I'd seen infiltrators in an opponent's defensive wall. Brazil placed two of their men on the end of the Czech wall when they were awarded a free kick just outside the penalty area. As the Brazilians peeled away, leaving a void at one end of the wall, Rivelino curled his left-foot shot through the space they'd vacated straight into the net.

I thought they were impressive but careless, and on the coach back to the hotel, Bobby Moore said, 'Brazil won't get a kick if they play like that against us.'

Our meeting with Brazil was considered to be the highlight of the qualifying rounds – the past champions against the World Cup holders. Most thought it would have made the perfect final. As a study in contrasting styles, there was probably no better match in the tournament, and even today the game is recognised as one of the most memorable in World Cup history.

Unfortunately for us, it all began to go wrong long before the kick-off. Our hotel in Guadalajara, an oasis of calm when we had visited the previous year, became busier and busier as the big day approached. Twenty-four hours before the match, fans began to arrive in vast numbers. A samba band played on the pavement, and all day and all night fans of Brazil drove round the hotel honking their car horns and chanting 'Brasil, Brasil'. If, as we suspected, it was an attempt to ruin our sleep, it worked well. Bobby Charlton and Gordon Banks hardly slept at all. Other players moved to different parts of the hotel in the middle of the night in the hope of finding some peace. Me? I slept through it all and woke fresh as a daisy, but when we kicked off at midday, several bleary-eyed individuals in our team were still trying to adjust to the glare. The sun was high in the sky. The temperature was 98°F. I'd got used to the altitude, but I don't think I ever fully adapted to the heat.

Alf had to make one change to the team. Keith Newton, kicked out of the match against Romania, was replaced by Tommy Wright. Alan Mullery was given perhaps the toughest task – marking Pele. This was the job Nobby Stiles had performed so diligently against Eusebio four years earlier. Brazil could score from practically anywhere, but Pele was the chief threat, as he demonstrated after just eleven minutes with a strike on goal that has rightly earned a revered place in the history of the game.

Carlos Alberto, the Brazilian captain and right-back, started the move when he struck a superb pass with the outside of his right boot. The ball swept around our left-back Terry Cooper into the path of Jairzinho, who crossed perfectly to Pele at the back post. He rose to meet the ball with a powerful downward header and was already shouting 'Golo' when Gordon Banks, with incredible agility, launched himself across his goal. He got one hand to the ball and turned it away, to the disbelief of Pele and everybody else. Forty years later, I still haven't seen a better save. It was almost supernatural.

Bobby Moore slapped Gordon on the back. 'Try and hold it next time, Gordon!' he said.

Gordon explained afterwards that Pele had looked at him in amazement, unable to believe the ball had not entered the net.

'I think golo,' Pele told him.

'I think golo, too!' Gordon replied.

When he tried to analyse it later, Gordon remembered the ball bouncing a few feet in front of him. Initially, he made contact with just one finger but rolled his hand using his third and fourth fingers to lever the ball away.

It was still goalless at half-time and in the cool sanctuary of the dressing room we all seemed to think that we could win it in the second half. Brazil obviously thought the same. On the hour, Pele, for once free of Mullery's attentions, slipped the ball into the path of the on-rushing Jairzinho who lashed his shot high into the net.

We fought on. Alan Ball squandered a scoring opportunity when he shot against the bar and Jeff Astle, replacing Franny Lee, drove a far easier chance wide of an empty goal. It was desperately disappointing but no shame to lose to the best team I ever played against. Since my dad told me I'd never be as good as Tom Finney I've been wary of making comparisons, but in my opinion Pele's Brazil that year were better than the Ronaldo-Rivaldo-Ronaldinho team that beat Germany 2–0 in the 2002 final in Japan.

Brazil has produced plenty of wonderful teams since 1970, but none that match this eleven: Felix, Carlos Alberto, Everaldo, Clodoaldo, Brito, Piazza, Jairzinho, Paulo Cesar, Tostao, Pele, Rivelino – and Gerson was absent because of injury.

Everyone acknowledges their technique, but there was a tough physical edge to them, too. I had the bruises to prove it at the end of the match. Jairzinho went over the top of the ball and raked my shins and I also had a dust-up with Pele just before the final whistle. He had a go at me and I retaliated. I lost my temper twice in that game and that was unusual for me.

Mullery had played Pele with superb aplomb and diligence

and Moore, with his tackles timed to perfection, showed why he was acknowledged as the world's finest defender. One of my favourite souvenirs of that match is the famous photograph of Bobby and Pele exchanging shirts and shaking hands at the end of the game. It remains a poignant illustration of the respect they had for each other.

After the 1966 World Cup final, it was the greatest match I played in. When people suggest that England in 1970 were better than the team of 1966 my reply is always the same – the best teams win the big prizes and the 1970 team won nothing.

At the end of the game I'd arranged to meet Kathy but that had to be delayed because Alan Mullery and I were selected by FIFA to provide urine samples. When you're as dehydrated as we were, that can be a long job. When I finally caught up with her, she was not in a good mood. She'd split her trousers on the way into the stadium and watched the match wearing the lightweight mackintosh she carried in case of rain. Bearing in mind the weather that day, she thought she looked conspicuous in a raincoat.

Brazil were far less impressive three days later when they beat Romania 3–2, but that result meant we needed only to draw with Czechoslovakia the following day to qualify for the quarter-finals. The Czechs had lost to both Brazil and Romania, so Alf decided to rest Ball, Hurst and Labone and replace them with Colin Bell, Allan Clarke and Jack Charlton. This was Jack's final England appearance.

We were terrible. We'd played well against Brazil and got nothing. This time we played badly but won. That's the way it goes sometimes. A sterile game, throughout which we were again jeered, was decided by a disputed penalty early in the second half. Colin Bell was the victim, brought down by Ladislav Kuna, the twenty-two-year-old Czech Footballer of the Year, who looked a promising successor to the great Josef Masopust.

I was convinced it was a penalty because when the Czech

slipped he fell on the ball and seemed to scoop it up into his arms while prostrate on the pitch. I immediately thought, 'Handball,' but later the French referee, Michel Machin, claimed that he gave a penalty because of Kuna's trip on Bell.

Whatever the reason was, the crowd whistled with derision as Allan Clarke lined up to take the penalty kick. He was ice cool as he placed his shot wide of the goalkeeper. In our team-talk, Alf had asked for a volunteer to take penalties should the need arise. Nobody stepped forward except Allan. 'I'll do it, Alf,' he said.

I was pleased for him. It was his first game for England, his wedding anniversary and his wife Margaret's birthday.

Our performance was an anti-climax after the way we had played against Brazil. I think Bobby Moore was the only one of us who played to his potential. He had to against the busy little striker Ladislav Petras. Even Banksie very nearly made a rare and costly error that day. Having survived a bombardment with coins and rubbish from our Mexican persecutors, he misjudged a swerving shot by Karol Dobias that moved deceptively in the thin air. The ball squirmed out of his grasp, hit the bar and spun up into the air. He was in a state of panic when he looked up because he couldn't see the ball. Luckily for him, it fell at the feet of Jack Charlton, who passed it back to our relieved goal-keeper. The back pass was allowed in those days.

We pulled Gordon's leg about it in the dressing room after-wards.

'I look at it this way,' said Banksie. 'It was past midnight at home and you lot had been so bad that I thought many of our fans would be dozing off in their armchairs. So I decided to liven it up a bit for them.'

A number of inquests followed our poor display but the most important thing was that we had come through the toughest of the four qualifying groups and now faced West Germany in the quarter-finals.

Czechoslovakia and Romania might have qualified for the last eight had they been drawn in other groups, but I felt the Czechs paid the price for arriving late in Mexico and not acclimatising properly. It was noticeable in their two early games, against Brazil and Romania, that they faded badly in the second half.

We were scheduled to play the Germans in Leon but before we left Guadalajara we watched film of their qualifying wins against Morocco, Bulgaria and Peru. Unlike us, they were not struggling for goals. They'd scored ten in those three games, Gerd Muller hitting seven of them.

We also visited the lush Guadalajara Country Club. The membership waiting list for this place was a mile long. It was luxurious and, after the incessant turmoil of our hotel, very relaxing – but not on the day we went. When we arrived, the pool area was dominated by a mass of the great and good from British football, including Don Revie, Joe Mercer, Billy Bremner, Johnny Giles and Roger Hunt. They'd had an impromptu kick-about before our arrival and the Mexican waiters were stunned by the skills of these 'supporters'. Apparently, Joe Mercer told them, 'If you think that was good, wait until the players arrive!'

We were in no mood for football, but it was still a lively afternoon, with Osgood and Astle speeding around the golf course in caddy cars. After that welcome break, the following day we travelled to Leon, a coach journey that took five hours.

We met the Germans three days after the Czech game and at some stage during those three days, Gordon Banks ate or drank something that disagreed with him. He was ill and missed the match. Some believe he was poisoned but I think that's a bit far-fetched. None of the rest of us complained of stomach problems, and if you were going to poison anyone in our team, you'd probably select a potential match winner, such as Bobby Charlton.

Initially, on the morning of the match, Gordon thought he would be able to play despite his upset stomach, and Harold

Shepherdson gave him a fitness test on a large green lawn outside our hotel. Banksie was diving from side to side, trying to convince the physio that he was fit.

'I'll be all right,' he mumbled, but I wasn't sure.

Later, Gordon was seen, white-faced, walking on the arm of the England doctor, Neil Phillips. He attended the team-talk, still looking awful.

'I can't be sure I'll get through it,' he said to Alf. That was enough. Alf never shirked the tough decisions.

'I'm not going to risk you,' he said.

It was a blow, but his deputy Peter Bonetti, Chelsea's outstanding goalkeeper, would probably have been first choice in any other World Cup team that summer. 'The Cat' took the news calmly but inside he must have been a little anxious. He hadn't played for six weeks and in the previous four years had made just six appearances for England. In those six matches he'd conceded just one goal, but he'd never played in a match of anything like this importance. Being asked to replace Banks at such short notice must have been something of an ordeal for him, although for the first hour, the absence of the world's greatest goalkeeper mattered little to us.

It was hot in Leon, which is higher than Guadalajara, but a refreshing breeze took the edge off the heat in the little 28,000 capacity stadium. England played with great composure and precision. We passed the ball well and played enterprising, fluid football. Franz Beckenbauer, no longer the callow youth of 1966, was still struggling to contain Bobby Charlton, now thirty-two and making a record 106th appearance.

After thirty minutes, Alan Mullery and Keith Newton conspired to open the German defence. Mullery crowned a flowing move with a thudding drive past Sepp Maier in the German goal. Five minutes after the interval, Geoff Hurst sent Newton away again. He hit a long cross from the right to the far post. The ball eluded Francis Lee but I got in front of my marker,

Berti Vogts, and side-footed it home – not one of my most spectacular goals but one of the most satisfying. With forty minutes remaining, we were leading 2–0 and the semi-finals were beckoning. We were clearly the better team and, as long as we kept possession and did nothing stupid, I thought we would run the clock down and deny the Germans their revenge for 1966.

Never underestimate the Germans, though. They were a fine side. Apart from Beckenbauer, other high-class players included Gerd Muller, Uwe Seeler, Vogts and my old adversary Wolfgang Overath. Just as we were beginning to believe that the job was done, outside influences took hold of the unfolding drama on the pitch. On the side, the two managers, Helmut Schoen and Alf, began to deploy their substitutes.

First, Schoen replaced Reinhard Libuda with Jurgen Grabowski, a winger with the pace to torment any full-back wilting in the heat. Full of running, he gnawed mercilessly at Terry Cooper and this gave the Germans fresh heart. Then despite the fact that Terry was struggling, Alf substituted Bobby Charlton and replaced him with Colin Bell. This was to be a key moment in the match.

With twenty minutes remaining, Beckenbauer advanced past Alan Mullery and sent a low, unexceptional shot goalwards. Bonetti dived but the ball slipped under his body. Nine times out of ten he would have stopped that shot. It was only the second goal we'd conceded in seven matches. Banks had played in the previous six.

Even at 2–1 I was still confident that we would win. A few minutes later, Harold Shepherdson signalled that I was about to be replaced, too. I gestured to the bench that Keith Newton had hurt a knee. Were they sure they wanted me off? Yes, they were. So, Alf sent on Norman Hunter in what I thought was a move designed to reinforce our defensive strength, but as I slumped on the bench – it was the first time I'd been substituted in an international – Alf leaned across to me and said, 'I want to save you and Bobby for the semi-final.'

That seemed like a reasonable idea at the time but, with eight minutes remaining, Brian Labone cleared the ball carelessly from our goalmouth, straight to Karl-Heinz Schnellinger. His cross was met by the stocky Seeler. With a mighty leap, Seeler somehow back-headed the ball over Bonetti, who was stranded out of his goal.

It was now 2–2 with extra time to be played and both substitutes already on the field. As I carried the drinks out to the lads on the pitch, I couldn't help but think of the similarities with 1966. We were even playing in red shirts, just as at Wembley that day, but the initiative was now Germany's. I think our last chance went when Geoff Hurst had a goal inexplicably disallowed by the extravagantly named Argentine referee, Norberto Angel Coerezza.

In the 110th minute, Grabowski flew past Cooper again on the flank and Johannes Lohr headed his cross back into the mouth of the goal where the squat, predatory Muller hooked the ball into the net. Colin Bell might have had a penalty a few minutes later and Keith Newton had a shot tipped over the bar by Maier, but I thought that, this time, it was all over for us, and it was. I remain convinced that we were the better team, but we were no longer world champions.

Most of the players were too exhausted to talk in the dressing room afterwards. I remember thinking to myself, 'My God, how did we lose that?' Alf joined us.

'You gave everything,' he said. 'I'm proud of you. Don't feel too badly about it.'

I felt sorry for him because we were the ones who had lost the match but he was the one who would have to face the music. The inquests started immediately. His tactics were dissected. His substitutions were questioned. Why did he leave Cooper on the field when he was clearly exhausted? Why did he put

Norman Hunter on? Why didn't he take a gamble on Peter Osgood?

I took some consolation from the words of the former Brazilian team manager, Joao Saldanha, who believed that England were the best team the new champions met in the tournament. His theory was that we had taken more out of ourselves in a tough qualifying group than the Germans, who had coasted through their games.

I left Leon the following day with Peter Bonetti to join our wives for a few days in Acapulco. Geoff and Bobby followed us. Peter never talked about the game but he must have gone over it hundreds of times in his mind. History has judged him harshly in the matter of Leon but I've always believed that it was an oversimplification to say that we would have won had Gordon Banks played that day.

16

'SORRY, I GOT IT WRONG, MARTIN'

I'm told that Alf Ramsey sat alone for long periods during the flight home from Mexico. He knew it was the closing chapter of the most memorable period in English football history.

It was certainly the end of his 1966 team of World Cup winners. Bobby and Jack Charlton and Nobby Stiles, all in the Mexico squad, followed the examples of Ray Wilson, George Cohen and Roger Hunt and retired from international football. Only five of the World Cup winners were to play for England again – Geoff Hurst, Bobby Moore, Gordon Banks, Alan Ball and me.

Alf made a point of flying home with his players. He had planned to return via New York where he wanted to visit his daughter and granddaughter, but he felt his place was with the players.

At home, most fingers were pointing at Alf and his decision to substitute Bobby Charlton and me. Did that cost us the World Cup?

Years later, long after Alf had retired, I was in the habit of visiting him at his house on the outskirts of Ipswich, where he'd originally made his name as a manager by winning the League Championship title in 1962. I lived in Brentwood, Essex, and my job often took me to Suffolk. When I was in the area, I'd try to call in on Sir Alf and his wife. Sometimes he was at home, sometimes he was out playing golf.

I was the only one of the 1966 team to live anywhere near him and he liked to keep up to date with the lads and their families. We used to have a cup of tea in the kitchen, where he would sit to write letters or sign the photographs people were still sending him. We had developed a good relationship over the years. We'd both lived and gone to school in Dagenham and both played for Spurs. He knew how grateful I was when he advised me about my transfer from West Ham to White Hart Lane just before the 1970 World Cup. By then, he knew as much about my game as anyone, although in the early part of my career he had been critical and, I think, made a premature judgement about me. I realise now that many of the qualities I had as a young player were not of the obvious kind. Apart from any other perceived flaws, Alf didn't think I could head the ball. I was astonished and disappointed when I heard this because heading has always been a big part of my game. Had he said at that time that my tackling was weak, I could have accepted it – but not my heading. I didn't let it affect me because I knew Alf was wrong. It simply reinforced my own belief that in football early impressions of a player are not always right.

I never challenged Alf over his early opinion of me, although when we met we talked a great deal about football. More often than not it was about some modern development in the game. He rarely dwelt on what we had both shared in the sixties and seventies.

Then one day, for no obvious reason, he started talking about 1970. Over the years, I noticed he became increasingly forgetful but he was able to recall all the events of that summer in Mexico quite accurately. With no prompting from me, he said, 'Of course, I was wrong to take you and Bobby off that day against West Germany.'

'Why do you say that now?' I asked him.

'I've thought it for a long time,' he replied. 'Everyone thinks I was wrong, don't they?'

I'd never heard him express that view before. It was quite true that people in the aftermath of the Mexico World Cup thought he'd made tactical errors, particularly with his substitutions against the Germans, but he'd never admitted that to any of his players. He never blamed any of us, either. He always said that he would shoulder the flak, and he did. He never publicly criticised any individual player. Loyalty featured high in the gospel according to Alf. He could quite easily have used the absence of Gordon Banks as an excuse for our defeat against West Germany but that would have implied criticism of Peter Bonetti. Although Peter received plenty of criticism, none could be attributed to the manager.

In his private conversations with me, he never blamed any individual apart from himself. He told me that he took Bobby and me off the field that day to save our legs for the semi-final. That is exactly what he'd told me on the bench seconds after I'd left the pitch. It's also what he told the media in the hours immediately after the match. At no stage did he admit that he'd made mistakes.

'If the same situation arose regarding the need for substitutes, I would take the same course of action,' he replied, when asked whether the substitutions had damaged England's hopes of beating the Germans. 'Calling off Bobby Charlton was fully justified in my opinion. At that stage the match was won, the Germans were finished and I was in a position where I could send on fresh substitutes in order to save men for the semi-final. The substitutes, Bell and Hunter, were not responsible for the turn of events.'

Alf told the press that England's defeat could be traced to poor defending.

'The first two German goals should have been prevented,' he said. 'I've not seen England give away two goals like that for a long time.'

When he had his heart-to-heart with me many years later, though, he said, 'I made two big mistakes that day, Martin. The first was taking Bobby off and the second was taking you off. We were winning 2–0 when I took Bob off and still winning 2–1 when I took you off. Had I kept you both on the field, I think we would have won.'

None of the players blamed Alf for what happened. We blamed ourselves. We were the ones on the pitch and we threw away a winning position.

I suppose that defeat was the beginning of the end for Alf, too. He didn't help himself on his return to England by stating quite categorically that we could learn nothing from the Brazilians. It was a reckless statement and he later tried to claim that he had been misquoted and misunderstood, but perhaps he was right. Perhaps we did have nothing to learn from Brazil. Could we emulate the spontaneity and fantasy of the Brazilian sun gods? Seriously? Could we? I'm not sure we could. Our traditional style of play was very different, and still hasn't changed much.

Brazil were spectacular in 1970, demolishing Italy 4–1 in the final. They had demonstrated marvellous attacking skills and having won the Jules Rimet Trophy for the third time were allowed to keep it permanently. Perhaps Alf realised that there was no realistic prospect of England producing footballers able to play like the Brazilians. Perhaps that was what he meant. We had our own strengths and they were greatly admired throughout the world. Alf was nothing if not a realist. It would have been churlish of him to belittle Brazil's achievement and I don't think he meant it in that way but, unfortunately, that was how the public interpreted his statement.

Another twelve years went by before England appeared in the World Cup finals again. By the time the 1982 World Cup came round, Alf was sixty-three and in retirement. He'd had a brief period managing Birmingham City after his shabby sacking by the Football Association in 1974 but I sensed he was disillusioned with football.

I continued visiting him for years, always in the same semi-detached house. I think he'd lived there since his time as Ipswich Town manager. Later, Sir Bobby Robson, who followed him as both Ipswich and England manager, lived in a house a few streets away.

It was sad watching Alf grow old because he'd played such a big role in my career. He was always friendly towards me and towards the others in the 1966 team – friendly but slightly aloof. The player-manager relationship remained intact till the end.

He died in April 1999. He was one of the most important and successful sporting personalities of the last century. I went to his funeral but was disappointed that so few of the game's establishment figures paid their last respects to a great English patriot.

17

MICH UND WOLFGANG

Losing the World Cup was perhaps the bitterest experience of my career. It wasn't something you could just shrug off. So, when we finally got home after our few days in Acapulco, we decided to take the children to Portugal to try to forget about football for a fortnight. We stayed in a lovely hotel, Donna Fillipa, at Vale de Lobo. We enjoyed it and we've been back many times, although in recent years the area has become a property speculators' paradise.

Any hopes I had of forgetting about the World Cup were quickly dashed when we bumped into Bobby and Norma Charlton, who like us had arrived in Portugal to relax a little before the new domestic season. A day or so later we met the Arsenal captain Frank McLintock and his family. It was all a bit unreal.

I reported back for training about three weeks before the new season started and almost immediately flew out to Majorca where Tottenham were playing in a pre-season tournament. It was an important competition for me because I wanted to get to know my team-mates better and continue to familiarise myself with Tottenham's playing style before the season kicked off.

The first match in the tournament was, believe it or not, against a West German side – FC Cologne. Both teams walked out on to the pitch before the game to be introduced to the crowd. We were in tee shirts and flip-flops. The Germans looked much more businesslike in their matching adidas tracksuits.

In the circumstances, the stadium announcer couldn't resist making reference to the football history between England and Germany and, specifically, the World Cup match between the two nations played just a few weeks earlier in Mexico. He mentioned Alan Mullery and me and then made a great fuss of Wolfgang Overath, who was in the Cologne side.

As we stood in the middle of the pitch, Overath smiled at me. He and I were never friends but I had great respect for him as a player. In my opinion, he was one of the most accomplished and talented of West German internationals. He never enjoyed the worldwide reputation that Franz Beckenbauer did, for instance, but he was acknowledged within the game as a midfield playmaker of similar influence. His 81 international caps, awarded between 1963 and 1974, give an idea of how highly rated he was by the Germans. He played in three World Cup tournaments – Germany finished as runners-up in 1966, third in 1970 and, finally, champions in 1974.

In Mexico, he was described as a cross between Einstein and a prima ballerina. He had strength, intelligence, wonderful balance, a great passing range and he could tackle like a demon.

Wolfgang and I were both born in 1943 and our paths crossed at critical stages throughout our careers, starting at Wembley in 1959 when we were fifteen and a huge crowd watched us play in the Schoolboy international when England beat West Germany 2–0. I was playing left-half and in direct opposition to me at right-half was Wolfgang Overath, of Siegburg, his home-town club.

Three years later we met again, this time in a Youth international match at Northampton Town's County Ground. By this time I was at West Ham. Other members of the England team included the Sunderland goalkeeper Jim Montgomery, the Leicester City centre-half Graham Cross and the Arsenal winger George Armstrong. Along with Overath, the West German team included goalkeeper Sepp Maier and defender Wolfgang Weber – all three of them destined for higher things in world football. On that spring day, though, the Germans were eclipsed by a superior England team. I'm pleased to recall that we won 1–0 and deserved more goals. I supplied our goal with a shot from about twenty yards.

We played against each other in the World Cups of 1966 and 1970 and now, in the sunshine of Majorca, we were doing it again. I caught him with a late tackle and was sent off for the first and only time in my career as Cologne beat Tottenham 2–0. The tackle was reckless but the Germans were taking the mickey. Cyril Knowles had already been sent off, we were chasing the game and they were happy to keep possession, taking full advantage of their extra man.

I suppose I was still irritated and frustrated by our World Cup exit and when Overath started teasing us – he was skilful enough to do that – I clattered into him. The referee had no hesitation in sending me off, and I had no hesitation in going. When I arrived in the cool shade of the dressing room, Cyril Knowles was sitting on the treatment table.

'What are you doing here? It's not over yet is it?' he said.

No, it wasn't over – nor was it over with Wolfgang. We played against each other yet again when Spurs were on their way to the UEFA Cup final in Rotterdam in 1973–74. We beat Cologne 5–1 on aggregate in the quarter-final and I scored in both legs. That showed him!

That was the last time we faced each other in competitive football, but it was not the end of the story. In 1996, I was approached by an intermediary who was interested in an item that had been slowly mouldering in my loft at home – Wolfgang Overath's 1966 World Cup shirt. This was about the time that Geoff Hurst became involved in a media-driven attempt to get the World Cup ball back from Helmut Haller, the German scorer of the first goal in 1966.

At the end of the game, Wolfgang and I had exchanged shirts. I didn't think much about it at the time but years later, I wondered whether I'd done the right thing. Anyway, Wolfgang had my shirt and I had his. Would we swap them back? I was happy to do so but, in the event, he couldn't find my shirt, so the deal was off. A few years after that, I came across Wolfgang's shirt again, still in my loft, and, along with other items of memorabilia, it went to West Ham to be exhibited in the club's museum. I guess he still has my shirt somewhere.

In all he played nearly 800 games for Cologne – his last was the German Cup final – before retiring in 1977 and becoming a representative for a sportswear company. He later spent four years on Cologne's board of directors and was then appointed club president.

As a player he was probably at his peak in the summer of 1970, and I guess he must have been disappointed to lose 4–3 in a thrilling semi-final against Italy in the Aztec Stadium. That game went to extra time and I reckon the match with us a few days earlier had drained the Germans physically.

I wish I had got to know Wolfgang. Apart from those intense ninety-minute periods when we were in direct conflict on the field of play, I've hardly had any other contact with him.

The defeat Tottenham suffered against Cologne in Majorca did little to lift my spirits but when we returned to London, we played Glasgow Rangers in a curtain-raiser to the new season and beat them 2–0. We played well, too.

The big football news as we prepared for the season to kick off was George Best's decision to sign an eight-year contract with Manchester United. The newspapers were full of speculation about his new salary. Most seemed to think he was going to be earning £10,000 per year, a small fortune in those days.

I remember this particularly because, at the same time, my old West Ham team-mate who'd played with me at junior level, Brian Dear, had been given a free transfer by Millwall and was about to sign on the dole. I was delighted shortly afterwards when Ron Greenwood decided to take him back to Upton Park.

Stag had played in the Cup Winners' Cup team of 1965, the year he distinguished himself by setting a goalscoring record with five goals in twenty minutes against West Bromwich Albion. He was a bit unpredictable in front of goal, though, and in his second spell with the club played just four first-team games. He was released at the end of the season after his involvement in the notorious Blackpool nightclub affair. It was not something Ron Greenwood could forgive easily. Jimmy Greaves, another of the group who went drinking the night before an FA Cup tie, played a few more games before retiring prematurely. I think the fact that Ron signed a new striker, Bryan 'Pop' Robson from Newcastle, and then tried to play Jimmy in midfield hastened his decision to hang up his boots.

When I lined up for the first match of the new season, though, Jimmy was there in claret and blue, grinning like a Cheshire cat. We kicked off against West Ham United in front of a crowd of 53,640 at White Hart Lane in August 1970. With four of England's Mexico squad on duty, this was the showpiece match of the first weekend of the season and was screened on Sunday afternoon's *The Big Match*.

Of course, the inevitable happened – Jimmy Greaves scored. Alan Gilzean had given us the lead in the thirty-first minute and within sixty seconds Jim had equalised for West Ham. 'Gilly' put us back in the lead but Peter Bennett's sixtieth-minute goal meant an absorbing match ended 2–2. All the goals were good, especially Gilly's diving header, but we'd failed to win our opening game. Jim had scored and I hadn't. The Tottenham fans were not impressed. I was beginning to think that it was going to take me some time to win them over.

The papers were still debating whether I was value for money at £200,000, although not all of them questioned the wisdom of paying that kind of money for me. Some felt West Ham had been wrong to sell me in part exchange for Jimmy Greaves. One of the East London papers claimed that the swap didn't make sense from West Ham's viewpoint. Jimmy, the paper claimed, was thirty and past it while I, at twenty-six, was widely considered to be one of the world's great players.

The comments were either flattering or offensive, depending on which newspaper I read. I tried not to let it trouble me but it is a fact that if a club pays a record transfer fee, you feel an extra responsibility. When we lost, I felt vulnerable. Our seventh game of the season was against Arsenal at Highbury. At that point, we'd won twice and I still hadn't scored.

It didn't improve at Highbury. Injury robbed us of two key players – Pat Jennings and Cyril Knowles – and Arsenal were gathering their strength for what was to be a formidable season for them. In a fitful, hard, fractious match, George Armstrong twice beat our deputy goalkeeper, Ken Hancock, to secure a 2–0 win for Arsenal.

After the match, as I walked out of Highbury's marble halls and down the steps to get on to the team bus, the waiting crowd on the pavement started howling abuse – Tottenham fans expressing their derision. Their theme was 'what a waste of money' with lots of invective and hostility thrown in. I was taken aback at the degree of anger they demonstrated that day. I'd not experienced anything like it at West Ham.

The supporters had paid to watch us play and if they didn't think we were pulling our weight, they were entitled to express their opinion – but I was pulling my weight. It just wasn't obvious to the fans that I was doing so. At West Ham, they had got used to the subtlety of my game. I was sure they'd grow to appreciate me at Spurs in much the same way.

I had no previous experience of a big North London derby

but, over the years I spent with Spurs, I came to realise how important this particular result was to the fans of both clubs. They felt the rivalry more intensely than the players because, if their team lost, the following day they had to face gloating workmates.

The abuse at Arsenal was the low point for me. The tide started to turn in my favour a few days later when I scored in a 3–0 win over Swansea in the second round of the League Cup at White Hart Lane. Then I struck again in front of our fans. This time we beat Blackpool 3–0 and I scored twice. Another goal came in a 1–1 draw at Derby and then 44,000 at White Hart Lane watched me score the only goal in a 1–0 win over Liverpool. The ten First Division matches following the defeat at Highbury produced eight wins and two draws. Suddenly, we were contenders for the title.

However, we were making the most exciting progress in the League Cup. We beat Sheffield United, West Bromwich Albion (I scored a hat-trick) and Coventry City to set up a semi-final clash with Bristol City of the Second Division in December. Manchester United and Aston Villa met in the other semi-final.

Bristol City, who just escaped relegation to the Third Division at the end of the season, proved to be difficult opponents. We drew the first leg 1–1 in Bristol, Alan Gilzean supplying our goal, and were made to work hard for a 2–0 win at White Hart Lane in the return leg.

As Villa, then a Third Division club, had surprisingly beaten Manchester United 3–2 on aggregate, we were strongly fancied to win at Wembley, which we did, but it wasn't easy. Villa had a big, powerful centre-forward in Andy Lochhead, who'd scored in both legs against United, and he kept Peter Collins stretched for the full ninety minutes in the final. They also had Bruce Rioch, a formidable Scot, in midfield.

We didn't play well and Steve Perryman had to hack one Villa shot off the line, but, in the final analysis, we had just a little bit more class. Two great, late goals from Martin Chivers won it and earned us a place in the following season's UEFA Cup, as the Intercities Fairs Cup had just been renamed.

Liverpool knocked us out of the FA Cup in a sixth-round replay at White Hart Lane, Steve Heighway scoring the only goal, but we managed to sustain a challenge for the First Division title into the last weeks of the season.

Our final home game was against our old friends from Arsenal, who were just two matches away from emulating Tottenham's double success when we met them on a Monday night early in May. For us, the humiliation potential was high. For Arsenal to achieve the first leg of the double, they had to secure the right result at White Hart Lane in their final First Division match of the season. They were locked at the head of the table with Leeds, who had completed their programme of matches. The mathematical permutations were complex but, basically, Arsenal needed at least a goalless draw to win the title. Defeat or a scoring draw would conclude matters in favour of Leeds United. Arsenal's priority, therefore, was to keep their goal intact.

The crowd numbered 51,992 and at least as many were locked out. That night north London came to a standstill. The match referee Kevin Howley, officiating at his final game before retirement, was forced to abandon his car and walk the last mile to the ground. The atmosphere inside was electric. We were determined to protect the legacy left us by the 1961 team and retain the distinction of being the only club to win the double in the twentieth century.

The game, tense and exciting, was the usual physical clash with no prisoners taken. I think we played the better football and after about thirty minutes I put a volley on to the top of the crossbar. Later, Alan Mullery and Alan Gilzean worked an opening for me and I hit a shot that Bob Wilson needed all his agility to save.

It was heading for a goalless draw when Pat Jennings punched away a shot from John Radford with just three minutes remaining. George Armstrong gathered the ball out on the wing and crossed it again. This time young Ray Kennedy rose powerfully and sent a header fizzing into the net.

Full of confidence, they followed that 1–0 victory five days later with a 2–1 win after extra time over Liverpool in the FA Cup final at Wembley. So, you could say they emulated Tottenham's achievement in the hardest possible way – by winning the First Division title in their last match of the season and the FA Cup in extra time.

Those two facts encapsulate that Arsenal side. They were not pretty to watch, but they were effective, efficient, disciplined and they worked hard. Tottenham always played the better football but Arsenal usually got the better results.

In 1970–71 they also reached the last eight of the Fairs Cup. In all, they used just fifteen players and some of them, including Bob Wilson, Frank McLintock, Pat Rice, Peter Storey, George Armstrong and Bob McNab, played between sixty and eighty games.

Frank was an outstanding leader and George a high-class winger who was unfortunate not to establish himself in the England squad. Charlie George was also a top-quality player, but what really set them apart was their work ethic. They were not unlike England in that respect. They were bloody hard to beat!

Three days after losing to Arsenal, we finished our season at Stoke. We were still battling with Wolves for a third-place finish but, as we had already qualified for Europe, the match result was largely academic. This became apparent when we arrived at Stoke to discover that Bill Nicholson wasn't with us. I'd never known an occasion before when the manager wasn't present at a first-team match. Apparently, he'd spent the day in Burnley trying to finalise the signing of their winger, Ralph Coates. He left kitman Johnny Wallis in charge.

A Spurs man through and through, Johnny was a portly, amiable figure who helped around the dressing room. He was enormously popular with the players and you can imagine the fun they had with him when he delivered his team-talk before kick off.

It didn't do us any harm. We finished the season on a high note, beating Stoke 1–0, and I was particularly pleased with the goal. I chased a high ball over the Stoke defence and as Gordon Banks advanced from his goal, I volleyed a shot that clipped the underside of the bar before bouncing into the net.

It was my fifteenth goal of the season. Only Chiv and Gilly had scored more. I'd made my point to any doubters left on the terraces at White Hart Lane.

18

'MINE EYES HAVE SEEN THE GLORY...'

'Glory, Glory, Hallelujah' was a rousing battle hymn adopted by Tottenham fans during the sixties. Their singing echoed around the rafters of the old stadium at White Hart Lane and a packed house in full voice lifted the spirits of the home side while sowing seeds of doubt in the opposition.

The hymn became the Tottenham trademark, particularly on big European nights. The fans sang their hearts out as the double winners progressed to the European Cup semi-final in 1962 and became England's first European champions in the Cup Winners' Cup a year later. From my experience, the only other fans to generate similar emotion were those on the old Kop at Liverpool when they sang 'You'll never walk alone' with such passion.

Tottenham and Liverpool shared with Manchester United the distinction of being among England's early successes on the European stage, although when I moved to White Hart Lane, big European nights were little more than a fond memory at the club. No member of the 1963 Cup Winners' Cup side was still at the club but several of my team-mates had been with Spurs for the best part of a decade. Pat Jennings, Cyril Knowles, Joe Kinnear, Alan Mullery and Alan Gilzean had joined Tottenham in the mid-sixties. The club had a reputation for spending big in the transfer market, but they did put some time and effort into developing youngsters. Phil Beal was one of these. Phil had joined Spurs as an amateur in May 1960, turning professional eighteen months later. Jimmy Pearce, a Tottenham boy, joined the club as an apprentice in 1973.

Everyone at the club wanted to experience big European nights at White Hart Lane and hear the fans singing 'Glory, Glory, Hallelujah' once more. It was a dream for us and it came true in 1971–72.

Our success in winning the previous season's League Cup meant that we had the chance to compete for the UEFA Cup, along with Leeds and Wolverhampton Wanderers, who qualified because of high finishing places in the First Division. We started like storm troops, beating little Keflavik 6–1 in a biting wind in Iceland. The match was distinguished only by Graeme Souness's brief appearance as a substitute.

Graeme was an outstandingly talented youngster in the same age group as Steve Perryman. They played together in the Tottenham side that beat Coventry City in the FA Youth Cup final in 1970, and Graeme contributed significantly to the unfolding drama in that four-match marathon. He scored the only goal in the first leg at White Hart Lane. He was booked in the second after a clash with Dennis Mortimer, sent off in a 2–2 draw in the play-off at Coventry and then scored the only goal to win the replay at White Hart Lane.

The Football Association banned him for twenty-one days and fined him £10 because of his dismissal and it still irks him that they denied him the winner's plaque that went to all his team-mates.

He was a very promising midfield player, but he was impatient. He thought he was worth a regular first-team place but Bill Nicholson didn't agree. Disgruntled and homesick, he went back to Edinburgh. Bill was disappointed with his attitude because he liked the qualities that the Scottish players brought to the game and I think he saw Graeme as an eventual successor to Dave Mackay. It didn't work out. Graeme returned to the club but Bill realised that he would have to release him.

I had a part to play in this. I realised that Graeme had the potential to become a great player and one day, on an England trip, I talked with Harold Shepherdson about the unhappy young Scot we had on the books at White Hart Lane.

As well as being one of Sir Alf Ramsey's backroom staff, Shep was assistant manager at Middlesbrough. They were looking for a Souness-type player and decided to buy Graeme, on my recommendation, for £30,000 in December 1972. He never looked back. I was delighted when he went on to have such a great career with Scotland and Liverpool, with whom he played in three European Cup finals.

Later, he became a successful manager. In fact, several players from that Spurs era, myself included, tried management when our playing careers finished but he was probably more successful than the rest of us.

Graeme didn't play in the second leg against Keflavik – a 9–0 victory with Martin Chivers scoring a hat-trick – nor did he get anywhere near the first team again before his transfer to Middlesbrough.

In the second round of the UEFA Cup we met Nantes. The first leg was played in France and the hospitality we received was exceptional. The night before the match the local mayor entertained the team and officials in a magnificent floodlit castle in the centre of town. If the idea was to lull us into a relaxed frame of mind, it wasn't entirely successful. We drew 0–0 and flew home thinking we'd done well but the next morning Bill Nicholson gave us a roasting in training. He was most critical of Martin Chivers, Alan Mullery and me. His words obviously hit home because a few days later we beat Nottingham Forest 6–1. I scored two and Mullers and Chiv were also on the scoresheet.

My goal in the return leg against Nantes at White Hart Lane secured us a place in the third round where we were drawn against Rapid Bucharest of Romania. Against them, we did the job at home in the first leg, winning 3–0. I scored the first one early in the game when Alan Gilzean flicked on a long throw-in from Martin Chivers. The long throw was a speciality of Martin's and provided us with a regular source of goals each season.

The Romanians demonstrated their displeasure in the second leg when they tried to kick lumps out of us. It was a vicious game but we won 2–0. Martin and Jimmy Pearce, a second-half substitute for the injured Alan Gilzean, scored the goals. Jimmy was on the field for just ten minutes. He scored a goal, had another disallowed and was then dismissed for retaliation along with the Rapid full-back Ilie Pop. I missed a penalty. After the match Bill Nicholson said, 'If this is European football, we're better off out of it. I haven't seen a dirtier game in thirty years.'

As luck would have it, we met another Romanian team in the quarter-finals. UT Arad were a more accomplished side than our previous opponents but we still won 2–0 in the first leg. Their little stadium was surrounded by houses and the locals removed slates from the roofs so that they could pop their heads through the holes to watch the match.

A 1–1 draw at home meant that we progressed to the last four with Wolverhampton Wanderers, AC Milan and Ferencvaros of Hungary. 'Glory, Glory, Hallelujah' echoed around White Hart Lane.

I thought we'd done exceptionally well, especially as we had been without Alan Mullery for four months. He was one of our most influential players and was desperate to get back in the side when we were drawn to face AC Milan, but he'd been out of action with a pelvic injury and the manager was reluctant to rush him back. Alan insisted that he would regain full match fitness only by playing first-team matches, so Bill Nicholson loaned him out to Fulham, the club where he had started his career.

As the first leg of the semi-final approached, Bill realised that we were heading towards one of those Easter fixture pile-ups that ruined the chances of so many English clubs in Europe. Our schedule meant we had to play five games in nine days – against Coventry, West Ham, Ipswich, AC Milan and West Bromwich Albion. Bill suggested a postponement to the Italians but they refused. To make matters worse, John Pratt broke his nose against Ipswich, two days before the Milan game, and Bill had to recall Mullers from Fulham because of a shortage of midfield players.

At White Hart Lane, a crowd of 42,000 welcomed him back like a returning hero. The fans loved him because he worked hard, was totally committed and urged greater effort from those around him. He was a demanding captain and once, after we'd lost against Chelsea without him, he tore into us at training. He could be very forthright and opinionated and some of the other big names weren't pleased with his outburst.

I thought he was a very good captain. He kept himself apart from the cliques that always develop in dressing rooms. I think he felt that he could lead the team more effectively if everyone recognised that his was an independent voice.

Alan's reputation went before him and Nereo Rocco, the AC Milan manager who led the club to European Cup triumph in 1969, immediately complained to UEFA when he heard that he had been recalled from Fulham. UEFA dismissed the complaint and Alan gave his usual 100 per cent in a hard game against a cynical Italian team.

They had their own Mullers in Romeo Benetti, a resilient, tough-tackling midfield player who was also a very good passer of the ball. He scored the opening goal and, for a while, it looked as though we might be in trouble. However, young Steve Perryman emerged as our hero, rescuing the tie for us with two goals. He was still learning the game but was to become one of the great names in Tottenham history.

Steve was just eighteen when I joined the club but he played with the maturity and confidence of someone far older. He loved facing players with big reputations. 'Don't worry about Johnny Giles,' he'd say. 'I'll look after him.' A natural-born winner, he should have got more than the one token England cap he was awarded against Iceland in 1982, but he was highly valued by a succession of Spurs managers and made a record number of league appearances for the club – 655 – between 1969 and 1986.

In his later years at the club he played right-back, but I thought he was best in the holding position in midfield. During my time at Spurs we played with three across the midfield – Steve in the middle, Alan Mullery on the right and me on the left. It worked well. We complemented each other perfectly and I don't think there were very many better midfield units in the game at the time.

Quite understandably, Bill Nicholson thought the world of Stevie P. I remember the big fuss Bill made after his two goals against AC Milan. The Italians were confident of going through, though, having scored an away goal, but Bill told us that he thought we could survive in the San Siro Stadium a fortnight later.

Steve played a key role in that game, too. Long before we got to the stadium in Milan, we sensed the intimidating atmosphere of the city. Although we left our hotel early for the match, the traffic was so bad that we arrived just forty-five minutes before kick-off.

The San Siro was packed with 80,000 fans and as we stepped on to the pitch we were greeted with fireworks and smoke bombs. We needed an early goal to take the sting out of the occasion but we were without Alan Gilzean. He was injured and Bill had asked me to play upfront alongside Martin

Chivers. The goal we needed came after just seven minutes. A shot from Martin was blocked and the ball flew out to Stevie Perryman. He took a few paces forward and then played it perfectly into Mullers' path. The captain ran to meet the ball and hit it first time. His shot instantly silenced the crowd, sweeping into the net beyond the diving goalkeeper, Fabio Cudicini, whose son, Carlo, was to play for Chelsea years later.

In the second half, Phil Beal gave away a penalty that AC Milan captain Gianni Rivera drove past Pat Jennings, but they couldn't get the second goal that would have taken the tie to extra time.

That memorable result was one of the best of my time at Spurs. Nereo Rocco congratulated us afterwards and while we celebrated in the dressing room we heard that Wolves had beaten Ferencvaros 2–1 at Molineux, setting up an all-English UEFA Cup final, to be played over two legs.

Wolves had been among the European pioneers in the fifties, but had never won a European trophy, while we were attempting to become the first English club to win two. Veteran Northern Ireland striker Derek Dougan led their attack, supported by the promising John Richards. They had plenty of experience in Jim McCalliog, David Wagstaffe and the former England midfield player Mike Bailey, who'd missed much of the second half of the season because of injury. Nevertheless, we thought we could beat them, and had done so handsomely at White Hart Lane a few months earlier, although we realised that our 4–1 victory in the First Division would count for little in a big European final.

Much of the pre-match build-up concerned the two big strikers – Martin Chivers and Dougan, a talented goalscorer but a bit of a showman. Martin emerged triumphant, his two great goals at Molineux putting us in a commanding position at the end of the first leg. In the dressing room afterwards Bill's coaching assistant Eddie Baily, who would often irritate Martin with his sarcasm, was fulsome in his praise.

'What can I say, Martin?' he shouted above the din in the dressing room. 'I'm out for the count. You've knocked me out.'

The sight of Martin in full flight would get you up out of your seat. A big, powerful runner, he could be a spectacular goalscorer when he was in the mood. I like to think that my arrival at the club had something to do with him regaining his best form. We established a good relationship, similar to the one I'd had with Geoff Hurst at West Ham. That 1971–72 season, he scored 42 first-team goals for Tottenham. For three or four years I considered him to be the best centre-forward in Europe and I was surprised that he didn't win more than 24 England caps.

A natural who made the game look easy, he had a long, loping stride, an impressive physique and was deceptively quick, but he didn't always make the most of his strengths. In training, Bill Nicholson used to ask our centre-backs, Mike England and Peter Collins, to goad him in the hope that it would make him respond aggressively.

I think Bill, who paid Southampton £125,000 for his signature, found him moody and difficult to handle at times, but the fans loved him – and still do. They remember him for his goals, his surging runs and his super-long throws. He remains one of the most revered figures at Spurs.

Martin and I had a free-kick routine that produced lots of goals over the years. I would address the ball at the free kick, take just one step back and flick it in quickly. Martin knew that if I took just one step back, the ball would come in early. This was the signal for him to start his run early and get in front of his marker. We used the routine in the second leg of the final against Wolves. I took one step back and, as planned, lifted the ball in early, but Alan Mullery had made the run, got in front of Martin and headed us in front.

Wolves battered us in the second half and although Wagstaffe equalised, they couldn't get the second goal that would have taken the match to extra time. Pat Jennings was in superb form and his contribution was as important as Martin's two goals in the first leg.

Pat was one of the world's great goalkeepers and enjoyed a fabulous career with Northern Ireland, Tottenham and Arsenal. Even today people ask me who was the better goalkeeper – Pat Jennings or Gordon Banks. It's impossible for me to distinguish between them. They were equally outstanding.

Pat would probably save us 15–20 points a season and could, almost single-handedly, win Cup finals. In fact, a single-handed catch in mid-air was his trademark. He could pluck a high ball from the air with astonishing grace, using just one of his out-sized hands. Unhurried and rarely flustered, his presence had a calming influence on the rest of the team and he was so reliable that when a ball dropped towards our six-yards box, you knew that he would catch it. All goalkeepers make mistakes, but Pat made fewer than most. He was a rock of a man and displayed an authentic element of genius in what he did between the posts.

He was certainly a key figure in the second half against Wolves that spring evening in May 1972, although even Pat recognised that the occasion belonged to Alan Mullery. It was particularly appropriate that Alan's goal played such a crucial role in our victory because it was his final game for Tottenham. When he carried the trophy around the pitch afterwards, waving to the fans, I don't know whether they realised they would not see him again in a Spurs shirt. That summer he rejoined Fulham on a permanent basis.

Mullery was one of the pivotal figures at Spurs, along with Pat, Martin Chivers and Alan Gilzean. Everyone loved and respected Gilly, both as a player and a person. He was a lovely guy, easy to talk to, never moaned and just got on with the job. He enjoyed a drink, but he always gave 100 per cent on the pitch and in training.

Is it the Kray Twins, or is it that equally feared partnership of Hurst and Peters?

My debut for Spurs after a record £200,000 transfer couldn't have got off to a better start than this: scoring the opener against Coventry in March 1970. (*Empics*)

In front of a crowd of over 53,000, I try to beat my old West Ham team-mate Bobby Moore in the first game of the 1970–71 season. (*Empics*)

They said I was sometimes too quiet on the field, but I was no push-over, as I show during our quarter-final UEFA Cup tie against Romanian side UT Arad.

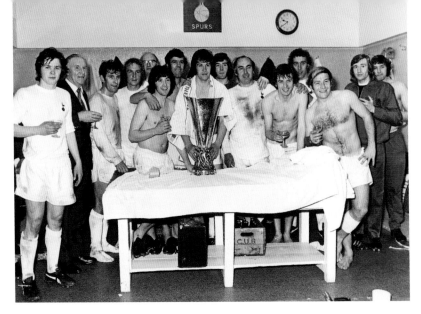

Celebrating our UEFA Cup final victory over Wolves in 1972.

Just four days before England's crucial World Cup decider against Poland in October 1973, I was in action in the north London derby – an unthinkable scenario today. (*Empics*)

Raising the trophy after winning the League Cup in 1973, beating Norwich 1–0 – it was my only trophy as captain, even though the game wasn't great.

A pensive moment on the training ground at Norwich.

Justin Fashanu looks on as I score in the first game of the 1978–79 season for Norwich against Everton.

Golfing buddies for the last thirty-three years: Ricky Jupp and Dave Readings during one of our trips to the Isle of Man.

One of the 1966 World Cup team's reunion events that have become special occasions for us all.

Our family: me, Lee Ann, Hannah, Kathy and Grant all together in 2003. (*Steve Bacon*)

My granddaughters Hannah and Meg on my 60th birthday.

My mother Mary and I go back to Roden, which was where I was evacuated to in the war as a toddler.

I would put him among the great touch players of that era. He was a subtle striker, who preferred to glance the ball with a twist of his head rather than thump it. With the deftest of touches he made a lot of goals for Martin Chivers and me. He wasn't a winger, but Bill Nicholson liked him to start wide on the right with Martin in the middle and either Jimmy Pearce or Jimmy Neighbour on the left.

Jimmy Pearce played for England Schoolboys and had a lot of ability. He worked up and down the left flank and scored a few goals each season, but he was a bit shy and I don't think Bill Nicholson was ever fully convinced that he was quite good enough.

Jimmy Neighbour, from Chingford, came into a similar category. He lacked a bit of confidence and seemed to play better if you sweet-talked him before kick-off. He was a talented boy, although his team-mates never let him forget his debut when he lined up to take a corner, missed the ball and instead kicked over the corner flag!

I don't think Bill ever felt he'd adequately replaced his double-winning winger Cliff Jones. He spent £100,000 on Roger Morgan, one of a pair of twins playing at Queen's Park Rangers, and although he was a good winger he was troubled by knee problems and had to retire early.

Perhaps Ralph Coates was the nearest he got to replacing Cliff. As coach to the England Under-23 team, Bill had watched Ralph score a great goal in Turkey and made a note to keep an eye on him. Four years later, Bill bought Ralph from Burnley for £192,000 – the highest cash fee at the time.

I sometimes wonder whether Tottenham's modern-day supporters fully appreciate the club's status and reputation in those days. Spurs were, for instance, the First Division's big spenders, easily able to eclipse the transfer budgets of Chelsea, Manchester United, Liverpool and Arsenal. In the early seventies, Bill Nicholson had three of the First Division's most expensive players in

Ralph, Martin Chivers and me. Arsenal's most costly player at the time was Peter Marinello, signed from Hibernian for £100,000. Chelsea's record capture, Tony Hateley, had cost the same amount from Aston Villa. Denis Law was Manchester United's most expensive acquisition at £116,000 from Turin.

As a club, Spurs were noted for their attacking prowess, although I sometimes thought this was a bit demeaning for our defenders. We had a back four as good as any in the business and in 1971–72 they kept 16 clean sheets in 42 First Division games.

Mike England was the key figure at the heart of the defence. A Wales international of enormous experience, he was one of the finest centre-backs of the sixties and seventies. At 6ft 3in he was particularly strong in the air and, between them, he and Pat Jennings would usually sort out most aerial threats. He was also dependable. For example, he played 38 of the 42 league matches that season. Of the outfield players, only Chivers and Perryman played more. For the best part of ten years, he and Phil Beal provided Tottenham with a durable centre-back partnership.

Phil made his debut in 1963, deputising for Danny Blanch-flower, and although he had a lot of injuries, he demonstrated a defiant, never-say-die attitude, which made him a favourite with the crowd when he finally established himself in the first team. He became an outstanding marker and was an unsung hero. Had it not been for Bobby Moore and Norman Hunter, I believe he would have been a regular in the England team.

You always had to be a bit careful when Phil was about because he had a reputation as a dressing-room joker. When a new player arrived at the club, he'd invariably call them on the day of their first match, pretending to be a reporter and suggesting an interview just before kick-off. He was good fun and immensely popular with the other players.

England and Beal dominated the two centre-back positions but if either were injured we'd call upon Peter Collins, who played his early football in the old Southern League with

Chelmsford City. He did a very good job whenever he was needed. I thought he had a great chance of becoming a top-quality defender but, sadly, he had to retire early because of ankle problems.

We also had the benefit of two of the best full-backs in the First Division – Joe Kinnear and Cyril Knowles. Both were high-class international defenders. Joe, who was born in Dublin but lived in Watford from the age of seven, won twenty-six caps with the Republic of Ireland between 1968 and 1976. Cyril, a Yorkshireman who spent a year with Manchester United as a boy, should have finished his career with far more than the four England caps he was awarded in 1968. I don't think Alf Ramsey was ever sure about him.

As everyone of a certain age will recall, Cyril was immortalised in song in 1973. 'Nice one Cyril' by The Cockerel Chorus spent twelve weeks in the pop charts, reaching number 14. Few players, before or since, have enjoyed the kind of cult status that Cyril had in football during those years.

A very popular figure in the dressing room, Cyril was always ready to catch out team-mates with some outrageous prank. He was as sharp as a needle and could quickly assess the potential for a joke. I remember watching this talent unfold during a visit to Portugal for a UEFA Cup tie against Setubal in 1973. The players were eating together when Phil Beal was called away to the telephone. In the few minutes he was away from the table, Cyril hatched a plot involving a fish with a couple of waiters. When Phil returned to the table one of the waiters explained that they had kept his dinner hot and placed a silver tureen in front of him. The other waiter whipped off the silver cover with a flourish. On the plate was a huge fish, head up looking at Phil, with a cigarette in its mouth. Phil's face was a picture! He knew immediately who was responsible. Later that day someone sneaked into Cyril's bedroom and placed the same fish under his pillow.

Bill Nicholson had bought Cyril as a nineteen-year-old from Middlesbrough and acknowledged that it was a bit of a risk, but he repaid the £45,000 fee many times over. He had a wonderful left foot, loved going forward and was fearsome when he tackled opponents.

When he finished playing, he managed Darlington, Torquay and Hartlepool but was forced to retire through ill-health. Sadly, he died in August 1991 at the age of forty-seven.

Like Cyril, Joe Kinnear enjoyed the same reputation as a mickey-taker. They were both noisy and boisterous in the dressing room and helped set the tone among the players. It wasn't all fun, though, and when we had to work, they worked like everyone else.

Joe probably didn't push forward quite as much as Cyril but he was outstanding defensively and always performed to the maximum of his ability. He originally joined Spurs as an amateur from St Albans City and was given his chance with a first-team place in 1966. He never looked back and, rather like Graeme Souness, was later to enjoy a distinguished management career, most notably with Wimbledon.

The other influential first-team personality was Johnny Pratt, a Hackney boy. He had joined Spurs as an amateur on the recommendation of Terry Medwin, who'd played in the double-winning side. John was a competitive, energetic midfield player who could deputise in midfield or in the back four. He was an invaluable member of the squad and while he never made one position his own, he played around 400 games in his ten years with the club.

John was a players' player who would patrol uncomplainingly from box to box. There was nothing very glamorous about his game and he used to say that if the fans were moaning at him, it was taking the pressure off the rest of us. He was probably right.

You could rely on him totally. He would always give 100 per cent and it was a shame that when his big chance came in the

1973 League Cup final, he had to leave the field in the first half because of injury. He was an opinionated, gritty character who later coached at Tottenham and became assistant manager.

It was a rare Johnny Pratt goal that gave us some hope against Leeds United in the sixth round of the FA Cup at Elland Road in March 1972. Having beaten Everton 2–0 at Goodison Park in the previous round, I fancied that we might get to Wembley but Leeds were at their majestic best and beat us 2–1, Jack Charlton and Allan Clarke supplying the goals. They went on to beat Arsenal 1–0 in the final.

At least in the League Cup we'd reached the semi-finals where we'd played two titanic matches with London rivals Chelsea. We lost the first leg at Stamford Bridge 3–2 but still thought we would turn it our way once the fans got behind us under the lights at White Hart Lane.

Martin – who else? – put us ahead in the first half but soon after the interval Chelsea began to gnaw at our defence. They had some really skilful attacking players in Peter Osgood, Alan Hudson, Charlie Cooke and Peter Houseman. They equalised through Chris Garland but then Hudson gave away a penalty. At the time, I was the Spurs penalty taker. As I lined up to take the kick against Peter Bonetti in the Chelsea goal, I recalled a conversation I'd had with him when he'd told me that he could always tell where I would place the ball when I took a penalty kick. For a couple of seconds I wasn't sure what to do. He was smiling at me because he was obviously having the same thought. In the end, with the tension in the 52,755 crowd rising, I struck it hard to his left. He tried to save it but didn't have a chance really.

So, we were ahead again but two minutes from time disaster struck. Chelsea were awarded a free kick out on the wing and Hudson curled the ball into the crowded penalty area as if he was delivering a corner kick. Cyril Knowles swung at it, intending to boot in into Row Z, but missed completely. It flew past him and through Pat Jennings' legs. Pat knew very little about it.

Chelsea held on to the 2–2 draw for the last few seconds and progressed to the final on a 5–4 aggregate. I was very disappointed. Before the match I'd set my heart on winning because West Ham were playing Stoke in the other semi-final and a Spurs–West Ham final really appealed to me. As it turned out, that semi-final went to a second replay with Stoke eventually winning 3–2 at Old Trafford and, surprise, surprise, unfancied Stoke beat Chelsea 2–1 in the final at Wembley.

At least we finished the season in sixth place – good enough for a UEFA Cup spot these days. Although Arsenal finished one point above us, we had the satisfaction of avenging our costly defeat at White Hart Lane at the end of the previous season. This time we went to Highbury and won 2–0. Mullers, in his final league game for the club, scored our first goal. Ralph Coates scored the second.

19

TEARS OF A CLOWN

It seems incredible now but in the spring of 1972 Ron Greenwood left Geoff Hurst and Bobby Moore out of his team specifically so that they'd be fresh for England's critical European Championship qualifying tie against West Germany. West Ham were in fifteenth place in the table, with relegation a growing threat, when Ron decided to rest Geoff and Bobby for a game against Arsenal at Highbury to help Sir Alf Ramsey. It's almost impossible to imagine any club making such a sacrifice for the England team today.

Seven days after Arsenal beat West Ham 2–1, Geoff and Bobby, rested and injury free, faced the Germans at Wembley. Ron's well-meaning gesture meant very little in the final analysis. England were not often comprehensively outplayed but we were that day. Derby County defender Roy McFarland was injured, so Alf asked Bobby Moore to play as a conventional centre-half. It didn't work – great player that he was, he wasn't a centre-half.

Uli Hoeness, exploiting Bobby's uncertainty in his man-marking role, gave Germany the lead but Francis Lee equalised in the second half. Then six minutes from time, Bobby tripped Siggi Held and the French referee Robert Helies awarded a penalty. Gunter Netzer, the man of the match in my opinion, scored from the spot and just before the end Gerd Muller hit a quite magnificent third goal for the Germans.

The blond figure of Netzer dominated the game, but the Germans weren't short of star names. Their line-up also included Beckenbauer, Schwarzenbeck, Breitner, Wimmer and Grabowski. They became only the fourth continental team to beat England at Wembley, following Hungary (1953), Sweden (1959) and Austria (1965).

I remember Geoff trudging off towards the end to be substituted by Rodney Marsh of Manchester City – the only occasion during his England career that he was taken off like that. It was his forty-ninth game for his country, and also his last.

A fortnight later we tried to overhaul the two-goal deficit in the second leg in West Berlin. This time, Alf adopted a more defensive strategy with Peter Storey and Norman Hunter in midfield. I was a substitute and eventually replaced Norman. The match ended goalless, which went some way to restoring our pride, but we were out of the competition. Germany beat Belgium in the semi-final and Russia 3–0 in the final. Many of their team played significant roles two years later when they won the World Cup.

As for England, only four of the 1966 team now remained in Alf's squad – Gordon Banks, Bobby Moore, Alan Ball and me. It was a time of change. The papers were suggesting that England were no longer a major power. Few would have argued when Northern Ireland beat us 1–0 at Wembley in the Home International Championship. Once again, Alf left me out of the starting line-up and put me on the substitutes' bench.

I'd now played fifty-four games for England and was approaching thirty. I realised that my international career might stretch to the 1974 World Cup, but not much farther. Happily, my form with Tottenham remained consistent and, as if to remind people that I was still around, I scored four goals in the opening three games of 1972–73 and all four when Tottenham beat

Manchester United 4–1 at Old Trafford in October. For a change, Bill Nicholson played me out on the right that day in the position usually filled by Alan Gilzean. Afterwards the media asked me how I scored all four and I explained that I was simply in the right place at the right time – four times!

I suppose it was quite an achievement for a midfield player – in fact, it would have been an achievement for a striker, too. When I take on speaking engagements in the Manchester area, I always drop it casually into the conversation and many people don't believe me. Well, it's true! Ask Bobby Charlton. He scored the United goal that day. In fact, he was United's top league scorer that season with just six – yes, six – goals. United finished in eighteenth position and Bobby played his last game for the club in a 1–0 defeat at Chelsea. It was a poor season for Bobby to end a great career. During seventeen years with Manchester United, Bobby played 606 league matches.

It was also the last season for his brother Jack. They'd finished their England careers together in 1970 and three years later bade farewell to the First Division at the same time. Jack made his 629th and last league appearance for Leeds in a 3–1 defeat at Southampton. He left the field before the end, having pulled a hamstring. But for that injury, his last game may well have been Leeds United's ignominious 1–0 defeat by Sunderland in the FA Cup final at Wembley.

Such was the status of both players that, within weeks of their retirement, Bobby was offered the job of manager of Preston North End and Jack was offered the same job with Middlesbrough.

Thoughts of management were still some way in the distance for me. Tottenham finished the season respectably in eighth position and I was delighted to contribute a total of twenty-four goals, my best goalscoring season for Tottenham. Only Martin Chivers scored more.

My most important goals came in the Cup competitions. I

scored in a 1–1 draw at Liverpool in the fifth round of the League Cup and, after we'd beaten them 3–1 in the replay, I scored against Wolves in both legs of the semi-final.

However, there was no doubting the hero of the final. This honour went to Ralph Coates, who had previously scored just four goals since his big-money signing from Burnley in May 1971. Ralph was a great professional and became a very popular figure at White Hart Lane, although he suffered all the usual mickey taking when he arrived. His choice of sweaters often produced lots of sniggering in the dressing room. Anything that stamped you as different was a target for dressing-room jokes – clothes, hairstyle, accent, new car. A new player, especially one from the north, unsure of how things worked in London, was always an easy target. Ralph was no different. When we were having shooting practice, everyone would stand in the goal when it was Ralph's turn because, they said, it was the safest place to be!

He scored against Norwich in the League Cup final, though, illuminating an otherwise indifferent occasion. We were clear favourites even though Norwich, despite a protracted fight against relegation, had beaten Arsenal and Chelsea on their way to the final. The game was drab and goalless when John Pratt was injured late in the first half, allowing Bill Nicholson to usher Ralph from the substitutes' bench. Even today, fans remember him for his goal, which gave us our second League Cup triumph in three seasons and maintained the club record of never having lost a final.

The occasion remains particularly memorable for me because it was the one and only time I lifted a major trophy at Wembley as captain. I enjoyed being captain at Spurs but, to be honest, the team didn't need much in the way of leadership. We had experienced players and some strong personalities. I'd speak up when necessary – but it wasn't often necessary.

A few days after the League Cup final we turned our attention to the UEFA Cup. We'd beaten Lyn Oslo, Olympiakos and Red Star Belgrade to reach the quarter-final where we were to play Vitoria Setubal of Portugal.

We'd been playing well in Europe, although coach Eddie Baily had given us a terrible roasting in the dressing room after our 6–3 win over Lyn in Oslo. 'How could you concede three goals to them?' he demanded.

Red Star were an outstanding team, managed by Miljan Miljanic. I remember Bill becoming very friendly with Miljanic, who at one point in the seventies toyed with the idea of joining Arsenal as manager. He knew his stuff and after two truly tremendous games against his team we began to think we had a good chance of actually winning the competition. We now had players with substantial European experience. Martin Chivers, for instance, seemed to be scoring goals for fun. By the time we faced Vitoria Setubal he'd already scored seven in the UEFA Cup.

However, the Portuguese team were no pushovers. We won the first leg 1–0 at home with a goal from Ray Evans, but were trailing 2–0 in the return. We needed an away goal and were piling on the pressure. I could sense the desperation in the Setubal defence. At one point, one of their players tossed a handful of sand into Pat Jennings' eyes when we were lining up for a corner. It was unusual to see Pat lose his temper, but he did on that occasion. In the event, Martin rescued the situation. He hit a thirty-five-yard free kick that thundered into the net and gave us the tie on the away goals rule. Now all we had to do was beat Liverpool in the semi-final.

Liverpool were just coming to the boil. They'd signed a youngster from Scunthorpe called Kevin Keegan. They had Ray Clemence in goal, big John Toshack at centre-forward, Steve Heighway on the wing and the vast experience of Ian Callaghan, who'd been with me in the 1966 squad.

Alex Lindsay, their left-back, scored the only goal in the first leg, and we returned from Anfield thinking that we could win the tie at White Hart Lane. Two days before we met, Liverpool clinched the First Division title by beating Leeds 2–0. They were on a high, and they wanted revenge for their quarter-final defeat by us in the League Cup. It was all set to be a great night of European football, and so it was.

In front of a crowd of 47,000, everything seemed to be going our way when I opened the scoring to draw level on aggregate. Then Heighway hit the critical away goal for Liverpool. I scored a second, running on to a long throw from Martin Chivers, but it wasn't enough. This time Liverpool were the beneficiaries of the away goals rule. It had been one of the most spectacular matches I'd played in and afterwards Bill Shankly, the Liverpool manager, said, 'For both teams to give that sort of performance at this stage of the season after more than sixty games was unbelievable.'

Liverpool, who used just fourteen outfield players through-out the season, went on to beat Borussia Monchengladbach 3–2 on aggregate. Keegan scored two in the 3–0 win at Anfield. It was the start of the Keegan phenomenon. Kevin was in the process of becoming a European superstar. Unlike George Best, he went to great lengths to protect his image and this attention to detail helped him later in life when he hung up his boots and went into management.

I never considered him to be a classy or stylish player, but he had enormous energy and the ability to make the most of his talents. He became a prolific goalscorer, an inspirational England captain and was twice voted European Footballer of the Year.

Alf gave him his international debut against Wales at Ninian Park, Cardiff, in November 1972. It was Alf's hundredth match in charge and the 1–0 win opened England's World Cup quali-fying programme. We had to negotiate a route past Wales and Poland to qualify for the 1974 finals in West Germany.

The team was changing. Emlyn Hughes, Colin Bell, Martin

Chivers and Roy McFarland were becoming more influential, and two young goalkeepers, Peter Shilton and Ray Clemence, were rivals to succeed the great Gordon Banks. Gordon had been pretty much unchallenged as England's first choice since 1964, but his magnificent career had suddenly been cut short by a car crash in which he lost an eye.

Now Keegan was pressing his claims. He retained his place for the second leg against Wales at Wembley but had a poor game in a 1–1 draw. He was absent when England played Scotland at Hampden Park in February 1973 to mark the Centenary of the Scottish FA. Bobby Moore, winning his hundredth cap, and I were both reinstated. I'm pleased to say that England won 5–0. Three months later, Bobby and I were still in the team when we beat Scotland 1–0 at Wembley in the Home International Championship. I scored my twentieth and last goal for my country.

That result was particularly encouraging because we were due to resume the World Cup qualifying campaign against Poland in March. The Polish team was still mostly made up of the amateurs who had won the gold medal at the Munich Olympics but, before facing them, we played a warm-up match in Czechoslovakia, which we drew 1–1. Then we travelled on to Chorzow, a grim city in the Silesian coalfields.

Within seven minutes of kick-off, Alf's plans were in disarray. A badly defended free kick bounced off Peter Shilton, hit Bobby Moore and flew back past Shilton into the net. England were a goal down. Two minutes into the second half, Bobby tried to dribble the ball out of defence and lost possession to Wlodzimierz Lubanski, who scored a second goal for Poland.

It got worse. We seemed unable to respond. Frustration set in and tempers frayed. I was fouled and, while lying on the pitch, was kicked by their midfield player Leslaw Cmikiewicz. Seeing this assault, Alan Ball took great offence and came running to my rescue. He made the mistake of grabbing the Pole by the throat at which point he became only the second England player to be sent off in a full international.

So it was a disconsolate group that left Poland the following morning to continue England's end-of-season tour. We flew to Moscow where we beat the Soviet Union 2–1 and then moved on to Turin where, four days later, we lost 2–0 to Italy.

The build-up to the second leg with Poland, in October 1973, was dominated by questions about Alf's future. Among the media an assumption had taken hold that if England lost, Alf's time as manager would be over. The players were aware of it and some of us resented the way Alf was being set up for a big fall.

Early in the new season the Poles beat Wales 3–0 and this meant that they needed only to draw at Wembley to qualify for the World Cup. We prepared for the game with a friendly against Austria at Wembley. After his indifferent game in Chorzow, Bobby Moore was left out and I was made captain. It was my sixty-third cap and I was easily the most experienced player in a team that included Southampton's Mick Channon, playing his ninth game, and Sheffield United's Tony Currie, playing his fourth.

Tony was commanding in midfield, passing the ball with fluency and precision and contributing to one of England's best performances for a long time. We won 7–0 with Allan Clarke and Channon scoring two goals apiece. The other scorers were Martin Chivers, Colin Bell and Currie.

The Poland match was just three weeks away and the papers were full of speculation about the make-up of Alf's team. Would he retain faith with the side that put seven past Austria, or would he recall Mooro?

My own form was good. Four days before facing Poland I played in the Spurs side that beat Arsenal 2–0, a game, incidentally, that marked Liam Brady's debut. Alf was at the match, checking on Martin Chivers and me. In the end, he decided to field an unchanged team and I continued as captain, which was a great honour. In all I captained England four times – against Wales (o–o), Austria (7–o), Poland (1–1) and Portugal (o–o), Alf's last match in charge.

Tina Moore was furious that her husband had been overlooked for the Poland match and made her views clear. Bobby, unmoved by it all, sat on the substitutes' bench on what turned out to be an eventful evening.

We started with pace and confidence but, despite our three proven goalscorers, Chivers, Clarke and Channon, the night was not to belong to us. It was to belong to the Polish goalkeeper Jan Tomaszewski. Before kick-off, the Derby County manager Brian Clough, one of the most outspoken TV pundits of the time, described Tomaszewski as 'a clown'. He couldn't have been more wrong.

Yes, we missed a lot of chances but the Polish goalkeeper saved everything we fired at him and in doing so, secured a place in World Cup folklore. He produced a string of spectacular saves to frustrate wave after wave of England attacks. We hit the woodwork twice and had four chances cleared off the line. The corner count – 26 to 2 – reflected England's domination of the match.

Yet, amazingly, Poland took the lead after an hour, stunning the 100,000 crowd. Many blamed Norman Hunter for the Poland goal. When the ball fell to him in a wide position on the halfway line, he tried to evade winger Gregorz Lato instead of taking the easier option and hitting the ball upfield. A clever little player, Lato nicked the ball off Norman and began running straight at our goal. He drew Roy McFarland towards him and then passed inside to Jan Domarski, who was racing towards the edge of our penalty area. Emlyn Hughes didn't get close enough to make a tackle and Domarski's low shot went through his legs and under Peter Shilton's dive.

I've never thought it fair that the burden of responsibility fell on Norman for a mistake he'd made on the halfway line. We had chances to rectify the mistake and failed. I think Peter Shilton knew in his heart that 99 times out of 100 he would have saved the same shot. What it meant on that tumultuous night was that we had to score twice to qualify with little more than thirty minutes remaining. It was looking desperate and in such circumstances desperate measures are sometimes required.

With about twenty-five minutes left, I swept down the right and cut into the Poland penalty area where their left-back Adam Musial tackled me from the side. He barely touched me but I went flying. I dived. I threw myself over. It wasn't a penalty, but the referee didn't see it that way. Vital Loraux, from Belgium, put the whistle to his lips and blew. He gave us a glimmer of hope but Allan Clarke's coolly taken penalty kick was too little, too late.

In the final moments, Bobby Moore, typically committed, was pleading with Alf to send on Derby's winger Kevin Hector. The week before, the Poles had lost a warm-up match to Holland and the Dutch victory was largely due to the pace of their wingers. Kevin was fast and direct and could cross the ball well. With two minutes remaining, Alf sent him on for his debut and he nearly achieved immortality. His header from a corner was cleared off the line and Allan Clarke stabbed the rebound wide.

I was shattered at the end. We could have played for a month and not scored. Tomaszewski was shedding tears of joy. As I left the field, the referee put a sympathetic arm around my shoulders. For a second I wondered whether I should confess that I'd tricked him with my dive in the penalty area but I didn't say anything. No one realised. I'd never cheated like that before and I never did again. England were desperate and my act had been spontaneous, something I thought was necessary in the heat of the moment.

In the dressing room afterwards, Alf said that we could have done no more. 'You gave everything,' he said. There was no suggestion from him that he would quit.

The disappointment was magnified for me because, with Bobby's international career rapidly drawing to a close, it had occurred to me that I might have been England captain had we qualified for the final tournament in 1974. At least I'd played in two World Cups, though, unlike Chivers, Channon, McFarland, Madeley and Currie – not only did they miss the 1974 World Cup but also the 1978 tournament.

The newspapers the next morning were full of gloom and despondency. 'End of the World' was one headline. Many theories emerged in the days that followed and most drew the same conclusion – Alf would have to go. Some argued that his tactics were too negative, that he didn't know how to use substitutes and that he simply couldn't cope with the demands of the modern game. Nobody seemed to acknowledge that we had overwhelmed the Poles and would have won comfortably but for bad luck, the inspired goalkeeping of Jan Tomaszewski and an outstanding performance from their 6ft 3in centre-half Jerzy Gorgon.

A month later Alf was in a subdued mood when we gathered for a friendly international against Italy. Norman Hunter was missing because of injury and Bobby was back as captain for his 108th cap, a record until it was broken by Peter Shilton, who played 125 times. Bobby was thirty-two and knew that evening that he would never play for England again. It was fitting that such a fabulous career should end at Wembley but sad that it ended in a 1–0 defeat.

England's golden age was slowly coming to an end.

20

CHANGING TIMES

On 1 May 1974 the Football Association sacked Sir Alf Ramsey. He was fifty-four. Of his 113 matches in charge, he'd lost just 17, and the FA have been trying to find a worthy successor to England's greatest manager ever since.

Failure to beat Poland and qualify for the World Cup gave those who were waiting to ambush him the excuse. I think he had an uneasy relationship, for instance, with the influential vice chairman of the FA, Professor Sir Harold Thompson. Professor Thompson, who later became FA chairman, was a distinguished expert in infrared spectroscopy, but not known for his tact. Once, Alf asked him to put out his cigar because he was blowing smoke into the faces of the players. Alf's friends were inside the dressing room. He made no secret of that. Those outside he simply tolerated. Only a winning manager can get away with that.

The FA gave him just two more matches after the 1–1 draw with the Poles – a 1–0 defeat by Italy followed by a 0–0 draw in Portugal. For the Portugal game, Alf belatedly decided to introduce some new faces, including Phil Parkes, Trevor Brooking, Mike Pejic, Martin Dobson, Dave Watson and Stan Bowles. I was captain again that day but didn't realise that it would be Alf's last match in charge.

I was deeply shocked when I heard that he'd been sacked, as were the rest of the lads. We spent much of the day on the telephone talking to each other. The 1966 team were unanimous in believing that Alf had been betrayed by the FA. From a personal point of view, not only was he still the best man for the job, but he was also a central pillar in my career. Whether or not the FA were justified in sacking him for England's failure to qualify for the World Cup, I felt his departure could have been handled in a more gentlemanly fashion. There was no need to treat him so shabbily.

The reaction of some newspaper critics made you laugh. They'd been baying for Alf's head for months and the instant he was sacked some of them turned on the FA and attacked them for their heartless actions. The people who had pilloried Alf now made him a martyr.

The FA's official statement at least acknowledged the debt they owed Alf. It read, in part: 'We wish at this time to record our deep appreciation for all that Sir Alf has accomplished and the debt owed to him by English football for his unbending loyalty and dedication and the high level of integrity he has brought to world football.'

Alf said nothing. He simply asked the FA for a few days' grace to inform his family before they released the news. Then he went abroad on holiday before the official announcement was made. Plenty of newspapers offered him money to tell his story but refused them all. He was a man on integrity all right. No one could dispute that.

Kathy was a bit tearful when she heard the news. Alf had played a big part in our lives for eight years. The players' wives didn't always see eye to eye with the manager over things like hotel accommodation and travel plans, but they all recognised that their husbands had great respect and affection for him. I wondered when I would hear that clipped London accent again.

The FA appointed Joe Mercer as caretaker manager and advertised the job. The former manager of Manchester City, Joe was working at the time as general manager of Coventry City and had no interest in the England job on a long-term basis.

His first task was to prepare a squad of players for the Home International Championship and a three-match tour of Europe. A genial, popular man, who had played five times for England in the thirties, Joe had no worries about long-term responsibilities. He had the job for five weeks and seven matches and said, 'We're all going to have a laugh.'

He didn't select me for the Home Championship matches against Wales and Northern Ireland. I wasn't surprised. I was thirty-one and, along with Alan Ball, represented the last of the old guard. This was the start of a new era and I didn't expect to have much part to play in it.

Also, I had other things on my mind. Although Tottenham's domestic season had been indifferent – we'd finished eleventh in the First Division and made early exits from the FA and League Cup – we'd marched purposefully through Europe once again. It was our third consecutive season in the UEFA Cup and, as in 1972, we'd reached the final, where we were due to play the accomplished Dutch side Feyenoord over two legs.

Bill Nicholson reckoned that 1973–74 was his worst season as manager of Spurs. It was hard to disagree with his assessment because we didn't get out of the bottom half of the table until the last match of the season. I was again the second highest scorer, but this time with just six goals from thirty-five league matches. Compare that to my record in Europe – eight goals from twelve matches. The first two came in round one when we demolished Grasshoppers of Zurich 9–2 on aggregate. I hit another in the second round when we beat Aberdeen 5–2 on aggregate.

Then we had to make an exhausting journey to Tbilisi in Georgia, deep in the south of the Soviet Union. We arrived late and sat down to eat in our bare, functional hotel at 1 a.m. The Georgians were enormously hospitable and invited us to watch a display of Cossack dancing.

A crowd of 42,000 watched the match. Dynamo Tbilisi had some technically talented players, particularly David Kipiani, whose career was to be cut short by a broken leg. We drew 1–1 and then beat them 5–1 at White Hart Lane, when I scored twice.

I added another in the first leg of the quarter-final as we beat Cologne 2–1 in Germany, with Wolfgang Overath in the Cologne side. I scored again in the return when we won 3–0.

In the semi-final we faced a team from East Germany – this was during the Cold War before the Berlin Wall came down. Lokomotiv Leipzig had required a penalty shoot-out to knock out Ipswich in the quarter-finals. They had drawn 1–1 on aggregate.

Leipzig was a bleak city that I was pleased to leave after winning 2–1 in the first leg. Ralph Coates and I scored the goals. In the second leg we won 2–0 with Martin Chivers and young Chris McGrath scoring.

Bill Nicholson warned us that Feyenoord would be our toughest opponents. He prepared thoroughly, watching them in action. He also watched the Dutch national side because they included four outstanding Feyenoord players – Wim Rijsbergen, Wim Van Hanegem, Theo de Jong and Wim Jansen.

Three days before we were due to play Feyenoord at White Hart Lane, I was summoned to England's cause. Joe Mercer had recalled me to the side for the Home Championship match with Scotland at Hampden Park and for the European tour. He'd selected a young, inexperienced team against Scotland, including David Nish, Mike Pejic, Colin Todd, Keith Weller and Frank Worthington. Stan Bowles, the talented but temperamental Queen's Park Rangers striker, had been in the squad but walked out when substituted against the Irish. As Joe quickly learned, managing England wasn't all fun and games.

By this time, Emlyn Hughes was emerging as the long-term successor to Bobby Moore, so he led the team out as captain. For my part, I was just delighted to be back, winning my sixty-seventh cap for my eighth match against the Scots. I loved playing against them because I normally scored – five goals in all, which is not bad for a midfield player – but this time we were in for some special barracking.

The Scots had qualified for the World Cup and a 94,487 Glasgow crowd kept reminding us that we hadn't. To make matters worse, Scotland took the lead when Pejic scored an own goal. Then, unbelievably, Nish scored an own goal – they beat us 2–0 with two own goals.

The little matter of Feyenoord in the UEFA Cup final was now top of the agenda, and 41,000 fans witnessed another of those breathless, 'glory, glory' nights. Heavy rain and a wet pitch undermined our rhythm but we took the lead through Mike England. We were a bit fortunate when Joop van Daele scored an own goal and although Wim Van Hanegem scored a brilliant free kick, we were hanging on to a 2–1 lead with four minutes remaining. Then Theo de Jong hit the equaliser.

The return leg in Rotterdam was an intimidating prospect. Bill Nicholson chose the same team, with me playing upfront again. A crowd of 62,988, including many thousands from north London who'd travelled across on the ferries, filled the huge three-tiered Feyenoord Stadium.

We started well, had most possession and looked in control until just before the interval when Wim Rijsbergen scored. It now looked a lost cause. In the dressing room at half-time, Bill tried to convince us that we could still overturn the result, while outside, unknown to us, a full-scale crowd riot was developing. At one end of the ground, in the middle tier where the Tottenham fans were massed, fighting had broken out and was very quickly getting out of hand. Bill was asked to make an announcement over the public-address system and pleaded with the fans to behave and not let the club down.

The players were unaware of the extent of the trouble until we left the dressing rooms for the start of the second half. The long corridor leading up to the pitch was beginning to fill with injured supporters and medical staff. By the time the Italian referee Concetto Lo Bello blew his whistle to restart the game, the police had regained control on the terracing. In all, seventy fans, mostly from Spurs, were arrested and 200 people were treated for injuries.

Although hooliganism was a common occurrence in English football, it was the first major example of crowd violence in Holland. What made the whole unedifying business truly disturbing for Bill Nicholson was the fact that his daughter Jean was in the crowd. She had travelled to the match with our supporters in a motor coach.

At the time I didn't know why or how the trouble started and I still don't know. In those days, it was assumed automatically that the English fans were responsible for any trouble on the terracing, but the Spurs supporters had absolutely no reputation for that kind of thing. They had travelled around Europe for three consecutive seasons without a hint of a problem.

Bill viewed it as a national disgrace. When he got home, he made sure that the club chairman Sydney Wale wrote to the Feyenoord club and the Rotterdam police apologising for the behaviour of our supporters. In his book, *Glory, Glory – My Life with Spurs*, Bill made it clear that the crowd trouble in the Feyenoord Stadium that night contributed to his decision to retire. It was particularly sad that his last major final should end in disgrace – and defeat. I don't think the rioting fans distracted us or caused us to lose focus. Feyenoord were simply the better team on the night. They scored a second goal through Peter Ressell to secure a 2–0 victory, 4–2 on aggregate. It was the first time that Tottenham had lost in a final.

The following morning I left my Spurs team-mates and flew

from Rotterdam to Sofia to join the England tour. England had drawn 1–1 with East Germany in Leipzig as Spurs were losing to Feyenoord, and had two more matches to play. I arrived on the morning of the match against Bulgaria, with little chance of being selected, and watched England win 1–0. Frank Worthington scored the goal.

The following day we flew to Yugoslavia. At Belgrade airport, Kevin Keegan was marched off by police. He had been among a group of players larking about around a luggage carousel. Joe, bandy legs and big smile, needed all his charm and diplomacy to extricate Kevin from an ugly situation. At one stage, the England players were refusing to fulfil the fixture with Yugoslavia but common sense prevailed. Kevin was released and played against Yugoslavia, scoring in a 2–2 draw. When I wasn't selected, I knew that, with the Leeds manager Don Revie lined up to take over, my international days were over.

Now Alan Ball was the sole England survivor from 1966. He played a further six games under Revie, winning his seventy-second and last cap in a 5–1 win over the Scots in May 1975.

The new England era quickly unfolded under Revie. He had performed miracles at Leeds United, transforming them from an anonymous under-achieving Second Division club into League Champions and a team of internationals. If you let them play, they could be brilliant. If you wanted a physical battle, they would happily oblige.

It was clear from the outset that Revie's priorities were different from Alf's. I was among the 80 present and potential England players summoned to a bonding session in Manchester. He told us that he would negotiate a better financial deal with the FA. They eventually agreed to pay £100 for a draw and £200 for a win on top of the £100 appearance money.

He tried to replicate the cosy family atmosphere he had created among his player at Leeds. He also courted the media. He began a campaign to get the Football League secretary Alan

Hardaker, an old adversary, to postpone fixtures on the Saturday before an international match.

I suspected that all this would have very little to do with me and I was right. He didn't pick me for his first game in charge – Czechoslovakia at Wembley – and I didn't blame him. He had to look to the future and Tottenham's results early in 1974–75 didn't help my cause.

We lost our first four matches and, at the end of August, were stuck at the bottom of the table. It was the worst start to a season by Tottenham since 1912. My goal, in a 2–1 defeat by Manchester City, was the only one we scored in those opening four games.

Twenty-four hours after that defeat Bill Nicholson announced his resignation. He had been with the club for 39 years, 16 as manager. Bill hadn't even told his wife, Darkie, that he'd had enough. She heard about it on the radio.

Numerous reasons were put forward for his decision to leave. These included contract disputes with players, his failure to buy new players when it was clear they were needed, the defeat and crowd trouble in Rotterdam, his deteriorating relationship with Martin Chivers and Tottenham's appalling start to the new season. All of them may have been contributory factors but he told those close to him that he was tired, needed a rest and was finding it difficult to adapt to the changes in the game. He told the media, for instance, that new players were reluctant to join Spurs because the club refused to give them under-the-counter money. He claimed that players were asking for at least £7000 in cash before agreeing to sign.

One of his problems, which he later acknowledged, was his inability to delegate. Eddie Baily was a loyal and energetic assistant on the training pitch and in the dressing room, but Bill would insist on doing all the administrative jobs himself. He ran the club from top to bottom. In all his years as manager, he never had a long holiday. He worked in his office at White Hart

Lane every Sunday and kept his small house close to White Hart Lane so that he didn't waste time travelling to and from work every day.

Bill agreed to stay on for a fortnight while the club looked for a successor and when, two days after his announcement, Derby County came to White Hart Lane, we beat them 2–0, both goals being scored by Jimmy Neighbour. How ironic! It was our first win of the season against a team that would be crowned First Division champions nine months later.

After the match, Phil Beal and I asked to see Bill in his office. We told him that the players didn't want him to leave and asked him to reconsider his decision. He seemed surprised. Perhaps he thought some of us wanted him to go. Most of the players had signed a petition, which I organised, urging him to reconsider. Only one player refused to sign, because he believed Bill had been trying to sell him. Later that evening I went on television and told Jimmy Hill that the Spurs players wanted him to change his mind.

He didn't, though, and after what he'd achieved in the game, you had to respect his decision. I was saddened by this sudden development. I had the greatest respect for Bill and felt we had a good rapport. After all, he'd taken a big gamble when he'd broken the transfer record to sign me from West Ham. Under his leadership, I'd enjoyed a lot of success at Spurs and he had made me captain.

In many ways, he was similar to Alf. He cherished such old-fashioned values as loyalty and humility, qualities that were vanishing from the professional game. Even so, Bill was always very protective towards his players. He treated us all equally with firmness and understanding but I know that months of protracted contract talks with some key players had frustrated him.

We had a few mickey takers and jokers in our dressing room and Bill didn't always appreciate their humour. He disliked swearing and asked the players to watch their language if children turned up at our training ground at Cheshunt.

He was clearly sickened by the increase in soccer hooliganism and I knew he felt players were becoming more mercenary. Such great players as George Best and Bobby Moore had lifted footballers from the back of the cigarette card and turned them into TV personalities and superheroes. You can trace the roots of the celebrity status enjoyed by today's footballers back to those years in the early seventies.

So, Bill followed the example of his good friend Ron Greenwood, who a few days earlier had decided that he no longer wanted the responsibility of first-team management at West Ham. Ron was fifty-two. 'I'm becoming increasingly angry at the way the game is developing,' he said at the time.

Ron remained at West Ham with the title of general manager, helping with the scouting and signing of players. I was delighted when he persuaded the club to hire Bill, claiming that his experience, especially of European football – West Ham were in the Cup Winners' Cup in 1975–76 – would be invaluable.

Within the space of a few weeks, the three men who had helped shape me as a player had all become victims of the changing demands of professional football – Alf Ramsey, Ron Greenwood and Bill Nicholson. Bill Shankly also resigned after fifteen years as manager at Anfield. The game was changing, but not necessarily for the better. It seemed to me that professional football was losing men of integrity and substance. I don't suppose that any of them – not Alf, Bill, Ron nor the great Bill Shankly – could have coped with modern football and all the baggage that millionaire players and their egotistical agents and lawyers dump on the desks of managers these days.

Tottenham's choice of new manager reflected the changing game. Bill, I know, favoured either the former Spurs captain Danny Blanchflower or the captain of Leeds United, Johnny Giles, as his successor. The board ignored his suggestions and, instead, appointed Terry Neill. It was a surprise choice. At the time Neill was the manager of Hull City in the Second Division and part-time manager of Northern Ireland, for whom he'd won fifty-nine caps as centre-half and captain between 1961 and 1973. Most of the caps had been awarded during his long-playing career with Arsenal.

That's why the Spurs fans and players were surprised by his appointment. He was an Arsenal man. Even Bill was shocked. He'd been in the front line of the rivalry between the two North London clubs for a long time and knew that our fans would take a very dim view of the appointment of a former Arsenal captain.

Terry's other handicaps were his age and inexperience. He was just thirty-two, making him the youngest manager in the First Division at the time. Some of the players in the Spurs dressing room were older. He would have to win them over, as well as the fans.

Bill Nicholson was always going to be a tough act to follow, whoever got the job. Terry's appointment was confirmed on the day that Middlesbrough beat us 4–0 in the League Cup at White Hart Lane. I didn't play, but sat and watched among a paltry, disillusioned crowd of 15,216.

I was back in the side a few days later when Terry took charge for the first time. West Ham were the opposition. It was strange listening to a new voice in the dressing room. He liked to use a blackboard to illustrate points. On that occasion he was smiling at the end because we won 2–1 but victories were few and far between. I think he felt that he was having problems introducing new ideas to players set in their ways. Kinnear, Knowles, England and Perryman had been with Bill for the best part of a decade, and Terry gradually came round to the idea that the best option for him was to get rid of the old heads. He had thirty-two professionals on the staff, many experienced internationals, and they were blocking the progress of Glenn Hoddle, Chris Jones, Steve Walford and other younger players.

In his first season he released ten players, including Mike England, Joe Kinnear and me. He and I didn't hit it off. He said later that I'd disagreed with his views about how the game should be played. That wasn't true. I might have had my own thoughts but I certainly didn't share them with him. I wouldn't have had the temerity to tell the manager how to play. I thought I would stay with Tottenham for the rest of my career. I had no thoughts of moving until he started leaving me out of the first team or substituting me. Slowly I realised that I was no longer valued in the way I had been by Bill Nicholson.

Terry had some good points, but I didn't feel coaching was one of them. When you'd worked with Greenwood, Nicholson and Ramsey, Terry Neill seemed a bit shallow by comparison.

I played my last match for Tottenham on 22 February 1975, against Leicester City at home. We hadn't won a home match since early December. Sadly, we didn't win that day either. Leicester beat us 3–0. We slumped to nineteenth in the table and were facing an almighty fight to avoid relegation. I wasn't involved.

A fortnight later I was transferred to Norwich City for £50,000. I didn't want to leave Spurs – I didn't want to leave London – but it was clear that Terry Neill didn't want me and I felt I needed to make a new start.

On the day I signed for Norwich, Kathy and I went to Wembley to watch England play West Germany in a friendly. I smiled when the captains shook hands – Alan Ball and Franz Beckenbauer. They were the only two of the 1966 cast list still involved at international level. England won 2–0, the first win over the Germans since the great day. It all seemed a very long time ago.

21

THE CALL OF THE COUNTRY

A warm welcome and an optimistic dressing room awaited me at Norwich, contrasting sharply to the baleful atmosphere I'd left behind at White Hart Lane. In the end, Tottenham needed to beat Leeds in the last game of the season to avoid the drop into the Second Division. They won 4–2 but it was only delaying the inevitable. Two seasons later, after Terry Neill had joined Arsenal as manager, they were relegated.

From the outset, Norwich were an absolute joy. On the day I signed in March 1975 they were third in the Second Division, pushing hard for promotion. John Bond, the manager, had convinced me that my first taste of football in the Second Division would be brief.

'With you in the team, promotion is practically guaranteed,' he said in his bullish manner.

He didn't really need to sell the club to me. I already had a good feeling about it. I had happy childhood memories of Norfolk because that's where we used to go on the train from London for our family holidays. Now, with London a regular target for IRA bombers, inflation and unemployment raging and the dustmen on strike, Norfolk struck me as a safe and peaceful haven for my family. Norwich seemed the ideal stage for the final chapters of my career. I was thirty-one.

Contract negotiations with John were simple. We knew each other well from our days together at West Ham. We'd played in the same team for about four seasons when he was a senior professional and I was a youngster making my way through the ranks. He made me a good offer and I accepted – on one condition. 'If you ever nick my sausages again, you know what'll happen!' I told him.

He laughed. He knew full well what would happen. In 1962, when we were touring with West Ham in Ghana, culinary matters became the priority each day. The quality of the food on that trip was, well, suspicious! The only meal we could rely on was sausages and chips and we ate that every day.

One day John decided to exercise his seniority and stole my sausages. I saw him take them from my plate and when I politely asked him to return them, he threw them at me and laughed. As one of the youngest members of the squad I didn't feel that I was in a position to make a big issue of this but I resolved to make him aware of the error of his ways.

I waited until training the next day and nailed him with a tackle that would have stunned a water buffalo. It hurt him. At that moment he knew – everyone knew – the price to be paid for nicking Martin's sausages. He never took liberties with me again and, over the years, we became good friends.

When I arrived, Norwich had ten matches still to play. It was a high-quality Second Division that season with Manchester United, Aston Villa, Sunderland, West Bromwich Albion, Bolton and Southampton all vying for the three promotion places.

I made my debut against Manchester United. They'd led the table since September, which wasn't surprising when you studied the make-up of Tommy Docherty's team. It was packed with internationals, including Stuart Pearson, Martin Buchan, Lou Macari, Sammy McIlroy, Gerry Daly and Alex Stepney, plus future England winger Steve Coppell.

Seven weeks earlier, Norwich had knocked United out of the

League Cup in the semi-final and the pain of that defeat was still raw for Docherty and his players. Having drawn 2–2 at Old Trafford in the first leg, Colin Suggett's goal at Carrow Road was enough to clinch Norwich a place in the final against Aston Villa. Ten days before I joined the club, Villa beat Norwich 1–0 at Wembley.

My new team-mates realised that it was going to be a difficult debut for me, but I'd always enjoyed visiting Old Trafford – and it wasn't that long since I'd scored four there. In the event, it was a good start. A crowd of 56,202 watched a thrilling game that ended 1–1. On the train back home that night I was told that Spurs had lost 3–0 at Middlesbrough with the boy I recommended to them, Graeme Souness, scoring twice.

I played in all ten remaining games and we lost just two, one of them against Fulham at Carrow Road. It was good to see Bobby Moore that day. I'd played against him before for Tottenham, but I didn't see so much of him now. We had a chat about old times before the game. At thirty-four, he was still an influential figure at the heart of the Fulham team, along with another old friend, Alan Mullery. They were both still enjoying their football, and in a very good mood after beating us 2–1. A few days later they beat Birmingham City in the FA Cup semi-final and then faced West Ham. They lost 2–0 at Wembley but that must have been a lovely day for Mooro.

The Fulham defeat knocked Norwich down to fifth and raised a few eyebrows. They'd spent most of the season in the top three. Now the promotion bid was suddenly in jeopardy. The fact that I hadn't scored didn't help. I sensed some unease among the fans. Some thought I was a flash Londoner who'd turned up late in the day just to take the money and run. That was never the case, and they eventually realised that – I spent more than five years at Norwich and enjoyed every minute.

Wins against Leyton Orient and Sheffield Wednesday put us back on track. After the 1–0 win over Wednesday on a cold, snowy night at Hillsborough, John's assistant Ken Brown took me to one side and said that I needed to improve my tackling, which took me aback. Ken was another former Hammer whom I'd played alongside in the sixties and I was offended by his remarks. I never shirked a challenge and I asked him to tell me specifically when in the game he thought I'd been less than fully committed. He couldn't come up with an answer. I told him that I didn't agree with his assessment. I wasn't the perfect player by any means, but I'd never pulled out of a challenge and I wasn't about to start.

With three games left, John shrewdly decided that the club would appeal against Phil Boyer's pending suspension. He'd been sent off in a goalless draw with Sunderland just before I joined. The timing of the appeal to an independent tribunal meant that he would be available for the critical final matches. When we beat Nottingham Forest 3–0, I scored my first goal for the club and Phil hit two. Then, in the penultimate game, he scored again as we beat Portsmouth 3–0 at Fratton Park to clinch promotion. I scored the third goal. United were champions and Villa finished runners-up.

In the dressing room after the match, John Bond reminded me of what he'd told me on the day I signed.

'I said you wouldn't see much of the Second Division,' he smiled.

On the return journey, I managed to persuade John to divert the team bus to a popular pub in Chigwell, Essex, where we celebrated our triumph. I knew The Retreat well. It was where I had enjoyed my stag night.

I was pleased for John and Ken. They'd joined Norwich together from Bournemouth in December 1973, replacing Ron Saunders. When they took over, the club were bottom of the First Division, having won just two of twenty matches. Sadly, they couldn't halt the decline and the club were relegated. Now they had returned to the top flight at the first attempt.

I was pleased, too, that Tottenham had avoided relegation but I was now entirely focused on ensuring that Norwich retained their First Division status. I'd been staying in a hotel on the outskirts of the town but that summer I moved the family from Essex to Norfolk. We bought a large, old farmhouse with a pool and an acre of garden in the village of Sprowston, just north of Norwich, surrounded by open countryside. We sent the children to private schools and found stables for Lee Ann's horse, Checkers.

It was very different from the East India Dock Road and my childhood in London. We were now country folk and our lifestyle began to change. Kathy found it quite hard to adapt. She'd left behind lots of friends and sometimes felt lonely when I was away with the team. Without the social demands of London, though, I found I had more time at home with the family. I was never a big drinker or party-goer but the Tottenham players were a very sociable bunch and we'd often drift off to a pub or club, especially when we returned to London late on a Saturday night from a match in the provinces.

I was regularly invited to functions and Kathy and I were often guests at dinners organised by the East London Businessmen's Association. A friend of ours, Jimmy Quill, an Arsenal supporter whom I first met at the 1970 World Cup in Mexico, often took us to his pub, The Globe, in Mile End Road. Sometimes, after matches, I'd go there with Phil Beal and Johnny Pratt. I'd buy the first round at the bar and then not touch my wallet again because everyone else in the bar plied us with drinks. I'd have a couple of lagers but my favourite drink in those days was Mateus Rose.

Occasionally, we'd have a really late night in a club but these were rare. I remember being with Terry Venables once when a scuffle developed on the dance floor. He got pushed into the band and sent the drum kit flying all over the place. Little happened in those days, though, to generate the kind of sleazy tabloid headlines that nowadays proclaim some misdemeanour by a Premiership star.

I was drunk just once. After a very good 1–1 draw with Dynamo in Tbilisi in the 1974 UEFA Cup, the host club took us all to a bar, high on a mountainside. I had too much to drink and had to go back to the hotel where I collapsed on the bed. It was the only time that happened and I'm not proud of the memory – especially as I was the Spurs captain at the time.

At Norwich, initially at least, I had none of the responsibilities that went with the captaincy. In fact, joining a smaller club had lifted many pressures. The expectation levels were not as high as they had been at White Hart Lane. Tottenham is a huge club and each season we were expected to win one of the major honours. Expectation then was even higher than it is today. At Norwich, as I was soon to learn, simply surviving in the First Division was a notable achievement.

I eventually succeeded Duncan Forbes as captain and enjoyed the responsibility. John Bond allowed me to change things on the pitch, something I would not have done at Tottenham. Changing the tactical system at Norwich usually involved modifying my own role in the team. I had the freedom to make that type of change during a match, which was quite a compliment.

I knew how tough it was going to be the following season and the opening-day defeat – 3–0 against Manchester City – simply confirmed my fears. By the time we drew 2–2 at Tottenham in the fifth game of the season, we were sixteenth in the table.

Slowly, we came to terms with the new challenge and, ultimately, I thought we did remarkably well that season. We had some really impressive results, such as 3–0 at Leeds, and some real shockers. Losing 2–1 to Fourth Division Bradford City at Carrow Road in the fifth round of the FA Cup was a major disappointment – they scored with the last kick of the match. In the next round Bradford went out to Southampton, who progressed to the final where they beat Manchester United.

I was happy because, not surprisingly, John Bond encouraged the team to play much like West Ham had under Ron Greenwood. We were an attacking side and we could always score goals. Ted McDougall hit 28 that season. I was second highest scorer with 13 and was quite proud of the fact that Ted and I were the only players to have appeared in all 42 league matches.

John was a good, imaginative coach who had adopted the gospel according to Greenwood during his time as a West Ham player. Ken Brown had also worked under Ron's tutelage. They thought a lot about tactics and how to get the best out of the players they had available to them. John would often alter team strategy because he felt that we would benefit by presenting opposing teams with different tactics. Survival in the First Division was the priority and everything John did was geared to that. If he felt we were likely to struggle against certain opponents, he would devise a tactical plan that gave us an edge.

I was often a key figure – he moved me about the team regularly. I was never fast enough to be a successful front striker, but I did play upfront with Ted MacDougall at Liverpool in November that season. Ted and I were instructed to play out wide rather than stay together in the centre of the field as twin strikers would normally do. As a result, Liverpool's centre-backs, Phil Thompson and Emlyn Hughes, didn't really have anyone to mark. This caused considerable confusion in the Liverpool defence and while they were sorting it out, Ted and I scored a goal apiece.

Colin Suggett also scored in a remarkable 3–1 win. We were jubilant. It was unusual for Liverpool to lose at Anfield and five months later they lifted the First Division title for the ninth time.

On another occasion, John played me as a sweeper against Nottingham Forest. Brian Clough's team were on their way to the 1978 title and it looked as though we would do little to stop them. We were three goals down in the first half when the manager decided to abandon the sweeper plan and move me back to my normal midfield position. It was a masterstroke. The match ended 3–3.

We finished tenth in the table in 1975–76, one point below Spurs. John Bond was triumphant. Such was the sense of achievement at Carrow Road that Kathy and I decided to host a party to celebrate the fact that we had avoided relegation.

We invited John and Ken, all the players and their wives. The club chairman Sir Arthur South came with other members of the board. It was a wonderful evening at the end of a very hot day. The players were jumping in and out of the pool, or dancing. I hired a jukebox and it seemed to play nothing but a succession of Abba records – 'Waterloo', 'Mamma Mia', 'Fernando'. Everyone enjoyed themselves.

The following seasons we finished 16th, 13th, 16th and 12th. We accepted that the prospects of winning the title were remote. Liverpool and Nottingham Forest were the big guns, but that didn't stop us dreaming. That, after all, is what sport is about.

John ensured that we always made the most of our talent. In 1979–80 we started the season like a runaway train. We won our first three matches against Everton, Spurs and Leeds, scoring ten goals. I particularly enjoyed the win against Spurs. They had Ossie Ardiles, Ricky Villa and Glenn Hoddle in their team and they played us off the park in the first half. Then we found a bit of rhythm and beat them 4–0 with goals from Kevin Reeves (two), Justin Fashanu and me.

Top of the table at the start of September, we were still fourth in January. Then the English winter began to gnaw at our momentum. At least, I like to think that's what happened. Frozen pitches meant that over a period of six weeks we played just one First Division game – against Liverpool at Carrow Road – but it was a classic. They were the defending champions and leading the race once again, much as you'd expect with a team that included Ray Clemence, Alan Hansen, Phil Thompson, Graeme Souness and Kenny Dalglish.

I scored the first goal of the match after sixty-five seconds. David Fairclough, 'supersub' as he was known, equalised and scored another before Kevin Reeves levelled the score. Then, soon after the interval, Fairclough completed his hat-trick. Young Justin Fashanu drew Norwich level again with an epic strike from outside the area, but late goals by Jimmy Case and Dalglish gave Liverpool a sensational victory and put them two points clear at the top of the table.

Liverpool went on to win the title again but that 5–3 defeat was the turning point of the season for us. We won just four more games, slipping from fourth to twelfth. It was frustrating at times but John encouraged us to play with freedom and the quality of our football attracted praise.

In my first three seasons, John played me mostly wide on the left and then he moved me into the centre of midfield. Once, against Forest, he tried me as a spare man almost in the right-back position. It made little difference to me where I played. I seemed to get more scoring opportunities from wide positions and, in 1978–79, finished as the club's top marksman with twelve goals.

Natural wear and tear took its toll but I was very lucky with injuries. My form remained consistently good throughout my time at Carrow Road and in October 1979, after I'd had a particularly good game in a 4–1 League Cup win over Manchester United, I was flattered to read of suggestions that I should be recalled by England. I was a couple of weeks away from my thirty-sixth birthday and, even though Ron Greenwood was now in charge of the national team, I knew that such a recall was unrealistic. I hadn't played for England for five years, but in the match against United, playing just in front of our back four, I clearly eclipsed their England internationals Ray Wilkins and Steve Coppell.

I wasn't really surprised when John Bond suggested that Ron Greenwood should be thinking of reinstating me for the European Championship finals in Italy the following summer, but when Alan Mullery, then manager of Brighton, took up the call, some newspaper columnists weighed in with their opinions. Alan said, 'Age shouldn't stop Martin playing for England,' and Fleet Street's finest followed that by claiming I remained ten years ahead of everyone else!

However, despite that late surge, it was an inescapable fact that my playing career was slowly coming to an end. Alan Ball was still playing but was seriously considering moving into management. Eventually, he accepted a job as player-manager at Blackpool.

I guessed that I would have to stay in football when I hung up my boots because I had no other skills or training. Today, a player with my kind of career would be worth a fortune and would never have to work again, but there was no question of me not working. When I stopped playing I'd have to find a job. Almost subconsciously, perhaps preparing myself for a future as a coach, I'd been helping advise and encourage some of Norwich's young players, the best of whom included Kevin Bond, the manager's son, Kevin Reeves, Greg Downs, Mark Barham and Justin Fashanu.

Just as at any other club, some of them would make it and others would fall by the wayside. One thing I did notice was the changing attitude of some of the young players in the Carrow Road dressing room, merely a reflection of the changing values in society, I suppose.

When I was a young player, I was interested only in improving my skills and fitness. I was devoted to my job. I wanted to be the best. At Norwich, I realised that some of the youngsters were less interested in training and more interested in what they would be doing after training. Some of them had real talent but didn't apply themselves in the way that was necessary if they were to become good footballers. I didn't say anything at the time because I didn't think it was my place but I did try to set a good example on the training field. After all, I felt that John had signed me not just to play but also to act as a role model for his younger players. Some, though, simply didn't have the right attitude.

Justin Fashanu in particular was not one of these. He started his career like a meteor and for a time looked as though he might become a great player. He was a Barnado's boy, just sixteen when John gave him his first-team debut in a 1–1 draw against West Bromwich Albion in January 1978. A good, young centre-forward, he was strong and willing to learn, which was an important point in his favour.

He and his brother John came from Hackney and had trained as boxers. Justin had a muscular physique and quickly learned the value of brute strength when challenging for the ball. Unfortunately, he could be a little over-enthusiastic. I saw him bring down more than one centre-half with his elbows, and clearly remember him knocking out the Leeds defender Paul Hart, who was no lightweight.

John Bond played to his strengths, knocking high balls upfield for Justin to win and touch on to Kevin Reeves, who darted about picking up the pieces. They had the look of a good striking combination.

Justin was also a goalscorer and will always be remembered for the fabulous volley he hit from outside the box against Liverpool in our 5–3 defeat in the winter of 1980. A recording of that remarkable long-distance strike regularly crops up on TV when they're showing the greatest goals of all time.

Justin's potential was recognised by England at Under-21 level and after scoring 34 goals in 90 appearances for us, the club decided to sell him. Brian Clough, the manager of Nottingham Forest, paid £1 million for him in August 1981. It was Justin's big chance but Clough, inexplicably, wanted the ball played to his feet, which was the one truly weak area of his game. He scored three goals in thirty-two appearances in his first season at Forest, and was labelled a misfit, a title he didn't deserve.

Sadly, his life went downhill after that. He'd made a remarkable impression as a youngster but he couldn't sustain it. A complex boy, he had problems we weren't aware of at the time. I don't think many at the club realised he was gay because he'd often be seen in local nightclubs with a trophy blonde on his arm. He was just thirty-six when he hanged himself in a lock-up garage in London, having fled the United States where he was facing accusations of sexual assault on an underaged boy. The Norwich players of that era were really sad when they heard about Justin. Although a bit brash, he was popular and, in other circumstances, may have had a long and rewarding career.

Players were often reluctant to leave Norwich. Kevin Keelan, for instance, spent seventeen seasons in the first team. Born in Calcutta, where his father was serving with the British Army, he became an outstanding goalkeeper and a Norwich legend.

Duncan Forbes was another loyal servant. An uncompromising Scot, he spent eleven seasons in the heart of the Norwich defence, giving 110 per cent every time he pulled on a Norwich shirt. He wasn't the most accomplished player but he could stop others playing. Dave Stringer, from Gorleston in Norfolk, was another long-serving centre-back. He stayed for thirteen seasons and also had the kind of attitude I admired.

John Bond inherited these players but his masterstroke when he arrived at Carrow Road was the twin signings of Ted MacDougall and Phil Boyer. He signed Ted from West Ham in part exchange for Graham Paddon in December 1973, and two months later reunited him with his old side-kick Phil, signed from Bournemouth for £145,000. This deadly duo operated like Batman and Robin in opposition penalty areas. In their first full season together for Norwich, they scored forty-one goals between them.

Ted and Phil had played together for York City and Bourne-mouth and at both clubs had enjoyed a fruitful goalscoring partnership. John knew them because he had been their man-ager at Bournemouth.

Ted could be temperamental. He'd get really upset during a match if the wingers were not giving him the service he needed. You couldn't complain because he was a natural goalscorer and took his job seriously. I knew that if I got the ball in to the near post, he'd be in front of his marker and get a strike on goal.

I think John got the best out of him at Norwich. It was while playing at Carrow Road that he won seven caps for Scotland, and Phil was capped for England while at Norwich.

After John sold Ted to Southampton for £50,000 in September 1976, he took the former England and Chelsea striker Peter Osgood on loan from Southampton. Ossie played just three games for Norwich before returning to the south-coast club, but he's since told me that John Bond was the best of all the coaches he worked with.

John would sometimes consult me if he was looking for players to strengthen the squad. He seemed to value my opinion and I was probably influential in the capture of two former Spurs players – Jimmy Neighbour and Martin Chivers.

Jimmy played for Norwich for three years before moving on to West Ham but Martin managed just eleven games. John asked me about Martin before signing him from the Swiss club Servette. At one time, Martin had been the best centre-forward in Europe and, although his best days were probably behind him, he started really brightly when he joined us. He scored four goals in the opening seven matches of the season. Then he was injured and never really recovered. His last game was a 6–0 defeat at Liverpool in February 1979. A couple of weeks later, John released him and he joined Alan Mullery at Brighton. Although his stay had been brief, Martin was with Norwich long enough to appreciate the very special atmosphere the club generated. It was a true community club and, although I won no trophies, my time at Carrow Road was as rewarding as the years I spent with West Ham and Spurs. Not many people realise it, but I spent longer with Norwich that I did with Spurs.

We had great team spirit and John Bond ensured that it was a happy dressing room. The Carrow Road ground, on the banks of the River Wensum, had been home since 1935 and they had preserved many of the values of the two local schoolmasters who founded the club in 1905. The green and yellow strip was one of the most readily identifiable in the Football League and every schoolboy knew the answer to the question, 'Which football club is called The Canaries?'

You can imagine, therefore, how surprised I was to learn of the changing circumstances of Tony Powell, whom I played alongside for almost six seasons. For much of that period, Tony and I roomed together when the team stayed in hotels.

'Knocker' Powell was a centre-back who, as you'd expect, was good in the air. I used to partner him when we had head tennis competitions during training and we'd annihilate the opposition. He'd played for John Bond at Bournemouth before following him to Norwich. A good-looking boy, he had a lovely blonde wife, Marilyn. When they married in 1972, John was the guest of honour.

In March 1981, Tony left Norwich and signed for San Jose Earthquakes in California. I heard no more about him until bizarre stories began to circulate about the former Norwich City centre-half who had started a new life in San Francisco. Eventually, details began to appear in the Sunday tabloids. He and his wife divorced and the last I heard he was working as a receptionist in a seedy hotel in Hollywood.

As far as I was concerned, he was a team-mate, and a good one. I have nothing but good memories of the lads I played with. They were a great bunch and although I was a World Cup winner with a big reputation, they made me feel part of the club.

I had my leg pulled a bit by the lads when I went to Buckingham Palace to collect the MBE from the Queen. It was a wonderful family day. Kathy and the children were there, and so were my mum and dad. The Queen asked me how long I'd been playing and what club I was playing for now.

My team-mates decided to mark the occasion by forming two lines and clapping me on to the pitch when we next played at Carrow Road. It was nice, but I was embarrassed by the fuss.

In October 1978, they all turned out when the club organised a testimonial match for me. I was honoured that the club thought me worthy of a testimonial. At that time, these games were usually awarded to players who had given ten years' service.

Sir Alf Ramsey brought an England XI, including many of my old World Cup team-mates, to play Norwich at Carrow Road. A crowd of 18,426, bigger than the average home gate that season, went to the match and helped make it one of the most memorable nights of my career. The England team was Springett, Stiles, Hollins, Greaves, J. Charlton, Moore, Ball, Hunt, R. Charlton, Hurst, Peters. Ken Brown, a useful centre-half in his playing days, made a brief cameo appearance as substitute for Jack Charlton.

The Norwich team, 4–2 winners on the night, was Keelan, Bond, Davies, Ryan, Hoadley, Powell (Sullivan), Neighbour, Reeves, Downs, Mendham, Paddon.

I was delighted to see so many of my old mates. Jimmy Greaves played out of his skin and refused to take any expenses. George Cohen turned up but was unable to play, having just undergone serious surgery. I owed a special debt to Johnny Hollins, whom I asked to play just twenty-four hours before the match.

I felt I could have stayed at Norwich for a long time but the end came upon me suddenly. In July 1980, during pre-season training at Mousehold Heath, John Bond took me to one side and told me that he was about to join Manchester City as manager. This was news to me – and to everyone else when it was finally made public. He wanted me to know because Sheffield United had called him to ask whether I was available for transfer. They wanted me as player-coach. John knew that I was thinking of coaching in the future and he didn't want me to make a decision about my career unaware that he would soon be leaving Carrow Road.

22

THE BLADES

I'd enjoyed my time at Norwich and, looking back now, realise I was a fool to leave. I felt privileged to have played for such a fine club and still enjoy going back to Carrow Road. Their fans voted me the best player ever to pull on a Norwich shirt and that meant a great deal to me. However, at the age of thirty-six I had to look to the future. I'd been playing well but how much longer could I continue? Sheffield United wanted me as player-coach and when I met their chairman John Hassall at a hotel in Peterborough, he explained that they wanted me eventually to take over as manager from Harry Haslam. It sounded ideal.

Harry was a lovely man but his health was failing. He was sixty when I agreed to join him at United. He'd had a long and chequered career. Rejected by his home-town club, Manchester United, he'd played briefly as a full-back with Oldham, Brighton and Leyton Orient before turning to coaching with Gillingham. He managed Barry Town, Luton and Sheffield United and had been an intermediary when Tottenham manager Keith Burkin-shaw signed the Argentine World Cup stars of 1978, Ossie Ardiles and Ricky Villa. Harry was exceptionally well connected in Argentina and had paid River Plate £160,000 for Alex Sabella, whom Sheffield United later sold to Leeds for a big profit just before I arrived.

Harry put me straight into the first team and on the opening day of the season we won 3–0 at Carlisle with two of the oldest men on the field supplying the goals. Bob Hatton, the much-travelled striker then aged thirty-four, hit two and I scored the other one.

Although we won comfortably, I have to say that my first taste of Third Division football was not encouraging. Three days later we beat Chesterfield 2–0 – I scored again – and Bob scored when we beat Oxford United 1–0. After three straight wins, we were top of the table, and Harry was all smiles.

Strange as this may seem, it was not easy for me at this level. Running was not my game. I was just too old for the box-to-box stuff, and was more interested in using my guile and experience to open up defences with passes. The trouble was that few of my new team-mates were on the same wavelength. I could see a pass, but no one would respond. I could move into space, expecting the ball, and nothing would happen. This was not football as I'd been taught to play it.

I talked to Alan Ball about it. By then, he was player-manager of Blackpool and when we met them in September we were second in the table. We won 4–2, Ballie and I playing against each other. His view of football in the lower divisions was similar to my own. I realised then that it would become increasingly difficult for me to maintain my own standards, satisfy my own sense of professionalism and, at the same time, make a useful contribution to the team.

Gradually, Harry came to the same conclusion and so did the board of directors. I guess they decided to bring forward their long-term plan because in the New Year, Harry was moved upstairs and I was promoted to manager. By that time, we were slipping into the lower half of the table.

I played the last Football League game of my career against Gillingham at Bramall Lane on 17 January 1981 and a crowd of 8778 shared the experience with me. We lost 1–0 to a

Gillingham side that had a young Steve Bruce in the heart of their defence. After 722 league matches, I decided it was time to focus on management, so I hung up my boots and set about ensuring Sheffield United remained in the Third Division.

What a task that turned out to be! I had sixteen matches left. We won just three of them. I realise now that I simply didn't have the experience for that situation. I needed some advice and practical assistance. Harry Haslam couldn't provide as much help as I thought he would do. I tried to get Cyril Knowles to join us but he wasn't interested. I also tried to sign Peter Morris, an old friend from Norwich, but he didn't want to be a number two. He was managing Peterborough at the time.

We needed to strengthen the squad, too, but the only player I was able to sign was the former Republic of Ireland striker Don Givens. I bought him from Birmingham for £5000 and he played in the last eleven games of the season.

Although our results were dire, we reached the last day needing a draw to avoid relegation to the Fourth Division. The final game was at home to Walsall, who were also in serious trouble. They needed to beat us to stay up, so it was a real nail-biter.

I spent the week preparing the players, and in the dressing room before the game I mentioned the tendency of one of their more experienced players to go flying spectacularly in the penalty area whenever tackled. I stressed this to my centre-half John MacPhail in particular.

'Be careful when you tackle him,' I said. 'If he can get a penalty out of it, he will.'

With five minutes remaining the match was goalless. We were safe, Walsall were down. Then what happened? The player went over in the box, the referee awarded a penalty and Donald Penn – appropriate name I thought at the time – scored. Two minutes later we were awarded a penalty. I stood on the line wringing my hands. 'Score this and we're safe,' I thought.

Hold on, though. What's happening? The player designated to take our penalties, John Matthews, once of Arsenal, was refusing to take it. So up stepped Don Givens. My heart was in my mouth as he struck the ball. He hit it well enough but the Walsall goalkeeper Ron Green saved it. I couldn't believe it. You couldn't make it up. We were down. For the first time in the club's history, Sheffield United were relegated to the Fourth Division.

The fans didn't blame me and I don't think the club blamed me, either, but it was not a happy time with the Blades. As well as lacking the knowledge necessary for the job at that level, I was not prepared for the bitter rivalry between the United and Sheffield Wednesday fans. This affected the children at school, particularly Lee Ann. Sometimes when Kathy and I were out shopping, we were shouted at by Wednesday fans. On one occasion, someone spat on the pavement in front of us. We just weren't used to that sort of thing.

The saddest memory of that time, though, concerns the sudden death of young goalkeeper Keith Solomon from viral pneumonia. He was just nineteen when he collapsed at training one day. I followed the ambulance to the hospital but there was nothing anyone could do.

We'd signed him from Truro. He'd been playing local football in Cornwall while working for the railways, and one of our scouts had spotted his potential. He was a charismatic lad with good hands and good positioning sense. He could have made it as a goalkeeper.

My first match after taking charge of the team was against Leeds United in a friendly. I decided to put him on the substitutes' bench. He came on for the last twenty minutes and I remember thinking, after he died, that at least I had given him a taste of first-team football. We won 1–0. I nearly put him in the team for the next match, which would have been his league debut, but he was having a problem with his ankle. So he never played in the first team. Three weeks after that friendly match he died.

At Lee Ann's school a couple of days later, a boy who was a Wednesday fan said to her, 'I see one of your pigs died last week.' She was a mild-mannered teenager but she lost it completely that day. She got hold of the boy by the hair and pounded his head against a desk.

We inaugurated a memorial trophy for Keith Solomon and I took the team down to Truro for a benefit match. The two clubs still meet from time to time, and in the clubhouse at Truro a memorial plaque hangs in his honour.

23

BY THE SEASIDE

The late spring of 1981 was one of the few seriously low points in my football career. The rest of the world was preparing for the marriage of the Prince of Wales and Lady Diana Spencer but I was not happy. I was not used to failure and Sheffield United's relegation hit me hard.

I was convinced that, given the opportunity, I could prove myself in management and, initially at least, I was determined to redeem myself at Bramall Lane and lead United back to the Third Division at the first attempt. I realised that Sheffield United had enormous potential. I was just one year into a three-year contract and had no thoughts of resignation until the new chairman, Reg Brealey, called to say that he wanted to talk about the future of the club. He'd just replaced John Hassall, the chairman who'd appointed me a year earlier.

He came round one afternoon and Kathy and I showed him into our lounge. She and I had discussed the likely outcome of the meeting before he arrived. Obviously, the sack was an option that we had to face. I knew that relegation was a disaster for the club but I hadn't taken charge of the team until January. You could hardly describe it as my team, either. I'd inherited all the players bar one, Don Givens.

It was my first job in management and I thought I deserved

another chance. Mr Brealey didn't think so – at least not with
Sheffield United. Kathy was the first to recognise this. When he
left us after an amicable meeting she said, 'He's giving you a
way out. They want to make a change but he doesn't want to
sack you.'

She was absolutely right. Just as I didn't want to be tagged a
failure in management, he didn't want to be known as the man
who sacked a World Cup hero. When I spoke to him the following day, we quickly agreed a satisfactory severance deal that
included the purchase of our house by the club. It was a lovely
large house in an affluent suburb high on a hill, but Kathy was
delighted to leave it behind. 'It's above the snow line!' she used to
tell her friends in London. We'd decided to move back to Norfolk.

My departure, by 'mutual agreement', was big news, particularly in Yorkshire, and before the details were made public,
Kathy went to stay with friends in Norfolk and I went to Belgium
with my two old mates Ricky Jupp and Dave Readings to play
golf for a few days.

I told Ricky and Dave that although I was probably wrong
to accept the job in the first place, once I'd said I would do it I
was totally committed to making a success of it. Failure had
been a bitter disappointment. I still wanted the chance to show
what I could do in football management. Sheffield United had
given me a taste of the pressures and problems, and I wanted
more. I hoped I'd get another opportunity, but I had to get a
job of some sort. There was no question of sitting back and
counting my money.

Kathy and I thought about taking a public house, a popular
move among many former footballers at the time. Pubs and
insurance were the two lifelines many ex-players clung to in the
days before Sky TV and the Bosman ruling ensured that most
big-name stars retired as millionaires. Geoff Hurst had a pub on
the outskirts of Stoke-on-Trent. Bobby Moore had also invested
in pubs and a country club, with limited success. Our applica-

tion for a pub was refused – I don't think we'd have made very good publicans anyway.

The problem came back to convincing a club that I'd make a good manager, but the boys of 1966 had not covered themselves in glory in that respect. Geoff, for instance, had been sacked as manager of Chelsea just a few weeks before I left Sheffield United. Bobby had been floundering about between business ventures and low-key football jobs. His three-year contract as manager of Oxford City having been terminated, he went to Hong Kong to manage Eastern Athletic. At about this time, Nobby Stiles lost his job as manager of Preston North End. Bobby Charlton's brief career at Preston was already history.

In management terms, Jack Charlton and Alan Ball enjoyed the best careers. Jack managed Middlesbrough, Sheffield Wednesday, Newcastle and the Republic of Ireland. Alan was in charge at Blackpool, Exeter, Southampton, Portsmouth and Manchester City.

If nothing else came along, I thought I could probably pull my boots back on and play at a lower level for another season. I'd had offers in the past to play abroad. I spent one summer playing for Australian club Frankston City, just outside Melbourne, and my old West Ham team-mate Noel Cantwell had tried to persuade me to go the United States to play for his club in Boston. I could have coped with football at that level. Fitness was never a problem for me. Once I stopped playing I still made sure that I ran a couple of times a week and, even today, I'm only a few pounds over my playing weight.

Perhaps the most tempting offer came from Bobby Moore. He called me during the summer of 1981 and asked whether I'd go to play for his club in Hong Kong. The money was good, but it was a long way from home. We'd just moved to the village of Salhouse on the Norfolk Broads and we'd have had to take the children out of school had we accepted Mooro's offer.

Colchester, then in the Fourth Division, offered me the chance to make a comeback as a player. I was interested until I talked to their manager, Bobby Roberts. He wanted me to play at the front and I suspected that I wouldn't be able to do that. I had to say, 'No'.

Secretly I was hoping that Norwich City might offer me a job on the coaching staff. Ken Brown had succeeded John Bond as manager and I thought that he might consider giving me a job. Perhaps I was a bit naive. When I heard nothing from Norwich, I came up with a cunning plan. At least, I thought it was cunning! Cardiff City had just asked me whether I'd be interested in playing for them. I rang the local Norwich evening paper anonymously, offering them this snippet of news in the hope that they would print it. My theory was that if they ran a story along the lines of 'Cardiff want Peters' it might excite a bit of interest at Carrow Road. I was so desperate to get back into the game that I would have gone to Norwich to coach the kids. Sadly, nothing came of my devious plan.

Instead, out of the blue one day, I had a telephone call from a well-known Norfolk businessman, Jimmy Jones, whom I'd met during my playing days at Carrow Road. He had a proposition to put to me. He was the chairman of Gorleston FC. They played in the Magnet and Planet Eastern Counties League. He wanted me to play for them each Saturday and work for him during the week. He ran a company, based in Great Yarmouth, called J and J Leisure.

'I want you to do a bit of PR work for me during the week,' he said, 'and I know that if you play for Gorleston on Saturdays, you'll double our attendance figure.'

It sounded OK to me. The salary was hardly a fortune, but at least it was a weekly wage. Some weeks, I did nothing but play and train on two evenings. Other weeks I'd make personal appearances in pubs and clubs where Jimmy had an interest.

A popular seaside resort with a long, sandy beach, Gorleston is just south of Great Yarmouth. The team played at the Gorleston

Recreation Ground where the average crowd was about 200. Apparently, this figure doubled for my debut and most of the club's we visited enjoyed big increases in their gate figures.

I played throughout season 1981–82 at centre-back and still managed to score four goals. They were a great bunch of lads, managed by former professional Ronnie Piper. We finished the season in third place. Our top goalscorer was a former Northern Ireland centre-forward, Sammy Morgan, who had played for Port Vale, Aston Villa, Brighton and Cambridge.

Ronnie Piper and I established an immediate rapport because he had once played for Tottenham. He was my age, came from Lowestoft and had spent a short spell as an amateur with Arsenal before joining the staff at Tottenham under Bill Nicholson. He had made just one first-team appearance in 1962.

Jimmy Jones, who is now in his second spell as chairman of Gorleston, had spent thirteen years on the board at Norwich. He's one of those benevolent enthusiasts without whom football at the lower levels would probably struggle to exist.

During this period I also coached in holiday camps in such places as Skegness and Clacton, but I was slowly coming to the conclusion that I was not about to be swamped with job offers from the professional ranks. It was hard to believe but it looked as though I'd had my one and only stab at management. I had to come to terms with the fact that, after nearly a quarter of a century, professional football was no longer going to be a significant part of my life.

Geoff Hurst had been facing a similar crossroads in his career when he was offered a job by Motor-plan, an Essex-based company that administered used-car warranties, underwritten at Lloyd's. Geoff accepted the initial offer to join their sales force but was so successful that, after an interlude coaching in Kuwait, he negotiated a new position as sales director and purchased 19 per cent of the company.

He'd asked me once or twice whether I'd be interested in

joining him but each time I'd told him that I wanted to return to full-time football. Then, in 1984, Kathy started to complain that I was hanging around the house too much.

'You're getting under my feet,' she said. 'Why don't you get yourself a proper job?'

So, although I knew nothing about the warranty business, I called Geoff and said, 'When can I start?'

Ron Pleydell, the chairman of Motor-plan, agreed to see me and we agreed a six-week trial period. I travelled around the country with reps discovering how the business worked and quickly realised that it wasn't as daunting as I feared. I have to be honest and admit that being a former England footballer opened doors that may otherwise have remained closed. I was also reaping the benefits of a good image. Having avoided any controversy in my playing career, I found companies and individuals eager to associate their product with my name.

Once the trial period ended, I joined Motor-plan full time and returned to Essex to live. It was September 1984. My new job involved travelling around the country, visiting garages and opening new accounts for the company. Booted and suited, up at 6 a.m. Monday to Friday, overnights in motels, it was a taste of the real world. For the first time I was not pulling on a tracksuit as either player or coach. I wasn't convinced that I would enjoy the nine-to-five routine that shapes so many lives but I was determined to give it a try.

Although my status as an ex-footballer helped at times, in the final analysis, past sporting glories counted for very little. The only results that mattered in the business world were those that appeared on the account sheets. It was a lesson I learned quickly. The profit and loss columns dictated everything else.

When I started they paid me about £12,000 a year but once I got my feet under the table and had enjoyed some success opening new accounts, I asked for a pay rise. They said they'd give me a bonus of 25p for every policy sold by an account holder I'd introduced to the company. It didn't sound much at the time but it proved to be quite lucrative. Every month I'd check the list of new accounts against the list of new policy holders. The more they sold, the more I earned. It was some consolation for the nights I spent in motels up and down the country.

Although I had no connection with the professional game, I still played in charity matches. Motor-plan sponsored Dennis Waterman's Showbiz XI and Geoff and I were regulars. Warren Clarke, the actor, was a frequent team-mate, along with Dennis of course. It was good to play at weekends. I have to admit I missed involvement with professional football. I guess that when you're fortunate enough to have enjoyed the career I had, much of what follows must be anti-climactic.

Occasionally, I went to a professional game as a spectator, but I avoided the celebrity circuit. I was more likely to see old team-mates at golf days than at football matches. Golf was already a passion and I was influential in inaugurating the Motor-plan company golf day.

Eventually, Motor-plan sold out to Diamond Group Holdings in 1989 and when they collapsed, London General Holdings, a subsidiary of AON, acquired the company. Geoff and I survived all the changeovers. I was with them for a total of seventeen years. Then suddenly on 1 July 2001, I was summoned to the company offices in Middlesex and informed that I was to be made redundant.

'Sorry, but unavoidable,' said the chief executive, Roger Powell. As I left, still bewildered by the news, he said, 'Remember the golf day tomorrow, Martin. You will be there won't you?'

24

BACK TO WHITE HART LANE

Kathy likes people to be polite and courteous so when she picked up the telephone at home one autumn day in 1998 and realised the caller was eating she was not impressed.

'Is Martin there?' said the voice at the other end of the line.

'No,' she replied, 'he's not. Are you eating?'

'Yes,' said the voice, 'I am.'

'What are you eating?' she asked.

'A pizza,' was the reply. 'Look, if Martin's not there, would you kindly ask him to ring Alan Sugar when he gets back.'

Kathy related the story to me when I returned to our home in Shenfield, Essex.

'Perhaps he was hungry,' I said. 'He's a busy man after all.'

I called Alan Sugar on the number he had left.

'Would you come in and see me?' he asked. 'I want to put an idea to you.'

A couple of days later I went to see him in the chairman's office at White Hart Lane. Much to my surprise, he asked me to join the Tottenham board of directors. I didn't have to give it much thought. For a former player who retained a great affection for the club, it was an honour to be asked to go on the board. In fact, I think I was the first former player to be invited on to the Spurs board.

Hunter Davies, who explored the inner sanctum of seventies White Hart Lane in his book *The Glory Game*, wrote that getting into the Athenaeum club in London was easy compared to getting on the board at Spurs. 'The Spurs board is a very tight little circle,' he wrote.

That had changed. In the seventies, the same families had supplied Tottenham directors, such as vice chairman Arthur Cox, since the turn of the century. Sidney Wale, the chairman, had been a director since 1957 and his father Frederick had been chairman before him. That kind of boardroom stability disappeared in the decade between Mr Wale's departure and Alan Sugar's arrival in 1991. In that time, Spurs had three different chairmen – Arthur Richardson, Douglas Alexiou and Irving Scholar.

Alan Sugar, who had saved Spurs from imminent financial disaster when he took over, explained to me when we met that he wanted someone on the board to represent the views of the club's fans. He thought I had an affinity with the supporters and would therefore be in a position to voice their hopes and fears at board meetings.

I'd already been back at the club for about five years, associating regularly with the fans, when Alan asked me to go on the board. In 1993, when Gerry Francis was in the early days of his management, the club asked if I would host an executive lounge at White Hart Lane on match days. Martin Chivers was doing something similar. I really enjoyed the commitment. It meant that I saw all the home games and it also gave me the chance to meet a great number of Tottenham fans. I guess that was one of the reasons why Alan Sugar wanted me on the board.

A couple of years after I started at Tottenham, West Ham asked me to do the same for them at Upton Park on match days. As they usually played on alternate Saturdays, I was able to do both. If there was a clash, I always went to Spurs because they asked me first.

The West Ham crowd generated a very friendly, working-class atmosphere, although we always attracted a few celebrities. Nick Berry, Leslie Grantham and Ray Winstone were regulars at Upton Park.

Tottenham's match-day operation for their corporate and executive fans was probably sleeker and more professional. It was geared to enhance match-day profits and the club's success in this respect was recognised when they were voted the best corporate entertainers in the Premiership.

Meeting and greeting fans was something I gradually got used to. As a player years earlier, the thought of public speaking didn't appeal to me but, having stopped playing, I had to make a living and I realised that one way of doing this was by sharing my experiences in public. When I was approached by an agent, Dave Davies, and asked if I would fulfil a nationwide speaking tour with England's 1966 team I was a bit apprehensive. I'd never done anything like that before, but it was an earner – £500 a night.

Davies organised a tour of provincial theatres and clubs. Four or five of us would appear each time – Geoff, George Cohen, Gordon Banks, Alan Ball, occasionally Jack Charlton and me. The comic Ian Richards warmed up the audience, then we all had a turn with Geoff usually winding it up. Then there was a question and answer session.

I found standing on a stage looking into the spotlights quite intimidating at first but the audience was always receptive and welcoming. I remember getting a standing ovation that would have made Lord Olivier proud when we appeared at the Royal Theatre in Norwich – my home ground!

Not every theatre was full. When we appeared in Newcastle, traditionally considered a hotbed of football, the audience numbered thirteen. To make it a bit cosier we took the whole show into the theatre bar and the lucky thirteen had the time of their lives.

The most popular question we were asked, some thirty years after the event, was did Geoff Hurst's shot cross the line in the final? The other favourite themes invariably involved today's star names. How good is David Beckham? Would Paul Gascoigne have got in to Alf Ramsey's team?

Those stage appearances gave me the confidence to try after-dinner speaking, another little cottage industry for the 1966 team. I began to speak at sportsmen's dinners and picked it up as I went along. I still get invitations to speak at dinners. Mixing with fans at Tottenham and West Ham on match days helped because I would sometimes pick up fresh material, hear a funny story or some outrageous opinion that was taking root among supporters.

It was not difficult, as a match-day host, to reach the conclusion that the fans were very unhappy with Alan Sugar's choice of Christian Gross as manager of Tottenham. The amiable Swiss coach of Zurich Grasshoppers had little knowledge of the English game when he was appointed to succeed Gerry Francis in November 1997. He took over at a difficult time, with the club struggling just above the relegation zone, but his first match at White Hart Lane produced the worst home defeat since 1935. A clueless performance in the 6–1 thrashing by Chelsea suggested that he was going to find the challenge difficult.

Christian had been manager of the club for ten months when I joined the board of directors but on 5 September 1998, within a week of my appointment, Alan Sugar fired him. I knew nothing about it and played no part in his dismissal. One of my first tasks as a board member was to give my opinion about George Graham, who was selected to replace him. George had an outstanding managerial pedigree, having won six trophies in eight years at Highbury, including two League Championships. George was at Leeds United when Alan suggested to him that he might like to return to north London and take charge of Tottenham. When asked by Alan for my opinion, I pointed out the obvious – would the Spurs fans happily accept an Arsenal man as manager? Terry Neill knew the answer to that.

No one could question George's management qualifications, though, and after a lukewarm reception, the fans at White Hart Lane began to warm to him. The fact that results improved helped his position enormously. The fans could sense a greater urgency and competition for places among the players. Shortly after his arrival, Spurs won 3–1 at Liverpool in the Worthington Cup, then beat Manchester United 3–1 at home in the same competition, both impressive results. George led them to Wembley where they beat Leicester City 1–0 in the final – the club's first trophy for eight years. He also steered them to the semi-finals of the FA Cup that season.

During this period I probably saw more of Spurs than anyone except the manager and the first-team coaching staff. I watched all the home games and travelled to most of the away games. In many ways it was a privileged existence for someone who loved football. Visiting directors are invariably feted by the home club and offered lunch before the game. Going to Old Trafford, Anfield, Highbury and Stamford Bridge as a VIP was a real treat.

I attended monthly board meetings, which were surprisingly friendly and constructive. Alan Sugar was the dominant figure but he wasn't as gruff and humourless as he's sometimes portrayed. I got on well with him. He came from a similar background to me, having grown up in a council flat in Hackney and married at twenty-one. His wife Ann is a lovely lady and it's easy to see why they have been together for so long. I think they are both people who value those old-time family virtues that were once so common in east London.

Financially, Alan's big coup was providing the first affordable home computer and by the time he was forty he was the fifteenth richest man in Britain with a personal fortune of around £600 million – not bad for a former car-boot salesman. He obviously knew a bit about the power and effect of wealth. If the team were going through a sticky patch, for instance, he would often say, 'What can you do to motivate eleven millionaires?'

You always knew where you stood with him. He was quite straightforward and if you said something he disagreed with, he told you so. Maybe he is an acquired taste but I enjoyed working with him. Quite often you'd see a flash of cutting humour – 'Darren Anderton injured again? What is it this time? A broken eyelash?'

Sometimes during a match or at half-time he'd question me about the tactics. 'What was the point of doing that?' he'd ask. I'd try to explain the manager's point of view. I suppose in a way I was flattered to be consulted.

I could tell that he was a real fan because he took his responsibilities seriously. When results went against us, and the fans began to abuse him, he found that very hurtful – me, too. To sit in the directors' box listening to some of the stuff they shout at you is not very pleasant.

By and large, though, I enjoyed a good rapport with the Spurs fans and that's why Alan encouraged me to establish greater links with them. He was delighted when I introduced a regular forum for supporters. This involved a question and answer session with the manager or one of the players. These became very popular and were always packed with fans.

I also introduced a dedicated telephone line so that the fans could call the club twenty-four hours a day for news about tickets, injuries, fixtures or stories that had appeared in the papers. The club updated this each day, which I think became something of a chore for David Pleat. As the club's director of football, he was largely responsible for most of the news items. We tried to give our fans the big news before it reached any other media outlet, but it sometimes put David under pressure.

Obviously, there are some issues the club would prefer to keep private, especially when negotiating to sign a new player, for instance, but if the story broke in one of the newspapers, David would have to decide how the club should respond on the fans' telephone line. We could not always confirm our interest in a player but nor could we deliberately mislead our fans.

One of the biggest stories of my period on the board unfolded in the winter of 2001 when Spurs, under new owners, sacked George Graham. He'd enjoyed the support of Alan Sugar and the board but Alan sold his 40 per cent stake in the club to ENIC, an investment company, just before Christmas 2000. The new chairman, Daniel Levy, obviously had his own ideas about the way the club should be run. Results were indifferent – one win in eleven Premiership matches in December and January – and I sensed the pressure growing on George.

In mid-March, twenty-four hours after being told by the owners not to discuss financial matters with the newspapers, he was called in to see executive vice-chairman David Buchler. The fifteen-minute meeting ended with George's dismissal. In many ways I was sorry to see him go because he was developing a young, workmanlike side. The fact that three weeks later a new manager – Glenn Hoddle – took the team to Old Trafford for an FA Cup semi-final against Arsenal suggests to me that George was leading Spurs in the right direction.

I remained on the board under the new regime but never attended a board meeting because there wasn't one. David Pleat and I were the only previous members of the board who remained when ENIC took over.

I began to notice changes. For one thing, board members used to travel home from long-distance away matches on the charter plane with the team. Glenn stopped that. Overall, I got the feeling that he wasn't happy with my presence as a director. I'd known Glenn for many years. I was still at Tottenham when he joined the club as an apprentice in April 1974. He had a fabulous playing career and I always admired his skill and passing range, but I think I upset him when he was England manager.

Remember Eileen Drewery? Well, as I understand it, she was his friend, adviser and faith healer, and Glenn believed that her presence helped his players. They met, initially, because she was the mother of one of his early girlfriends. She helped him recover from injuries and began to devote more time to healing and counselling footballers. Several high-profile players sought her help, and in the build-up to the 1998 World Cup, Glenn introduced her to the England squad as an 'agony aunt'. She claimed to be an 'instrument of God whose power would help England win the World Cup'.

The Football Association, Glenn's employers, were sceptical and at one stage the International Committee expressed concern at the closeness of Eileen Drewery to the England squad. Glenn, though, was adamant about the benefits of a faith healer. 'It would become an issue if the FA tried to prevent me using Eileen,' he was quoted as saying.

Much of what she did in her faith-healing capacity within the squad remains shrouded in mystery, but after a goalless draw in Italy in a World Cup qualifier in October 1997, she made what I considered to be a ridiculously naïve remark. Basically, she said that she had used her powers to prevent Ian Wright scoring a last-minute goal in Rome because it might have triggered crowd trouble. When asked about her claim by newspapers, I replied with some derisive comments that were widely reported. I thought she had become a farcical figure and, as I told the newspapers, while England players would accept her if that's what it took to be part of the squad, in private they probably felt she was a joke.

Glenn and I had never been close friends – I'd see him occasionally at golf days – but from that moment he appeared to ignore me totally. Once, at Selhurst Park where Tottenham were playing Wimbledon, Glenn, who was England manager at the time, sat right in front of me, but he didn't say a word to me.

Eventually, in September 2002, I received a letter from Daniel

Levy asking me to make an appointment to see him at the club. I went along as requested and was told that Glenn was unhappy having me, a former player, on the board. In fact, the future of the board was in question. As there were only of two members left, he said, there was no point continuing with it and he asked me to resign. So my four proud years as a non-executive director at Spurs came to a sudden end.

Although I was disappointed, I was happy to continue in my role as a White Hart Lane host on match days. At the moment, I'm the host in the Platinum Club, which is the plushest and most exclusive lounge at the club, giving those who can afford it a really memorable experience. A champagne reception is followed by an excellent lunch or dinner, with visits by the club's high-profile personalities. I greet the guests and at some stage interview a player, which can be a challenge, especially if the player selected for the job has been dropped from the team recently. The players realise they are expected to say the right things – although it may not be what they are feeling at the time.

I enjoy the job and I'm flattered that fans still seem thrilled to meet me all these years after I finished playing. I'm still associated with the World Cup forty years later and I think all of us are slightly puzzled about why the 1966 team remains so popular. Perhaps it's because no other team has repeated our achievement.

At some point on a match day I leave the Platinum Club and visit other lounges. That can be a time-consuming operation because of the number of fans who want to stop and chat or ask for an autograph or a photograph. Even in Sainsburys, I am regularly stopped by people exclaiming, 'Good God! It's Martin Peters!' It happens to all the lads.

My closest rapport is with the fans of West Ham, Tottenham and Norwich. I always receive a warm welcome from them and those are the clubs whose results I always look for first. I was sorry that Norwich couldn't consolidate their place in the Premiership after winning promotion as champions in 2004, but I was thrilled by West Ham's return to the big-time via the play-offs in 2005.

After a period of turmoil, Tottenham finally began to make sustained progress under Martin Jol in 2005. The sudden departure of Glenn Hoddle in September 2003 resulted in months of uncertainty with David Pleat and then Jacques Santini taking charge before Jol was promoted to head coach in November 2004. Martin, originally appointed as assistant to Santini, was able to use his vast experience, gained in Holland, to rejuvenate the club and ensure that the players and coaching staff were focused on the challenges facing them. He took charge of the situation, introduced younger players and quickly won the respect of the squad.

Sadly, the club lost Frank Arnesen, the former Danish international who had discovered and developed a host of players for PSV in Holland. He was lured to Chelsea and replaced as sporting director by Damien Comolli.

There are plenty of reasons for optimism at the moment. Goalkeeper Paul Robinson is acknowledged as the best in England. He enjoys the benefit of playing behind two of the best central defenders in the Premiership, Ledley King and Michael Dawson. I think Ledley King should be England's first-choice centreback, while Michael Dawson is emerging as a potentially great defender, although he still has a lot to learn. He's a big, strong lad who attacks the ball positively and takes on moves down the middle with confidence. He tackles well and blocks shots, but needs to be a bit cuter, especially with defenders running around the back of him. To develop to international level he must also improve his technique because sometimes he allows the ball to bobble away when he should be able to control it with one touch.

Michael Carrick has improved immensely since his move

from West Ham but I'd still like to see him score more goals. I'd like him to get into the penalty box more than he does but I think he's benefited from the arrival of Edgar Davids, a player of vast experience who has made the Spurs midfield more solid.

Upfront, Jermain Defoe is an outstanding prospect. He's a natural, instinctive goalscorer but went through a period that faces most young strikers at some stage in their development. They can look terrific when they first arrive on the scene but the novelty wears off when defenders learn how to play against the newcomer. Jermain has to progress to another level and I suspect the coaching staff have told him to give his game a little more thought rather than shoot on sight all the time.

That advice might have put him off his game a little – he wouldn't be the first to suffer in that way. At Norwich, shortly after Jimmy Neighbour arrived from Spurs, I remember John Bond telling him to think a little more about what he was doing. A spontaneous, instinctive winger, Jimmy played his natural game in his first two matches for Norwich in October 1976. In both he slaughtered his marker – Alan Kennedy of Newcastle and Ian Gillard of QPR. Norwich won both games 3–2 and Jim was outstanding. Then, in training, John took him to one side and tried to feed him information – Jimmy was to lift his head and assess the options before crossing the ball because John wanted more passes to the near post. In the next game, it was obvious that Jimmy was thinking about the things John had put to him. Instead of playing his natural game he was trying to play to instructions. He wasn't the instinctive player we'd seen in the first two matches. The fraction of a second it took him to think about what he was doing gave his marker time to make a tackle. Jimmy was an experienced player at that stage in his career while Jermain is still learning about the game and will improve. I have no doubt about that.

It's important that, having rediscovered some momentum, Tottenham now hold on to their good young players because

Martin Jol has raised the expectancy level at the club. Once again, the Tottenham fans have high hopes of a return to the glory days, and perhaps this time their optimism is justified.

25

AND FINALLY...

I wanted England to win the World Cup in 2006 as much as any other patriotic Englishman but the fact that they didn't meant that the team of 1966 retained a unique place in the folklore of the game. That might not have been much consolation for modern heroes like Wayne Rooney and John Terry but for me, Geoff, Bobby, Nobby, Gordon and all the others it meant that our status as England's only World Cup winners was preserved for another four years at least.

England's quarter-final exit in Germany illustrated once more how difficult it is to win the World Cup and just how successful Sir Alf Ramsey was all those years ago in gathering together all the elements that produced a winning formula. The World Cup remains a target, a challenge and a dream for future generations.

For me the expectancy level in 2006 was unrealistically high. The general public, their enthusiasm fuelled by the media, clearly believed England had an outstanding chance to win the tournament. The whole nation was convinced England were good enough to win. Quite what they based their optimism on remains a mystery to me.

I felt we had a chance but I knew we'd have to play to our full potential to match the best in the world. There was little evidence in the build-up games to suggest we could produce the level of consistency necessary to win the World Cup. The 4–1 defeat in Denmark, the narrow 1–0 qualifying win in Wales and the woeful performance in the 1–0 defeat in Northern Ireland in another qualifier posed serious questions about England's preparations.

The loss of Rooney with injury just a couple of months before the tournament was also significant though it didn't seem to affect the nation's sense of optimism. It was clearly a gamble to take the Manchester United striker, who broke a metatarsal at Chelsea late in April. He had been in prolific form, scoring six goals in United's previous eight Premiership games and the nation expected him to light up the World Cup. His influence within the England team is such that many understood why Sven-Goran Eriksson was prepared to gamble on his state of readiness. But the United manager, Sir Alex Ferguson, voiced his doubts from the moment his young player was injured at Stamford Bridge.

Steve McClaren, Eriksson's successor as England manager, confirmed what many suspected some months after the tournament. He had been one of Eriksson's coaches in Germany and knew the fight Rooney had to get fit. 'In hindsight we asked too much of him,' he said on Sky TV many months after the World Cup.

Many observers realised Rooney was a long way from peak condition in Germany but it didn't seem to dampen the nation's optimism. I don't think I've known a time when expectancy levels were so high. I never felt that weight of public expectation in 1966 when England were the host nation and, as such, among the favourites to win.

What was so disappointing in Germany was not simply that we failed to win the tournament but that we didn't play well. After every game you could sense the despondency in people and the belief that we'd play better in the next game. It never happened. We had to play to our full potential to challenge the best and we didn't do that. Not everyone plays brilliantly in every game, I accept that. But to be consistently successful most of your players have to play to their full ability in most of the games.

We didn't all make outstanding individual contributions in 1966, but most of us played well in most of the games. Sometimes an individual, like Bobby Charlton for instance, would produce a genuinely brilliant ninety-minute performance but Sir Alf Ramsey credited our success to the quality of the team play and the willingness of the players to work for each other.

That is a characteristic of the English game and to be honest I thought it would have underpinned our performance in Germany. But I was disappointed with the quality of our team play. I was particularly disappointed with Frank Lampard and Steve Gerrard, two outstanding modern midfield players. I've always believed that they were good enough footballers as individuals to be able to play together successfully. That was never apparent in Germany.

Rooney's injury, of course, caused a tactical re-think. Eriksson changed the system, eventually opting for a lone striker and a holding midfield player, and I don't think this did either Lampard or Gerrard any favours. What also became apparent early in the tournament was Eriksson's failure to take enough strikers. I thought the inclusion of Arsenal's young striker Theo Walcott was a waste of a place. He didn't have the experience to justify a place in the squad. He is an immensely talented young player with a big future but he wasn't ready for the World Cup in 2006 and the fact that he didn't kick a ball supports my claim.

Rooney missed the first game against Paraguay, was summoned from the substitute's bench against Trinidad and Tobago and made his first start against Sweden in Cologne. When

Michael Owen was injured Eriksson played Rooney as a lone front striker – not his best role. England drew 2–2 with the Swedes and Rooney, still not fully fit, retained his position as the focal point of the attack against Ecuador.

I think he became frustrated in that role and I'm convinced that this contributed to his sending off in the quarter-final with Portugal. It was a thankless task; he was running into blind alleys and brick walls. He was playing against four defenders and as soon as he received the ball was tackled by one of them. If he ran with the ball he was outnumbered and almost inevitably lost possession. I think this frustration was gnawing at him when he was sent off.

In the circumstances, with neither Owen nor Rooney fully fit, I feel that England would have benefited from more attacking options. I think I would have taken Charlton Athletic's Darren Bent – he was the Premiership's top English scorer in 2005–06 with 18 goals – and at least given some serious thought to Tottenham's Jermain Defoe.

In the end England simply didn't have the firepower. A goalless draw with Portugal after extra time produced the dreaded penalty shoot-out. England are not good at penalty shoot-outs. Had he not been sent off for stamping on Ricardo Carvalho, Rooney would have taken one of England's penalties. Instead Lampard, Gerrard, Jamie Carragher and Owen Hargreaves shared the responsibility. Only Hargreaves managed to score while Rooney's United team mate, Cristiano Ronaldo, who had been involved in the sending-off incident, drove home the final nail in England's coffin.

It was an ignominious end for Eriksson – and David Beckham. The following day Beckham announced that, after six years, he was standing down as England captain. He assumed he would add to his 94-cap collection but McClaren, the new manager, ignored him in the months following the World Cup.

Over the years David Beckham did a very good job for England. He played the wide midfield role – the same position as me in 1966 – with great enthusiasm and industry. I think he lost a little of his edge following his move to Real Madrid but in his heyday he was outstanding. He was one of the world's finest dead-ball kickers and no one would ever question his commitment. For me he deserves a place alongside England's finest captains, but Bobby Moore remains the best and most influential. He was simply a better player than Beckham.

The Eriksson legacy? Well, in terms of qualifying for major tournaments he was a huge success. He arrived in 2000 with qualification for Japan in serious doubt. He salvaged that situation, registering the best win of his reign – 5–1 in Germany – along the way. He then led England to Euro 2004 in Portugal and the 2006 World Cup in Germany.

His record in tournament football is less impressive. I thought the quarter-final exits in Japan and Portugal were acceptable in the circumstances but the defeat to Portugal in the last eight in 2006 was unacceptable. In nearly six years we hadn't really advanced or learned anything very much at all. We were no further forward than when he took over. Yes, one or two good young players emerged but they would probably have come through anyway. We hadn't looked like a team in Germany and that was one of my biggest criticisms. Portugal beat England in a penalty shoot-out in Lisbon in 2004 and did exactly the same two years later. So we clearly hadn't learned much about taking penalties.

This is not a satisfactory way to decide important matches. I'd far rather see a replay but it would be impossible to fit into an already crowded fixture schedule. So I think it's essential that the new England manager ensures that his players can take penalties with confidence before the next major tournament.

I used to take them and didn't enjoy it. There is pressure, but you learn to control it. I would place the ball to the side of the goalkeeper. I struck the ball with the inside of my boot and tried to generate a bit of pace. I felt accuracy was the most important thing. Geoff Hurst used to hammer his, so did Martin Chivers. You can work at it in training and become something of an expert. I read a statistic at the time of the 2006 World Cup. The Germans had been beaten only once in 15 penalty shoot-outs. The only German player to miss a penalty in that time was Uli Stielike. They obviously work at it.

The Germans, who beat Argentina 4–2 on penalties in the quarter-finals, were beaten 2–0 after extra time by the eventual winners Italy in the semi-finals. Despite the lack of goals in the first 118 minutes it was a pulsating game decided by goals in the last two minutes from Fabio Grosso and Alessandro del Piero.

It was a marvellous advert for the game, demonstrating a level of sportsmanship not often seen in the tournament. Sadly, there was a lot of diving and cheating throughout the tournament and my abiding memory will be of Zinedine Zidane's astonishing headbutt on Italy's Marco Materazzi in the final. It was a sad final act by one of the world's great footballers.

Whether provoked or not by the Italian, it didn't excuse his behaviour that day. Apart from Diego Maradona in 1994, no football legend has departed the world stage quite so abjectly. Having provided the opening goal, Zidane's premature exit from the final in Berlin obviously didn't help the French cause. They lost 5–3 in the penalty shoot-out, with only France's David Trézéguet failing to find the net from the spot. It seemed unfair to me that after two years of qualifying matches and four weeks of intensive tournament football the final should be decided by a penalty shoot-out.

To be honest I didn't think Italy would reach the final. There was no outstanding team in the tournament and this meant that a disciplined, workmanlike team – like Italy – had a very good chance. An accomplished, well-organised defence was the platform for their success and in Fabio Cannavaro they had the player of the tournament. What he lacked in height he made up for with great athleticism and a mighty spring. He could out-jump most attackers. The more I saw of him the more I appreciated his talent. The fact that Italy conceded just two goals in the tournament – an own goal and a penalty – was due in no small part to the enduring excellence of the Italian captain.

Initially I thought Brazil might win, but after watching Argentina they became my favourites. They had outstanding individuals like Juan Riquelme, Hernán Crespo, Maxi Rodriguez and Lionel Messi – I'd have liked to see more of him – and played some of the best football in the tournament. They fashioned arguably the finest tournament goal in the 6–0 win over Serbia – nine players, 24 passes and one goal in 57 seconds of exquisite football.

Their 2–1 win over Mexico provided fantastic entertainment but tactical mistakes by their coach José Pekerman proved critical in the quarter-final with the Germans. They were leading 1–0 and in desperate need of a second goal to secure the game when he took off his best player, Ricquelme, and his proven goalscorer, Crespo. Within 60 seconds of Crespo's substitution Germany equalised and went on to win 4–2 on penalties.

For me, the penalty shoot-outs and the attempts by players to con referees spoiled the tournament. FIFA's crackdown on reckless tackling, diving and other dubious tactics produced 345 yellow and 28 red cards, both records. In the early group games it looked to me as if FIFA had instructed referees to remove all physical contact from the game. Fortunately referees seemed to take a more tolerant attitude from the second round onwards.

A hard, crunching tackle is part of the game and it would strip the sport of so much of its appeal if all physical challenges were outlawed, but I think cheats, those who dive and try to con referees, should be automatically booked. However, I do recognise that it is difficult for referees to distinguish between a dive and a legitimate fall as the result of a tackle.

Germany marched on to face Italy in Dortmund while France met Portugal in Munich. As for England, they limped home. At his final press conference Eriksson summed up his reign quite aptly. 'The first two quarter-finals were good enough,' he said. 'But this is not good enough. If you look at the four teams in the semi-finals we should be one of them.'

Sven handed the poisoned chalice to his assistant Steve McClaren. Not everyone thought the Middlesbrough manager was the best choice as England manager. Certainly not the Football Association because they tried to appoint Portugal coach Luiz Felipe Scolari before turning to McClaren. But the new England manager impressed me immediately by deciding to appoint Terry Venables to his coaching staff. On paper it looked like a very productive partnership. Terry has vast experience and, of course, led England to the last four of Euro '96. He's a bright, innovate coach, no one's 'yes' man: he says what he thinks. Managers tend to surround themselves with cronies when they accept a new job, but Terry doesn't belong in this category. It was a bold move by McClaren and, initially at least, looks a good one.

One of McClaren's first tasks was to establish a system of play that would draw the best out of England's big reputation players – notably Lampard, Gerrard and Rooney. As Rooney was suspended for the first three matches of 2006–07, following his sending off at the World Cup, McClaren began his reign without him. Defoe joined Peter Crouch up front in the opening game at Old Trafford, a 4–0 win over Greece. Crouch scored twice, quickly lifting spirits after the disappointments in Germany. Then England beat Andorra 5–0 in the opening European Championship qualifying tie – Crouch and Defoe scoring two apiece – and followed that four days later with a 1–0 win in Macedonia.

It was an encouraging start but in October 2006, with Rooney back in the side, England faced Macedonia, again at

Old Trafford. This time it was a different story. Macedonia defended well, kept possession and caused England problems. A goalless draw meant two home points dropped.

Four days later England met Croatia in Zagreb. McClaren switched to an unfamiliar 3-5-2 system. It was a disaster. Croatia had never lost a competitive match at home and they never looked like losing this one. They beat England 2–0. Crouch and Rooney, playing together up front, didn't get a kick.

The marking by England's defence was lamentable and an uncharacteristic mistake by Gary Neville gifted Croatia their second goal. His back pass hit a divot, deceiving goalkeeper Paul Robinson, who started the match bidding to equal Gordon Banks's record of seven consecutive clean sheets. Robinson completely misjudged Neville's back pass, missing the ball with his attempt at clearing it. The ball continued its journey into the net. Robinson was widely criticised afterwards but I felt that a defender of Neville's experience should have ensured that his back pass was wide of the goal. If it bobbles in those circumstances it goes for a corner – not an own goal.

Neville has been one of England's greatest defenders but the call-up of Manchester City's young right-back Micah Richards for the next game – a 1–1 draw in Holland in a friendly – suggested that his days in the international team may be coming to an end. Richards made an impressive debut and with other young players, such as Aaron Lennon, Kieron Richardson and Theo Walcott, may have an increasingly significant role to play in the qualifying campaign for the 2008 European Championship. With Beckham unlikely to return, Tottenham's Lennon has a real chance to stake a claim on England's right flank. He could be a future star because he's the type who can beat defenders and create havoc in opposing teams. He needs, though, to improve the quality of his passing and learn that sometimes an early pass is more effective than trying to beat another defender.

At the start of the tournament most people felt that England would qualify comfortably. It would, after all, be a real shock if England failed to secure one of the two qualifying places from this group, containing Andorra, Macedonia, Croatia, Estonia, Russia and Israel. But dropping five points against Macedonia and Croatia has introduced an element of doubt early in the campaign.

My own feeling is that a sense of realism would do England no harm at all. The Eriksson years were as much about celebrity as achievement. Players' wives, for instance, seemed to make bigger headlines sometimes than the players themselves during the World Cup. I'm not critical of the fact that most of them stayed in a luxury hotel in Baden-Baden while their husbands and boyfriends prepared for matches in their mountain retreat, but I am critical of the fact that many of them spent their evenings in nightclubs and were photographed drinking and dancing on table-tops in the newspapers. How do players, preparing for big matches, feel when they see their wives out on the town? It's very distracting and not good for morale among the players.

I think Steve McClaren recognised this. One of the first things he did when he took over was to dilute the celebrity culture within the squad. The dropping of Beckham, the team's major international personality, immediately diminished media attention. The new England manager wanted to lower the profile of his squad, to get back to business and focus on the challenges ahead. He knows that for England the challenges remain as daunting as ever.

It'll be good for the England players to get back to Wembley. It was a shame that the 2006 World Cup final wasn't staged in the new stadium. That was the original plan when the Football Association, with full government backing, bid to be the host nation. I thought we put together a fantastic bid but, long before we knew the stadium wouldn't be ready, the Germans had pipped us to it anyway. Wembley is the spiritual home of English football and will surely stage the world's greatest football tournament at some time in the future.

I have great memories of the old stadium but, sad as it was to see the twin towers pulled down, the facilities were simply out of date. It was opened in 1923 and played a significant role in my life. As a kid in the East End I would always find a TV set somewhere on Cup final day. I have always remembered those finals by their popular names – the Matthews Final, the Trautmann Final and the Roy Dwight Final.

These were great sporting occasions for me and my pals. Football is as much about sportsmanship and developing skills at grassroots level as it is about huge transfer fees, vast salaries and the domination of the professional game by a handful of big clubs, and I fear that today we may be losing sight of this. The way Chelsea have been allowed to use their vast financial resources to undermine the spirit of the game annoys me. Football is becoming a charmless sport and deserves better.

I'm sure the Chelsea owner Roman Abramovich invested his millions with the best of intentions but a team that wins everything will eventually strip away the excitement and unpredictability that is an essential element in football. Even Chelsea fans would probably become bored if their team won every week.

On the other hand, the enthusiasm and wealth of rich benefactors can be hugely beneficial to the game. They are one of the reasons why Premiership clubs can now sign many of the world's greatest footballers. Gianfranco Zola, Thierry Henry, Dennis Bergkamp, David Ginola, Ruud van Nistelrooy, Cristiano Ronaldo and others have significantly enhanced the status of the Premiership. They have also introduced high-quality technique to the English game.

No one can dispute that some of the best foreign players are technically superior to the best in England. We have to look upon them as an example and try to learn from them. Sir Trevor Brooking, now the Director of Development at the Football Association, is trying to improve the skill level among players of primary school age. The belief is that if you coach kids properly when they are young enough, they will have those skills to call upon when they are strong enough to play at the higher levels. I don't think there is any susbstitute for skill whatever your position. You can be a tough, uncompromising fullback but you will be a better player if you can mix those qualities with skill.

Youngsters sometimes ask me who in the modern game plays like I used to play. They also ask what I was good at and what I was bad at. To be honest, I find it difficult to compare myself with any other individual. In many ways it's a fruitless exercise. Chelsea's Joe Cole has played several games in my England position on the left of midfield but no one would describe us as similar in style.

I always took pride in my technique and I thought I had good ball control. I could score goals, headed the ball well, could run all day and had a bit of an aggressive streak that became more apparent as my career developed. I wasn't quick but, rather like Bobby Moore, I compensated by thinking ahead and anticipating the flight of the ball and the movement of those around me.

The great thing I had in my favour was a love of the game. My enthusiasm for football was unconditional. I would play anywhere, anytime, with anyone. When I became a professional, I was first out for training in the morning and last back in the changing rooms. I played until I was fifty-three. One day after a charity match Kathy said to me, 'Your legs are beginning to look a bit thin, Martin.' She was right. My time was up.

I played for nearly half a century and still get a kick out of it when I see kids playing in the park just for the sake of it. We should be encouraging schools to include competitive sports on the curriculum, not to sell off playing fields. As a former England Schoolboy international I think I can talk with some authority about the importance of grassroots football for future generations.

I was a schoolboy when I went to Wembley for the first time in 1958. I went to watch Terry Venables play for England against Scotland in a schoolboy game. Terry was playing directly against a fiery little Scot called Billy Bremner. England won 3–1 and both those youngsters went on to have great careers.

The following year I went back to Wembley when I was selected to play for England Schoolboys against West Germany. That was my first big triumph, but the old stadium was also the backcloth for my despair in 1964 when West Ham played in the FA Cup final without me. In 1965 I was lucky enough to play in the European Cup Winners' Cup final at Wembley. Then came 1966 and all that. So Wembley holds many memories for me and I hope the new stadium can provide a future generation of footballers with similar good fortune.

Mine has been a fabulous career and I've enjoyed my time in the spotlight. I hope that today's kids view what my generation achieved in 1966 as a challenge, but we have to provide them with encourgament, support and a vision for the future. I know because I was once a little boy in the East End with a pair of football boots and a dream.

INDEX